Cyles' Feilds

lane

ye Strand

West house

Exter house

Wefter Savoy

Saltbury house

Ivie lane

Durham house

Yorke house

Cha. Croffe

Scotland Yard

Suffolk house

Graenes Ally

Harthorn Ally

Whit hall

D ITS SURROUNDINGS IN 1658

LONDON

Books by Mrs Robert Henrey

THE LITTLE MADELEINE (*her girlhood*)

AN EXILE IN SOHO (*her adolescence*)

MADELEINE GROWN UP (*her love story and marriage*)

A FARM IN NORMANDY (*the birth of her child*)

MATILDA AND THE CHICKENS (*a winter on her farm*)

A JOURNEY TO VIENNA (*the making of a film*)

PALOMA (*the story of a friend*)

MADELEINE'S JOURNAL (*London during Coronation Year*)

A MONTH IN PARIS (*she revisits the city of her birth*)

MILOU'S DAUGHTER (*a winter in the Midi*)

BLOOMSBURY FAIR

LONDON

By
MRS ROBERT HENREY

Water-colours by
PHYLLIS GINGER

LONDON: J. M. DENT & SONS LTD
NEW YORK: E. P. DUTTON & CO. INC.

D 116/9 m

FOR

DOROTHY SUTHERLAND

THE LONDONER IN THE COUNTRY

EXILED to bowers of beauty
  In upland valleys where
Cherry and apple blossom
Spill perfume on the air;
Surely I should be happy
Imprisoned here with birds
Who do not drag, when singing,
Our human chain of words?

Oh foolish and ungrateful,
Amid such wealth of song,
With freedom of the forest,
To find that still I long
To hear the heavy traffic,
To smell the airless street,
To see the tide of strangers,
The myriad unknown,
To feel that great heart beat,
And recognize my own.

                              Richard Church.

CONTENTS

THE FRONTISPIECE

Phyllis Ginger chose this group of shops in Old Bond Street to show what, until quite lately, was typical of the whole length of London's most fashionable thoroughfare. A chocolate shop in the centre. To the left is Corot, the dress shop, and to the right Fanchon who, with Delman on the other side of the road, is typical of the beautiful shoe shops in Bond Street.

This picture was made from the first-floor premises of Orlik Pipes, whose sign is a judge in wig and red robes. Under Orlik's are Marlborough, who show a different French painting every day —a Cézanne, a Manet, a Toulouse-Lautrec, and so on; Lenthéric, Paris powders and lipsticks; Wolf, a jeweller, and Lydia Moss, whose magnificent lingerie and blouses halt our steps as we walk slowly along this street where so many buildings were destroyed by air attack, but where so much remains to remind us of the eighteenth and nineteenth centuries. On the west side, to cross the street again, is Agnew where Old Masters beckon us—Constables, Van Dycks, and Rembrandts.

ILLUSTRATIONS

LONDON

WHAT IS LONDON?

FAMOUS AND MIGHTY is London, which for five years stood up proudly to what Mr. Winston Churchill once called 'long, monotonous days and long nights, black as hell.'

What exactly is London?

This great city, still the heart of an empire, is almost everything the human mind can imagine. Its aspect changes continually, not only according to the hour of the day or the night, but also according to whether we ourselves are happy or anxious or sad; rich or poor, ill or in good health; old, with long and picturesque memories to draw on, or young and breathing its glories and promised romance, love in home or shop or office, or opportunities for money or fame. Some still think of London in terms of those apparently beautiful years before the war of 1914, and when they go down the Strand they see pictures of Edwardian, or even late Victorian days. Others, when they pass through Leicester Square, remember a tune from *The Bing Boys* or think of a face or a building which is no more. The years between the wars, the Foolish Decade, were, for some, boom times—champagne, and *No, No, Nanette*; for others, black misery of the slump which followed the boom, or a nightmare of a growing cancer on the Continent. Almost as soon as the war of 1939–45 was over, a few of us, ungratefully, were tempted to think that London was a braver, better, more exciting place during the days of resistance, black-out, and bombs than in the drab dress of peace and going without, of grumbling and 'spivs.' But that it was a popular place was proved by the growing rush to nestle within its battered and dusty frontiers, and we clapped our hands at the sight of any new paint with a childish confidence in the future.

How large is London?

If you take it as represented by the Metropolitan police area, which includes the counties of London and Middlesex and parts of Essex, Kent, Surrey, and Herts, then the population of London was at the last census rather more than 8,000,000.

In this region there are 2,200,000 dwellings, of which *three-quarters* received damage of some kind or other during the air raids. Of these, 10,000 were destroyed or damaged beyond repair.

How much of London can we describe?

The woman who lunches in the giant Oxford Street store between two bouts of shopping has little idea of how the broker fares in Throgmorton Street. The housewife in Dulwich has probably never been to Hammersmith, and I, who live off Piccadilly, am sometimes tempted to think that Kensington High Street belongs to quite another town and that to buy a dress or a piece of ribbon there needs an excursion all on its own. Two people walking along Regent Street do not always look into the same shop windows, or if they do their interests may be caught by quite different objects. This book is merely what one mirror catches of a great big city, and mostly in the heart of it, the circuses and streets and squares which every tourist makes for, and which we who live within the sound of the traffic in Piccadilly quite unreasonably claim for our very own.

THE BATTLE

The battle so entirely changed the face of London that we must try to keep certain events always clear and fresh in our minds.

It was on 7th September 1940 that Goering, having told the German people 'This is the historic hour,' sent over 375 bombers and fighters in waves.

All those of us who were in London will remember that sunny Saturday afternoon when, soon after five, the sky became filled with tiny silver dots. I was sewing under a tree by the dell in Hyde Park, watching my baby in the pram. Though few knew it until the flames of dusk reddened the approaching night, this armada had dropped its bombs whilst it was still day on Woolwich Arsenal, on the gasworks at Beckton, on the docks at Millwall, on the docks at Limehouse and by Tower Bridge; at Rotherhithe, on the Surrey docks, and on the West Ham power station.

The day raiders had gone home by six o'clock, but at ten minutes past eight exactly the night raiders appeared, and by then the docks on both sides of the Thames were blazing furiously, and the new armada, guided to its target, dropped tons upon tons of high explosives and incendiaries on the immense riverside fires up and down London's dockland. Not until 4.30 a.m. did they return home, leaving fire and desolation in the dockside boroughs.

The following night (which was Sunday) the procession of bombers began again, and for nine and a half hours they continued their destruction. By Monday morning every railway line from London to the south was out of action.

For fifty-seven nights, without a break, an average of two hundred bombers attacked London. The alert would sound as dusk was falling, the anti-aircraft guns would open up, and soon the first thuds would be heard. The all clear would not be sounded until dawn.

These raids went on until the following May, by which time fifty thousand high-explosive bombs had fallen on the capital.

THE CITY

Just as the dockland suffered its greatest destruction at the beginning of the battle in September, so the City was altered for ever by the great fire-raid on Sunday, 29th December, when over a hundred planes showered incendiaries on the town's least defensible area. The entire area between St. Paul's and Guildhall was impassable while the flames burned until late the next day. The conflagration round Fore Street was abandoned to burn itself out, and the City is to-day the largest area of continuous air-raid desolation in Britain.

THE CENTRE OF THE TOWN

The plinth of Eros, the heart of the empire, the bull's-eye of so many nights' concentrated bombing, was never hit, but at three in the morning of the 10th September 1940, during the third night of the battle, a very heavy delayed-action bomb fell in Regent Street, within a few yards of Piccadilly Circus. Though made much less dangerous by Royal Engineers than it would have been, the bomb exploded the following evening at a quarter past six, breaking some plate-glass windows of shops in the Quadrant and chipping the façades of the Piccadilly Hotel and the Café Royal. Soon four thousand people on a peak night were to sleep under the plinth of Eros in Piccadilly Circus station.

Just before 10 p.m. on the night of 23rd September, Westminster's first parachute mine fell in Savile Row, opposite the new Central police station. St. Anne's Church in Soho was first damaged. The Queen's Theatre in Shaftesbury Avenue was hit.

On 7th October, No. 145 Piccadilly, former residence of the king and queen when Duke and Duchess of York, was hit, and so was the fire station in Shaftesbury Avenue.

The 12th October was the date of the disaster at the tube station in Trafalgar Square, near King Charles the First's statue. Another bomb fell in the centre of the National Gallery.

The 14th October: You cannot help thinking of this terrible night every time you walk up and down Piccadilly, because early in the raid St. James's Church was hit and set on fire, the rectory was destroyed, and the verger and his wife, trapped in the kitchen, were killed. On the

We are standing with our backs to the noble ruins of St. Mary-le-Bow (Bow Bells). Here the stonecutter plies his trade exactly as he did centuries ago. The roar of the traffic is dulled. Bread Street is merely a path between two rows of bricks. The wild flowers prosper on the fire-scorched earth and St. Paul's looks more magnificent than at any period since its building after the Great Fire of 1666.

B

other side of Piccadilly the Fifty Shilling Tailor's premises were ablaze, and all round the circus the rooftops were ringed with incendiaries. In Pall Mall the Carlton Club was hit, a great piece of stone hurtling down on an empty car in the street.

On 15th October, in an even heavier raid, a parachute mine at Alderney Street demolished 150 houses. At 3.30 a.m. (16th October), the south-west corner of Leicester Square was blown away by a parachute mine. Thurston's famous billiards house and the old Perroquet restaurant were wrecked, and while taxi-drivers were sheltering in the basement of a drapery store near by, their cabs were twisted and torn by blast, pieces being thrown up into the naked boughs of the plane-trees in the centre of the square, where Shakespeare's hand was blown away.

The 15th November was the date when Pitt's Head Mews in Mayfair and the Carlton Hotel in the Haymarket were hit, and on 11th December the largest unexploded bomb to fall in Westminster dug itself into a grass mound opposite the Dell in Hyde Park.

On 8th March 1941 Buckingham Palace lost its North Lodge, and on the same night took place the appalling tragedy at the Café de Paris in Coventry Street. Thirty-four people were killed and over one hundred injured.

Then came the terrible night of the 16th April—the historic 'Wednesday.' The north-east corner of Leicester Square was hit and the flames continued until well into the next day. A land mine fell in Jermyn Street. Another struck Newport Buildings in Shaftesbury Avenue, killing forty-eight and injuring eighty-three. The Shaftesbury Theatre was destroyed. Christie's auction-room was burnt out. Stone's Chop-house, historic eating-place in Panton Street off Leicester Square, was destroyed.

On 10th May came the Luftwaffe's final attack before it temporarily abandoned London. For five moonlight hours 300 bombers attacked the House of Commons, Westminster Abbey, the British Museum, the Law Courts, the

War Office, the Mint, the Mansion House, and the Tower. Happily, except to the House of Commons, the damage to these historic buildings was not serious. That night 1,436 people were killed and 1,792 injured.

THE FEBRUARY–MARCH RAIDS OF 1944

The February–March raids of 1944 were generally thought to be aimed against Norfolk House, St. James's Square, the headquarters of General Eisenhower, supreme allied commander, where the invasion of the Continent was being planned. There would appear also to have been an attempt to destroy No. 10 Downing Street, possibly in the hope of killing Winston Churchill. Four bombs were dropped in line—one in St. James's Park, two on the Horse Guards Parade, and the fourth in front of the Treasury, doing damage to the stone facing.

The attack on St. James's Square took place on 23rd February.

Norfolk House was not hit, but St. James's Palace, built by Henry the Eighth, was severely pockmarked and robbed of its clock; King Street, St. James's, with its many art shops, looked like a river of fire; and the London Library was badly shaken.

On 24th February a picturesque corner of Soho's Old Compton Street was blown away. On the trees in St. Anne's churchyard hung tattered garments from an old-clothes shop, and these fluttered in the cold night, illuminated by a huge column of fire rising from a burst gas main in the street. Winston Churchill arrived unexpectedly, and talked to rescuers whilst aged Italian women and swarthy Greeks crowded round him.

THE FLYING BOMBS

On Tuesday, 13th June, just after the invasion of the Continent, the first flying bomb fell at Bow, in east

London. On Sunday, 18th June, one of these missiles cut out over Westminster and dived down on the Guards' Chapel of Wellington Barracks during morning service; 119 people were killed and 141 wounded.

Other flying bombs fell in Constitution Hill, in the garden of Buckingham Palace, on the Regent Palace Hotel annexe in Brewer Street, Soho, in Aldwych, at the Dell in Hyde Park, and one grazed the east wing of Lansdowne House in Berkeley Square.

The Regent Palace Hotel annexe was hit at midday on 30th June, and the Aldwych disaster happened during the lunch hour of the same day. At Aldwych 46 people were killed and 399 severely wounded. Lansdowne House was hit on a Sunday morning in August.

In the first seven weeks, 5,340 flying bombs were launched on the country, killing 4,735 persons with 14,000 more or less seriously injured. In that period 17,000 houses were totally destroyed and about 800,000 damaged. A quarter of a million mothers with children were assisted to leave London. The weight of flying bombs from the night of 15th June to the night of 31st July totalled 4,500 tons.

THE V2 ROCKETS

The first V2 long-range rocket, having travelled at 3,000 miles an hour, so people said, fell at Chiswick on Friday, 8th September 1944. It was heard in Piccadilly. Though everybody talked about it, the Government tried to keep it a secret.

On Saturday evening, 2nd December, a V2 plunged into the mud of the Thames opposite the Savoy Hotel. Four nights later another fell on a public-house behind Selfridge's, and on Sunday, 18th March 1945, at breakfast-time, a V2 exploded at Marble Arch, killing a newspaper seller and the child he tried to shelter.

The last of these explosions was heard in London on 27th March 1945.

Altogether 1,050 rockets reached Britain, killing 2,754 people and injuring 6,523.

When, after the defeat of Germany, Mr. Winston Churchill spoke to the vast crowds gathered in Whitehall, he said: 'You have been attacked by a monstrous enemy, but you have never flinched or wavered. My heart goes out to the Cockneys. Any visitors we may happen to have here to-day—and many great nations are represented here in all those who have borne arms with us in the struggle—they echo my words when I say "Good old London!"'

THE ORIGIN OF LONDON

The bombs which during the various phases of the war of the air fell on London pounded equally Roman London, Saxon London, Norman London, Elizabethan London, Stuart London, Queen Anne's London, Georgian London, Victorian London, and the London of modern iron and cement buildings. The history of London is the history of England.

Of the rulers of London before the Christian era we know nothing, and, unlike Rome and Paris, we can point to no founder of London whose name is lost in the oozing mud of the Thames, which is said to have spread itself out like a vast lake. Brute, the Trojan, who was supposed to have founded London a thousand years before Christ, and King Lud, who would have been contemporary with Julius Caesar's invasion, are fanciful.

THE ROMAN INVASION

In 55 B.C. Julius Caesar and 8,000 men, having sailed from Boulogne, landed on an August Sunday near Romney Marsh. But this was merely a coastal survey, and the following year he arrived with twenty-eight many-oared triremes and 560 transports upon the same Kentish coast. From here he made for the first place where he saw that the river could be forded, and he probably crossed it at Brentford, but London does not appear to have attracted his attention. Caesar then left England and returned to meet his tragic end.

The inhabitants of this island were then a Celtic race who had passed through the ages of bronze and iron, and had been for some considerable time well skilled in metal work, having their own gold coins. Celtic London, if it existed, was probably in the Cornhill area.

A century after Caesar's invasion, from A.D. 43 to A.D. 50, the Emperor Claudius decided to resume Caesar's work, and he sent Aulus Plautius to reduce the island. London was his first objective, but at that time, of course, St. Albans was a more important city.

BOADICEA

The first specific mention of London is to be found in Tacitus. It occurs in his account of the revolt of the Iceni.

Boadicea, the widowed Queen of the Iceni, the Norfolk and Suffolk of to-day, welded together the still fierce Celtic tribes of those districts in a great rebellion against the Romans and Celts living farther south, and in A.D. 61 bore down on London. Tacitus (he was writing under Trajan in about A.D. 115-17) says that London was a place highly celebrated for the number of its merchants and the confluence of traffic. Boadicea's armies slew the citizens and allies of Rome, and the first recorded event of London is therefore its capture by a woman.

One imagines that London rose quickly from the ruins in which Boadicea left it. The Basilica on Cornhill was built in the first and second centuries, and was the largest in Britain. Towards the end of the third century, London stood as the starting-point of seven out of the fifteen or so great Roman roads in England. The most important was Watling Street, on which Cannon Street now stands.

THE WALLS

The walls were first built about 100–50 A.D.

At that time London was about three miles in circumference, and the main gates corresponded to Newgate, Ludgate, Bishopsgate, Aldersgate, Aldgate, and, perhaps, Cripplegate. The final Roman wall was high and built of ragstone with brick binding courses.

Fire which destroyed acres of the City has revealed new stretches of the Roman wall and one of its fine bastions, beautiful in the evening light, hitherto throttled by the maze of modern buildings.

Nineteen centuries of history began to unfold themselves.

The Roman level of Hadrian was about sixteen feet below the modern surface—the surface of red omnibuses and Victorian office buildings. The British Museum, the London Museum, the Guildhall Museum, several livery companies, and a number of learned societies became interested. The Roman and Medieval London Excavation Council was formed.

In the spring of 1947, at the Goldsmith's Hall, Mr. W. F. Grimes, keeper of the London Museum and director of excavations, gave news of a particularly colourful find. The bombed site of the Saddlers' Hall in Gutter Lane, north of Cheapside, provided stray pages from a story dating from the first century A.D. First came the huts of Roman-British settlers, about A.D. 70. Then other timber dwellings of native type, some with floors of clay or gravel. After this came probably six Saxon-Norman tanning pits lined with stakes, wattle, and planking, and so on until the Great Fire and beyond.

Meanwhile in other parts of the City more forgotten history was being dug up.

SAXON LONDON AND ST. PAUL'S CATHEDRAL

Except that Hengist, and Eric, his son, chiefs of the Saxon invaders, won a victory in 457 over the Britons who fled to London, we are told little about London after the departure of the Romans, until the seventh century, when Ethelbert, King of East Kent, built and endowed the earliest authenticated church of St. Paul's. Thus from the times of the Saxons to the present day, London's chief sanctuary of religion has stood overlooking the river, greeting the ships that sail into London.

When Sir Christopher Wren was building the foundations of modern St. Paul's which, by a miracle, stood firm throughout the Battle of London while all around it was cast down, he discovered Saxon stone coffins and Saxon tombs lined with slabs of chalk. Beneath were Roman lamps and Roman pottery kilns.

The Saxon kings were generous to St. Paul's, and the clergy obtained Tillingham, in Essex, as a grant from King Ethelbert. There is a tradition that King Athelstane once lived in Cheapside.

The Saxon St. Paul's, built and endowed by King Ethelbert in 610, lasted some three centuries. It was rebuilt twice before we come to the beautiful edifice of 1240, which every child knows about as being the St. Paul's of the Great Fire. Originally this medieval St. Paul's had a spire which was not only one of the marvels of London but of the whole of Europe. Henry the Eighth would have looked upon it when he was acquiring the palace of Whitehall from Cardinal Wolsey, and planning to build St. James's Palace. Queen Elizabeth particularly admired the lofty steeple and was much affected when it was hit by lightning, but in spite of her exhortations it was not re-erected.

This disaster destroyed the roof and melted the bells, but even before this St. Paul's had sunk into pathetic degradation. Beer casks, baskets of bread, fish, flesh, and fruit were carried through it, and mules and horses were tied to the columns. Soon after the spire was struck, a man who had provoked a fray in the church was set in the pillory in the churchyard, and had his ears nailed to a post and then cut off. Various proclamations did little good.

Thieves thronged the nave, and advertisements covered the walls. Ben Jonson lays the first scene of the third act of *Every Man out of his Humour* in the middle aisle.

This was the condition of St. Paul's when Queen Elizabeth drove through the Strand to hear a thanksgiving service preached at St. Paul's Cross after the defeat of the Armada, at which time she was residing at St. James's Palace.

The ruinous state of the cathedral caused James the First to appoint a royal commission, with Inigo Jones upon it, to inquire into the matter, but so little was done that Buckingham is said to have pilfered some of the stone to build his water-gate on the Strand embankment.

THE GREAT FIRE OF 1666

Charles the First was of a nature to appreciate the historic church and he commissioned Inigo Jones to supervise the repair of the cathedral, and more than £100,000 was spent on the work. To provide a covered shelter for those who had been used to saunter in the nave ('Paul's Walk') Jones designed the famous portico, well known from Hollar's etching, at the west end of the cathedral, the king himself bearing the full cost of this part of the work. But further repairs were stopped by the outbreak of the civil war, and horses were once again tethered in the nave. The Restoration would doubtless have brought the cathedral back to its ancient splendour. Indeed, Wren drew up designs for a rotunda and a lantern. Then came the Great Fire.

Bishop Sancroft preached in a corner of the ruins, just as in our time services were held within the stricken walls of Coventry Cathedral, but the damage was too great for St. Paul's to be restored. Charles the Second was of a mind to employ Perrault, the designer of one of the fronts of the Louvre, to build the new St. Paul's, but wisely he yielded to the opinion of those who wished Wren to carry out the work.

The new St. Paul's was not finished until 1710.

* B

By then the dome had its golden gallery and its glittering cross, and on the accession of the first of the Georges, all the court went in state to St. Paul's.

THE GREAT FIRE OF 1940

From the very first night of the Battle for London, because of the fires in the east which lit up the dome, St. Paul's Cathedral became a symbol of London's defiance.

But the battle had only just entered its second week when St. Paul's provided a human-interest story that thrilled the empire. A large delayed-action bomb hurtled down south of the granite posts on the night of 12th September, and buried itself twenty-seven feet deep. Of course, everybody knew that as soon as it exploded there would be nothing left of St. Paul's.

For three days men worked to dig it out. Then it was driven in state to Hackney Marshes on a lorry under the command of Lieut. Davies, a Canadian who became a national hero. Londoners marvelled, and felt that the action of Lieut. Davies and his colleagues was something to be proud of and to emulate.

The cathedral was never seriously damaged. All the time one had the impression that it was under divine protection. Even though a bomb fell on the north transept on 16th April 1941, something prevented an immense mine from exploding the same night when it landed gently a few feet from the eastern wall.

But it was the night of the Great Fire in the City—the historic 29th December 1940—that St. Paul's provided the most inspiring and terrifying sight that Londoners had ever seen.

Impressive photographs remind us how the cathedral was silhouetted against the red night sky, while everything round was crackling and falling. At times the dome seemed to ride the waves like a galleon, and the golden cross to scintillate above the reach of earthly harm.

Shakespeare says that the Tower was begun by Julius Caesar. Alfred the Great made a fortress here against the river. In its present form, however, it dates from William the Conqueror, since when succeeding ages have left upon its grey stones their grim stories.

Palace, castle, prison, place of execution. . . . Now we think of it in terms of beefeaters and Crown jewels and, in these days of peace, as Phyllis Ginger shows, picturesque crowds continue to visit it.

If you like to walk alone, you may go to church on Sunday morning, inspect the block, talk to the ravens, or simply lean over the parapet to look at the muddy river where Romans and Saxons tied up their boats.

Londoners could then imagine what must have been the terrific spectacle of the Great Fire of 1666, when the cathedral's predecessor was destroyed.

Did any modern Evelyn or Pepys wander through this nightmare, preparing an account of it for posterity? Alas, those who were in the City that night had doubtless other things to do. The Tower of London, Guildhall, and many a Wren church fought, that night, to exist, some in vain. The Cripplegate area, the Queen Victoria Street area, and the Wood Street area were red-hot furnaces. Paternoster Row, disappearing for ever—except for the tiniest piece—was singeing St. Paul's.

The Tower, which has been the background of all the most important scenes of English history, came through relatively safe. The story of the Tower is the story of London. The oldest building in the Tower is the White Tower, built by Bishop Gundulf under orders from William the Conqueror in 1078, and though two bombs exploded to the south of it, no damage was done. Fifteen high explosives, three flying bombs, and 153 incendiaries fell within its precincts during the course of the war. The northern bastion was destroyed entirely, but this was less than a hundred years old, and can be rebuilt as effectively in the present reign as it was first put up during the reign of Queen Victoria. A raven died from the effects of enemy action; another from old age. Three outlived the war. Rudolf Hess was imprisoned in the Tower from 17th to 20th May 1941, and three months later, on 15th August, Josef Jacobs, a German spy, was shot in the Miniature Range. The Crown jewels, and the valuable arms and armour, were removed to the north of the United Kingdom.

GUILDHALL

The Tower is the most venerable pile in London. As grimly as it has looked upon all the changing scenes of London since the days of William the Conqueror, it has twice watched the destruction of Guildhall, which was builded new in the fifteenth century. When to-day you enter Guildhall courtyard, you will pass on your left the ruins of the church of St. Lawrence Jewry, whose predecessor, like St. Paul's, was burned down in the fire of 1666, before which it had a history of at least 530 years. As in the case of St. Paul's, the new church was designed by Wren—the most costly of his City churches. At about 7.30 on the night of 29th December 1940, the southwesterly breeze which, at the beginning of the raid was only slight, had increased to gale force, and sparks from neighbouring buildings fell in showers over the church.

A few moments later an incendiary was seen in a corner of it, but, though it was immediately reported, help could not be sent for fifty minutes, by which time the fire had gained a hold and the steeple had crashed on the nave, while the wind was carrying fragments of burning wood towards Guildhall.

The Great Hall, the walls of which survived the fire of 1666, received the red-hot embers. Thomas Vincent, in *God's Terrible Voice in the City*, gives an account of this burning in 1666:

That night the sight of Guildhall was a fearful spectacle, which stood, the whole body of it together in view, for several hours together after the fire had taken it, without flames (I suppose because the timber was such solid oake) in a bright shining coale as if it had been a pallace of gold or a great building of burnished brass.

The first outbreak of fire in the Great Hall during the night of 29th December was seen at 8.30, but this was extinguished.

Soon afterwards more flames appeared, and though these were damped down, it was obvious that a great furnace was smouldering under the slates. Though a hose was carried to the roof, the water failed from lack of pressure and soon it was obvious that the hall was doomed. The firemen then tried to save the Council Chamber but burning fragments were falling from the roof, and when at 6.30 a.m. the flow of water increased it was too late.

The Guildhall Library, a relatively modern annexe built in Victorian Gothic to harmonize with the real Gothic of the fifteenth-century Guildhall, still exists and may be visited. The building was erected in 1873, but the library itself was founded in 1824 to collect material relating to the City of London, the Borough of Southwark, and the County of Middlesex. It had collected 130,000 printed books, 30,000 manuscripts from the fourteenth century onwards, and a large number of prints and drawings. Fire entirely destroyed 25,000 books and damaged many thousands, but though parts of the building were burned, the main structure was quickly repaired.

The chief treasures, such as the Shakespeare signature, were fortunately in the country, together with a rare map of London in Queen Elizabeth's time, which is now hanging once more above the beautiful fire-place in the study of Mr. Raymond Smith, the librarian. There is only one other known copy of this map, and it is to be seen at the Pepysian Library at Cambridge.

The map was made after destruction by lightning of the spire of St. Paul's Cathedral. A strange and entirely fanciful description of the origins of London is printed in a corner of the map, and this is what it says:

This ancient and famous City of London was first founded by Brute, the Trojan, in the year of the world two thousand, eight hundred and thirty two, and before the Nativity of our Saviour Christ, one thousand one hundred and thirty. So that since the first building, it is two thousand six hundred and sixty three years. And afterwards was repaired and enlarged by King Lud, but at the present so flourisheth that it containeth in length from the east to the west about three English miles; and from the north to the south about two English miles. It is also so plentifully peopled, that it is divided into one hundred and twenty two parishes that are in the Suburbs. It is planted on a very good soil; for on the one side it is compassed with corn and pasture ground, and on the other side it is enclosed with the river of Thames, which not only aboundeth in all kinds of fresh water fish, but also is so navigable, that it as well bringeth abundance of commodites from all parts of the world, as also conveyeth forth such commodities as the plentifulness of our country doth yield us; which both augments the fame thereof abroad, and also increases the riches thereof at home.

God prosper it at his pleasure Amen.

You will notice on this map that London Bridge (over-built with houses) alone spans the Thames. Few people realize that London Bridge, which in some state probably existed since Roman times, was the only bridge until the building of Westminster Bridge in the middle of the eighteenth century.

THE LORD MAYOR AND THE MANSION HOUSE

Everybody has heard of Dick Whittington and his cat.

He is the hero of every nursery.

Richard Whittington was the son of a Gloucester knight who had lost his money. According to fables, the lad, who was born during the reign of Edward the Third, was apprenticed to a mercer from whom he ran away, and it was while resting by a stone cross at the foot of Highgate Hill that he heard in the sound of Bow Bells the voice of an angel saying: 'Turn again, Whittington, thrice mayor of London.' Experts are not quite sure about the cat, though John Stow does tell a story that much resembles it. But Whittington was a real man, and was mayor of London three times, the first being a three months' tenure in place of a mayor who died in office.

He married the daughter of a west-country squire, became a wealthy merchant, supplied the wedding trousseau of the Princess Blanche, eldest daughter of Henry the Fourth, and also the pearls and cloth of gold for the marriage of the Princess Philippa. He became the court banker and lent much money to the chivalrous Henry the Fifth for making the siege of Harfleur, celebrated by Shakespeare. One of his many benefactions was the

building of the library at Greyfriars, and his executors—
notably the famous town clerk, John Carpenter—were
largely responsible for the first library at Guildhall. This
is thought to be the first library in this country to be
administered by a civic authority.

There were mayors long before Whittington.

The first mayor of London was installed, it would appear,
in 1191, but lord mayors are not mentioned till the sixteenth
century.

In olden times the lord mayors of London had no official
residence, but in 1739 the Common Council started to
build the present Mansion House, which was not completed
until 1753 when Sir Crisp Gascoyne took up residence.

The exterior of this building of Portland stone in the
very heart of the City is of Renaissance style, with a portico
of six fluted columns. It stands on ground where long
long ago there was a pair of stocks which gave its name
to a fish and flesh market, built during the reign of Edward
the First. To-day the Mansion House faces the Bank of
England, and underneath the traffic roundabout is the Bank
tube station, into which a heavy bomb crashed during the
nocturnal raids, causing considerable loss of life and
enormous structural damage.

None can serve the office of lord mayor unless he be an
alderman of London, who must previously have served
the office of sheriff. The lord mayor is elected by the
Court of Aldermen from two aldermen returned by the
Livery of London, in Common Hall (Guildhall) assembled,
on Michaelmas Day, 29th September, previous to which
election the lord mayor and corporation attend church in
state. On 8th November the lord mayor elect is admitted
into office publicly in Guildhall, having previously breakfasted with the existing lord mayor at the Mansion House.
After the swearing-in at Guildhall, when the lord mayor
publicly takes the oaths, accepts the sword, the mace, the
sceptre, and the City purse, he proceeds with the late lord
mayor to the Mansion House.

The next day is Lord Mayor's Day. The lord mayor used formerly to go to Westminster Hall by water, in the state barge, but now goes by land, and is presented to the judges of the King's Bench for the purpose of making his statutory declaration of office, after which he returns in state to Guildhall, where, in conjunction with the sheriffs, he gives a splendid banquet to the judges, ministers of State, ambassadors, and the Corporation.

During the war the lord mayor's procession was abandoned, and instead of a banquet at Guildhall, there was a lunch at the Mansion House, there being no facilities, since the nocturnal raid, to entertain amongst the ruins of Guildhall.

On 9th November 1944, Mr. Winston Churchill attended the function for the fifth consecutive occasion, and received an historic welcome from members of the War Cabinet, representatives of the defence services, General Koenig, military governor of liberated Paris, the burgomaster of Brussels, the Lord Chief Justice, and the Bishop of London.

In 1945 the procession was resumed, and the lunch was attended by the new Prime Minister, Mr. Attlee, who gave thanks to Almighty God, who had brought the country through such manifold perils.

THE CITY—A WALK IN 1945

Mincing Lane spells tea, coffee, sugar, rubber, and spices from the east.

In truth, the narrow lane no longer exists. There is merely a track bordered by two or three concrete buildings, scarred and pock-marked, in an area almost completely laid waste during the last raid of the Battle of London— 10th May 1941. There were houses here which burned during three nights and three days.

How impressive is this stricken site as you approach it from the river up St. Dunstan's Hill! As the narrow hill bends to enter Great Tower Street, one gives a little gasp of surprise to see this vast emptiness on the opposite side

of the street, where Mincing Lane is mapped out by rural
fences on the posts of which its name is nailed roughly and
askew.   Then, hesitatingly, one turns in the middle of the
street, in which there is hardly any traffic, to look back
whence one came—and there in all its beauty is the church
of St. Dunstan's-in-the-East, with the curious spire supported by four arched ribs and surmounted by a crowing
cock, and through the open walls of the church one guesses
rather than sees the swiftly flowing water of the Thames.
A century or more ago, when the rich tea-brokers of
Mincing Lane lived above their tasting rooms, they went
to church here on Sundays, and the Tower of London saw
an Easter parade.   Wren was very proud of this church,
which he rebuilt after the Great Fire; and being told one
morning that a hurricane had damaged many London
spires, he remarked: 'Not St. Dunstan's, I am quite sure.'
    A tug going down-stream with the tide hoots—once,
twice; and one turns suddenly eastwards, where the Tower
of London, visible as it has not been for centuries, mingles
its white-grey battlements against a winter sky with which
it appears strangely and beautifully to tone.   A City policeman with his corporation helmet stands firmly and silently
at the corner of Mincing Lane and Great Tower Street.   He
looks down sympathetically when one questions him, and
explains that having just been demobilized, he cannot
accustom himself to a beat with which he was familiar
before the war but which has changed so much since.
How august is the history of this Mincing Lane, which no
longer exists but as a track, marked half-way down by the
stalwart modern edifice of Plantation House, begun in the
late twenties but held up for a time by the great slump
which caused so many suicides on both sides of the
Atlantic.   At the outbreak of war three wings out of five
had been completed, and the site on which it was to extend
has been cleared by fire and high explosives.   Mincing
Lane owes its name to some houses belonging to the
'Minchuns,' or nuns, of St. Helen's, Bishopsgate Street,

and in old times there dwelt in this lane Genoese traders called 'galleymen,' who brought their wines to Galley Wharf down yonder in Thames Street, from which direction has always come the fishy smell of Billingsgate.

Pepys has a record of seeing Mincing Lane in flames on 19th June 1668.

Between two and three in the morning we were waked with the maids crying out, 'Fire, fire, in Marke Lane!' So I rose and looked out, and it was dreadful, and strange apprehensions in me and us all of being presently burnt. So we all rose; and my care presently was to secure my gold and plate and papers, and could quickly have done it, but I went forth to see where it was; and the whole town was presently in the streets; and I found it in a new built house that stood alone in Minchin Lane, over against the Clothworkers' Hall, which burned furiously; the house not yet quite finished; and the benefit of brick was well seen, for it burnt all inward, and fell down within itself; so no fear of doing more hurt.

The concrete of Plantation House, where the auctions are now held, proved what Pepys had noticed—that only the strongest buildings survive. In his days they needed to be of brick; now they must be of steel and cement. The Clothworkers' Hall burnt for three days and three nights during the Great Fire of 1666, and its successor burnt for the same length of time after the 10th May 1941 raid. Many treasures saved from the first Great Fire were lost in the second.

A tea and rubber broker, in his dark office in Philpott Lane (for gloomy City offices still exist on the fringe of open spaces) was waiting for the day when the Ministry of Supply would cease to be the sole buyer of rubber, and when the Ministry of Food would no longer be the only purchaser of tea. Like Pepys he had watched a mighty fire in Mincing Lane, but he pointed out that the flames had at least driven off the rats which formerly ate both the contents and the bindings of his ledgers.

This man had been on the roof of his old premises in

Mincing Lane during the first City fire of 29th December 1940, when the flames stopped short of the Eastcheap area. During successive nights of comparative calm he had amused himself by looking down, when the moon shone brightly, into old courtyards which, though he had worked in Mincing Lane since he was a lad, he had never suspected.

There were Queen Anne villas which, with the passing of time, had been encased in business façades, with the result that even those who worked in them hardly realized that these were once private houses in which families were brought up, whose oak walls and twisting staircases had echoed to childish laughter.

William James and Henry Thompson, brokers for nearly two centuries, had owned a villa in which their own forbears had lived, brought up a family, and gone to church at St. Dunstan's-in-the-East. Their villa had a garden and old trees, beautifully oak-panelled rooms, a spiral staircase with wrought-iron lamps in alcoves, fine kitchens, and a dial in the business room which, communicating with a vane on the roof, showed which way the wind was blowing, so that the partners could compute the progress of the tea clippers sailing for St. Katherine's Dock.

The fire of 10th May 1941 destroyed this lovely house, which stood next to the Clothworkers' Hall.

Men who had worked in the Lane for forty years or more, as so often their fathers had done before them, recalled the days when the tea merchants sent out travellers in their broughams to call on the grocers in the town with samples of tea, for the trade was not yet in the hands of large combines. The travellers were not always as serious as their top-hats would have one believe. If the grocer happened to say: 'This is not quite good enough for my customers. Have you nothing better than at three shillings a pound?' some crafty traveller might return to his carriage, and return with the same tea in another envelope, and exclaim:

'Smell these leaves, my good sir. What fragrance! I might manage some of this at *four* shillings a pound.'

Then the grocer would beam with pleasure and answer: 'Many thanks. That will suit me perfectly.'

Spices from the east, tea, coffee, rubber. Since the days of Genoese traders, Mincing Lane has dealt in eastern produce. The spices came first. Then came the tea, originally only from China; later from India and finally from Ceylon, which turned to tea after its coffee crop had failed from a disease which destroyed the plants. Rubber started to come from Ceylon some thirty years ago, where it was introduced by way of Brazil and Kew. There was romance in the street where once the nuns of St. Helen's had owned a row of small houses, and the waters of the Thames and the west wind which brought in the clippers made its fortune.

'I suppose,' said this broker, 'that a healthier Mincing Lane will rise on the site of the old one, but I hope they will keep it narrow. On sunny days most of the brokers —especially in rubber—liked to trade in the open air, and if the street is too wide, we shall be hampered by the traffic. Street trading comes in phases, depending to a great extent on the whims of certain brokers; for markets, like governments, depend on personalities.'

He opened the door leading to the outer office, where a man with a top-hat was bending over a heavy ledger. The man looked up, and the top-hat was ceremoniously removed. There was a merry fire in an old grate. The scene was quite Dickensian.

The winter's afternoon was already drawing in, but in Fenchurch Street there were daffodils and tulips and, behind frosted windows and on the pavements, shivering rose-trees and garden implements, all of which foretold the spring, and the interest of the City worker in his suburban garden.

In Threadneedle Street the great modern palaces of our banking institutions were ablaze with light, the high

From London Wall, a path overgrown with shrubs leads to this mighty bastion of the Roman Wall. Its magnificent curve stands triumphantly against the fenland. The civilization of modern times is reduced to moss-covered cellars disclosing Stuart, and sometimes Georgian or Victorian brickwork above a core of medieval masonry. Centuries have come and gone since Roman guards stood sentry here, and there is little to recall the passing of time but the tower of St. Giles's, Cripplegate.

Against this bastion was Barbers' Hall, which dated from 1381. It has disappeared completely, covered, with damp earth and chickweed.

windows of the Midland Bank protected by picturesque
but strong wrought iron, presumably to intimidate the
nocturnal burglar.   Its neighbour, the Bank of New South
Wales, reared its massive and glittering façade beside a low
corridor, ill lit and unnoticed by the busy crowd, leading to
all that is left of that medieval jewel, the Merchant Taylors'
Hall, whose great kitchen was built ten years after Agin-
court.   One enters this corridor with the feeling that one is
shaking off a century at each step.   The hooded wicker
chair, where the linkman once sat, half hides the fire-place
above which there are coats of arms in warm colourings.
and on either side of the distant archway, all in shadow,
are fine stone pillars and a staircase which is not of this age,
It is better to halt and to dream than to go forward from
here.   One is on the threshold of what once contained
glories from the fourteenth to the seventeenth centuries—
the largest hall possessed by any City company, the only
one preserving in perfect state its medieval features.   A
man sitting at a deal table in a makeshift office—it is the
light of his lamp which casts these provokingly picturesque
shadows—bends over a sheaf of papers beside the archway
which leads to nothing but the walls of the hall where
King Henry the Seventh was enrolled as a member of the
company.   Subsequently, on feast days, he sat openly
amongst them in a gown of crimson velvet.   This was the
company of craftsmen who, besides making the finery of
the day, sewed soldiers' quilted surcoats, the padded
lining of armour, and the trappings of war-horses.   The
total destruction of this magnificent hall robs Threadneedle
Street of a piece of old London sleeping beside its secluded
garden, and one thinks nostalgically of the great parlour,
drawing-room, and picture gallery with its seventeenth-
century panelling.
  Outside, in Threadneedle Street, a bevy of chattering
typists streamed out of a giant bank, their heels echoing
over asphalt which paves the centre of Roman London,
ground in which still perhaps lie hidden coins of Claudius,

Marcus Aurelius, and the Constantines. Now came a flow of employees from the recently nationalized Bank of England, rushing for the bus queues, or diving down into the tube station, which, during the raids, was the scene of one of the City's major disasters.

Poultry was blinking in the winter mist. A travel bureau had long since closed its doors owing to enemy action, and so had three consecutive shops, one of which had once sold Jaeger wool. Travelling, and the more attractively coloured knitting wools, were luxuries we eagerly looked forward to. On the opposite side of the street a maker of safes, strong-room doors, and locks was doing business at the corner of Old Jewry, where high explosives revealed traces of Saxon times. As Poultry merged into Cheapside a bank messenger stood waiting for an omnibus under half an angel carved in stone. A corrugated iron fence, creaking in the north wind, stretched as far as Ironmonger Lane, and through the joins one could see the ruins of the Mercers' Hall in whose records, Dick Whittington, a legend for five hundred years, is mentioned prosaically as a living person. This hero of our nursery days, by his wealth and charity, during the reign of Henry the Fifth, reflected great lustre on the Mercers' Company. The fairy-story atmosphere oozed from behind the corrugated fencing, tempting me to peep into the entrance where a porter stood warming his hands in front of a coal fire. Intrigued by my interest, he gallantly offered to show me round, leading the way along a newly bricked passage past the kitchen, where a woman was making toast which smelt good, and down a few steps into the ruins which were once the hall and private chapel of St. Thomas of Acre. As with the Merchant Taylors' Hall, nothing remains but the floor and the walls —the whole open to the sky. A basket of incendiaries came down on the ancient building in the early hours after the water supply had given out.

Outside in the street, the great modern building housing the Atlas Assurance Company quivered with the song of a

a thousand typewriters.   A stone figure carrying the world
on its shoulders overhangs King Street, and if the world
had fallen down during a raid it would certainly have
hurtled towards the city walls like a boulder hurled by
knights in armour.

Across Gresham Street is Basinghall Street, which skirts
the side of Guildhall, whose false Gothic battlements
give the narrow thoroughfare a medieval aspect, especially
as night falls.   Suddenly the passage twists and widens.
Here are more turrets, a building erected in the Dutch
style, a bright red pillar-box, and the columns of the Wool
Exchange.   A little farther on, through iron gates which
were still open, a carriage-way led to a delightful courtyard in the centre of which, and in front of an ochre portico,
grew a giant plane-tree whose naked branches looked in at
the highest windows.   Many solicitors have their chambers
here, reached by dark, winding staircases.

This was once a coaching inn, and the rooms communicated with each other along well-polished corridors.   We
might be in Exeter or Salisbury.   The windows are pic-
turesquely crooked and each floor slants like a ship in a
storm.   This pretty corner dates back to Ben Jonson's
time, even earlier.   A solicitor, whose forbears had
chambers here for a century, being on duty on the night
of the raid, looked out of his window to see his escape cut
off by a wall of fire which miraculously did not spread.
Thus was saved this quiet retreat.

After this one came upon a brightly lit shop selling
tobacco and sweets, and then suddenly—nothing.   The
town seemed to come to an end.   The road stretched
lugubriously into the infinite.   Was all beyond ploughed
fields and country?   One felt almost afraid to tread this
lonely path, to explore, by oneself, the unknown.   There
was only an occasional flicker of light, as if from a distant
inn or a wayside house.   A cottage, perhaps?   The January
wind howled over the flat, desolate country.

Now all the noise of the city was hushed, and one

regretted the warmth of the sweet-vendor's illuminated shop. In the distance, but coming nearer, was the sound of a horse and cart, the axles creaking in the night air. One recalled Juvenal's description of Umbricius leaving Rome to retire into the country, his cart wending its way heavily towards the Conduit Gate. The narrow road was marked out by low white fences. Soon it was cut by another whose name was painted in black upon the white wood and illuminated by a red hurricane lamp: LONDON WALL. Less than a decade ago, motor cars swarmed bumper to bumper, people thronged busy pavements. Now there was only this distant cart creaking, nearer and nearer. Not a human being was in sight. No friendly footsteps livened up this country road. Somewhere to the north-west lay the site of the Barber-Surgeons' Hall, whose ancient property included the bastion of the Roman wall against which it had stood since the fourteenth century. Its home was one of the few to survive the Great Fire of 1666. Perhaps this was no moment to search for the place where it stood.

Far to the left, on the fringe of civilization, a light flickered from a window.

After a few minutes' walk one discovered that this light was on the first floor of the Plough Inn, against Moorfields. 'This fen or moor field,' wrote Stow, 'stretching from the wall of the City betwixt Bishopsgate and the postern called Cripples gate, to Fensbury and to Holy well, continued a waste and unprofitable ground for a long time, so that the same was all letten for four marks the year, in the reign of Edward the second.'

Six centuries have brought it back to its original fen state with the wild chicory growing by the sides of the lanes marked out by wooden posts. The landlord of the 'Plough,' with shirt-sleeves rolled up, appeared to think it madness for an inquisitive female to cross the waste land in search of the Barber-Surgeons' Hall, but he left his bar and indicated the way across the desolate waste—back along

London Wall, towards the distant tower of St. Giles's, Cripplegate, illuminated by a single strong lamp in front of its wrecked porch.

Once again came the sound of wheels, this time from a post office van whose pony was trotting at a fine pace through the fens.

And so, not too bravely, I continued my journey.

At the corner of London Wall and Aldermanbury, an old man, looking rather like a medieval hermit, was standing at the entrance to a cavernous ruin illuminated within. At right angles five hurricane lamps marked the north porch of St. Alphage. When asked to help, the genial anchorite exclaimed:

'But with pleasure. Do you know who I am, madam? R. J. Evans, master die-stamper, bombed out from No. 10 Bartholomew Close, and now guardian of the City of London Corporation's Salvage Depot. Come in and see my treasures.'

He led the way into an ill-lit hall filled with medieval relics found on abandoned sites: three swords against a wall, all beautifully carved, one from Mark Lane, another from Seething Lane, and the third from Sise Lane; a female figure in stone from the Mercers' Hall, rows upon rows of painted church property plates, and a zinc tablet with the words: 'St. Alphage, Archbishop of Canterbury, martyred by Danish soldiers 1012, here buried.' The arms of the Coachmakers' Company: two coaches side by side, and one beneath, divided by red lines, a most exquisite model of Temple Bar from Guildhall, two street lamps which stood outside the gates of the City Carlton Club in St. Swithin's Lane, the glass globes also from this place which were covered with dust and grime; the portrait of a bishop with a benign expression from the City of London School; gas masks and pistols, rapiers and medieval lanterns, stained glass and stone statues. 'Lucky I'm a die-stamper,' he muttered. 'I've been painting the church property plates. The Barber-Surgeons'? But there's nothing left of it—nothing but the weeds that grow from the stones of the bastion—just as they did when the Romans manned it. There's another bastion come to light in Monkwell Street. We're back to the fens with the old landmarks—St. Alphage here, Cripplegate Tower, and the Roman wall.'

He walked out into the night.

'Don't you feel a bit eerie,' he asked, 'wandering from one graveyard to the next, on a dark night like this?'

'Just a bit,' I answered. 'What's this cavern you inhabit?'

It was a damaged modern building on which dimly appeared the words: FERGUSON BROTHERS; and leaning up against the side of it, lit up by those hurricane lamps, was the north porch of the church of St. Alphage with its high stone cross.

We turned into London Wall, that dark, quiet, mysterious country lane.

The hermit said: 'Until the reign of Henry the Eighth, the church of St. Alphage was on the north side of the road, where you see the garden with a piece of the Roman wall garlanded with dead ivy. When it came down, Henry the Eighth sold them a priory chapel on the opposite side of the road—the chapel of Elsynge Spital, which was soon renamed St. Alphage. The new St. Alphage escaped the Great Fire of 1666, but in Georgian times it was mostly rebuilt. That is why some thirty years ago people thought so little of it that the church, all except the fourteenth-century steeple, the vestry, and a new porch, was pulled down and the parish was merged with that of St. Mary the Virgin, Aldermanbury, which you can see to the south.'

'Why wasn't the whole church pulled down?'

The hermit answered importantly:

'Because St. Alphage came under the tithe rate and the other didn't. The rector received some £1,200 a year from the warehouses hereabout, and so the porch and the vestry were left standing. Otherwise the rector would have had no stipend. They fixed up the little piece that was left very nicely with chairs and an altar. All sorts of folks came to pray during the lunch hour. In winter tea was served in the vestry at a penny a cup, and in summer lemonade at the same price. It was a church and it wasn't a church, if you get my meaning. But now the great fire raid of 29th December has wrecked it and burnt it with everything else round here. In all the parish not one single building remains, so this time there really are no tithes for the poor rector. Incidentally his other church, St. Mary the Virgin's, Aldermanbury, the one that was no good for his salary, is wrecked also.'

'So what has happened to the rector?'

'Oh, he's gone—gone to another living. They'll pull down both churches, probably, and sell the land to help rebuild St. Giles's, Cripplegate, yonder. Come and look inside.'

There was a parterre of chipped memorial tablets and gravestones. A few remained intact, but there was nothing of the altar. Against a wall one read:

'Here lyeth the Body of Bridget Shorter—12th December 1709.'

There were rusty buckets and twisted iron.

An arch led to stone stairs twisting up to the tower. There was a beautiful flint wall, stronger than modern concrete. From dim chambers rose the acrid odour of charred beams, and in the vestry was an open hearth in front of which midday workers from the warehouses had sat happily reading the paper or knitting while tea was passed round at a penny a cup!

As we turned back into the stillness of the country lane, I thanked the hermit and left him.

To the south, the lights of the City were still burning in steel and concrete offices. Here there was nothing but the white glow of a rising moon and the fresh smell of verdure. Suddenly the path marked London Wall came to an end,

cut by the junction of Wood Street and Cripplegate
Buildings, but an uneven lane overgrown with shrubs
led to a mighty bastion of the Roman wall shining in an
unreal light. Its magnificent curve stood triumphantly
against the fenland, and all round was the civilization of
modern times reduced to moss-covered cellars disclosing
Stuart and sometimes Georgian or Victorian brickwork
above a core of medieval masonry. Centuries had come
and gone since the Roman guards stood sentry here, but
there was nothing to recall the passing of time but the
nearby tower of St. Giles's, Cripplegate and its battlements,
clothing the desolation within like the ruins of some
monastery one might come across during a walk over the
moors.

The Barbers' Hall, five centuries old, had gone, leaving
mounds of damp earth and chickweed on either side of
that part of the Roman wall on which it was built. This
was no land of the living. The figures of the past were
alone, quite alone, free, now that their heavy gravestones
had been blasted open, to walk out from their coffins and
examine this strange land so heavy with historic associations, so deserted by the living. The walls of St. Giles's
were licked by fire while Henry the Eighth was beautifying his palace of Whitehall. The turret where once
pealed a dozen bells was silent. Roman and Saxon, Dane
and Norman, Tudor and Stuart could meet by moonlight
on common ground. Here, after many a voyage and
many a battle, that old Elizabethan warrior, Sir Martin
Frobisher, was brought to rest after receiving his death
shot at Brest, here Oliver Cromwell was married, here were
laid multitudes of poor folk dying from the Great Plague;
here John Milton, author of *Paradise Lost*, was buried.
Hither came Pepys, after dinner, to see Chirurgeons' Hall
(the Barbers and the Surgeons made one at that time), to
visit their theatre after it had escaped the Great Fire.

A bright light acted as a beacon in front of the porch of
St. Giles's, and southward, little by little, the windows of

Armour House by the General Post Office went out, one by one. Northward was the only secular building to withstand the fury of the great fire raid, which in a few hours turned this throbbing city back from town to country, back six centuries and more. As I approached it, I read the words: *Fire Station, built in 1900.*

This is Parliament Square. In May 1937 it was floodlit for the coronation of the present king. Kings and queens and the highest dignitaries of Europe drove through the gay crowds to be received by the Speaker in the historic library overlooking the Thames.

In May 1941 a deliberate attack was made on the House of Commons and Westminster Abbey, the Commons Chamber was entirely destroyed by a fire which spread to the Members' Lobby and caused the ceiling to collapse. The roof of Westminster Hall was also set on fire.

In May 1945 Parliament Square was again joyfully floodlit, and vast crowds converged on it to hear that the war with Germany was finished. The House of Commons was illuminated as it had been for the coronation. Westminster Guildhall was bathed in orange light, which was reflected back on the plane-trees and the noble statue of Abraham Lincoln looking down on his khaki compatriots.

From the balcony of the Ministry of Health building in Whitehall, Mr. Winston Churchill was unexpectedly talking to the crowds: 'Good old London—London like a rhinoceros, a great hippopotamus saying : "Let them do their worst!"'

Then all the crowd sang with the Prime Minister :

'Britons never, never, never will be slaves.'

This picture was painted on a peaceful May morning after the war.

WESTMINSTER

THOUGH SUCCEEDING AGES have re-edified the Palace of Westminster, though it cannot trace its history back so far as the Tower of London, and though it has not been a royal residence since the reign of Henry the Eighth, it has played and continues to play a more important role in the life of this country than any other place on our venerable soil.

While the fortress-palace of the Tower of London slept under a warm May sun, it was under the battle-scarred roof of the Palace of Westminster that Winston Churchill announced to Mr. Speaker that Germany had surrendered unconditionally and that hostilities would end officially at one minute after midnight 'to-night, Tuesday, 8th May,' 1945.

A few yards from where the greatest of our captains spoke, the Chamber of the House lay burned out and open to the sky, ravaged by flames as so many historic halls and chambers had been on the same spot since the days of Canute, but the spirit of our land was never more magnificent—'this House of Commons which has proved itself the strongest foundation for waging war that has ever been seen in the whole of our long history.' Do you remember those words that echoed throughout the empire? 'Advance Britannia! Long live the cause of freedom! God save the King!'

After which, as had been the case a quarter of a century earlier when another great Prime Minister had safely guided the nation through war to prevent enslavement, the House, not being inclined for debate or business, but desiring to offer thanks to Almighty God, to the Great Power which seems to shape and design the fortunes of nations and the destiny of man, went in procession to the church of St. Margaret.

The Palace of Westminster lives while ravens croak under the shadows of the noble battlements of the Tower and while the halls and gardens of the Palace of Whitehall are hushed for ever. The great Gothic edifice that stands guard over the Thames and dwarfs the abbey is very little more than a hundred years old, built in the least inspired of Victorian times, but where it is built there has passed, in a series of brilliant pictures, the whole history of England, and for centuries and centuries processions of kings and warriors, nobles and princes of the Church have trodden the sacred ground between it and the abbey. Fires innumerable have destroyed its pillars, its beams, its paintings, and its tapestries, and massive walls have crumbled since the Saxon traitor, Duke Edric, was said by some to have been thrown from an upper window of Canute's palace into the Thames, but the Palace of Westminster is gifted with the genius of emerging stronger and more virile after each catastrophe, until it now seems almost immaterial that so much of the interior was destroyed in the great nocturnal raid of 10th May 1941. It continues to write history while architects pore over future embellishments.

Scarcely anything is known about the palace which stood here during the reign of Canute, except that it was destroyed by fire some thirty years before the Conquest. Its early history is therefore lost in the mists of time like that of the abbey, or the monastery of St. Peter, as it was then, where the monks fared sumptuously on the offerings of the Thames fishermen by virtue of the fact that the founder, having been ferried across the water by a fisherman, rewarded him with a miraculous draught of salmon, and an assurance that his fellow watermen would never want for fish, provided they gave one-tenth of what they caught to the new church.

Edward the Confessor rebuilt Canute's palace. He made it a structure of great strength and it stood on the site of Old Palace Yard. The annals of the palace and of the abbey begin with him, for, having built his palace where

he held his court, and on one occasion entertained there
very splendidly the high and mighty Duke William of
Normandy, he set about rebuilding the abbey, which had
suffered greatly from the ravages of the Danes. He pressed
on the work so earnestly that he appropriated to it a tenth
of his entire substance in gold, silver, cattle, and all other
possessions. From the windows of his new palace he
could see the progress of the magnificent building rising
in the form of a cross, which was to become the pattern
for church building throughout the kingdom. Meanwhile
he caused the parish church of St. Margaret to be newly
built without the abbey church of Westminster, for the
ease and commodity of the monks, because before that time
the parish church stood within the old abbey church in
the south aisle, somewhat to their annoyance. Thus the
spiritual meditations of the monks would not be broken in
upon by parochial duties or secular care.

North of it was the Sanctuary, which afforded a refuge
to those who were guilty of capital felonies, and this right
was retained by Westminster for several centuries.

Edward the Confessor was granted the privilege of seeing
his abbey church completed, but on Christmas Eve, 1065,
only a few days before St. Peter's was to be consecrated,
he was taken grievously ill, and tradition says that while
from every corner of the land came bishops and nobles to
attend the ceremony on Holy Innocents' Day, 28th December, its artificer lay dying in the room which, almost entirely
reconstructed and lavishly decorated by Henry the Third,
was to become known as the Painted Chamber. Here
Edward the Confessor was watched over by his Queen
Editha, and his unfortunate successor, Harold.

Already, however, he had granted to the monks a new
charter in which he recited the account of St. Peter's consecration, the ravages of the Danes, and the motives which
had prompted him to restore the sacred edifice to its former
splendour. From his sick-bed he listened to the great
throngs of people passing between the new palace and the

new abbey church and he dispatched Editha, his queen, to take his place at the consecration. During the first days of January 1066, a year that was to be amongst the most important in the history of our nation, he died, and in due course was laid in the rich tomb which is to-day the jewel of the abbey, venerated by countless generations.

Before the end of January, Harold was crowned in the abbey church whose stones shone bright and new, but when the bells next pealed for Christmas morning, that Duke William of Normandy, who had been so lavishly entertained by Edward the Confessor in the adjoining palace, came riding through the streets of London to be crowned King of England. Rows of soldiers, horse and foot, lined the approaches to the glittering new Westminster as William, now the Conqueror, attended by 260 of his nobles, clattered into view. At the opening of the ceremony one of William's prelates, Geoffrey, Bishop of Coutances, asked the Normans, in the French language, if they were of the opinion that their chief should take the title of King of England; and then the Archbishop of York asked the English if they would have William the Norman for their king. The shouts and cheers were so loud that the Norman cavalry without the abbey feared a revolt and began to set fire to the adjoining houses—whereupon the ceremony ended in some confusion. But this momentous coronation not only started a dynasty but established the precedent for our sovereigns being crowned at Westminster.

William the Conqueror, according to Stow, found Westminster Palace far inferior to princely palaces in France, and though it was new, added considerably to it. In 1085 we find him holding his court there at Whitsuntide, on which occasion he received the homage of his subjects, and knighted his youngest son, afterwards Henry the First. The law courts were held in the palace and the law students probably resided in the King's Court, but this appears to have annoyed the Conqueror's son William Rufus, who built the Great Hall in 1097. Three years later he, in turn, kept the Whitsuntide festivities very magnificently, using the hall he had just built. By this time the palace had become a very imposing edifice, and according to the monk Fitzstephen the palace was connected with the City by suburbs, and the bishops, abbots, and noblemen lived in beautiful houses, where they maintained magnificent establishments. Near the palace Londoners frequented a large cooking resort, at which dainties of every kind could be had.

Henry the Third, the successor of King John, made large additions to the palace. He had been crowned in the abbey when only ten years old, wearing on his head a plain circlet of gold because the crown had been lost by King John in the Wash. During his reign he organized great festivities at the palace, and on his marriage to Eleanor the ceremonials surpassed in splendour anything which up to that time had been seen in England.

In the fifth year of his reign the king began the new work of Our Lady's Chapel in the abbey, whereof he laid the first stone; and in the year 1245 the walls and steeple of the monastery church built by Edward the Confessor were taken down and, according to Stow, the abbey was enlarged and made more comely; and in order to pay for it, the king appointed a mart to be kept in Westminster.

A great part of the abbey as it now stands—the eastern part with the choir, to some distance beyond the transept, we owe to Henry the Third, though the work was not finished until after his death and though a serious fire, kindled in the lesser hall of the palace, spread to the abbey, doing considerable damage, in 1299. Henry the Third also caused the body of Edward the Confessor, that before lay at the side of the choir where the monks sang, to be removed with great solemnity and placed in a rich shrine at the back of the high altar. At the conclusion of the ceremony the king gave a magnificent banquet in his palace.

In this reign also we find the first assembling of the Commons.

The birth of a body of citizens and burgesses was the result of the king's need for money and his weakness in public affairs.

Parliaments of lay nobles aided by bishops and leading abbots of the monasteries were summoned from time to time by the Norman kings and sat in Westminster. They constituted, of course, a single body. Henry the Third had a Parliament to meet him at Westminster in 1225, and there Hubert de Burgh had asked for a grant to help the king tide over a financial crisis, but as the reign continued a scarcity of provisions had made things progressively worse, and the barons, who had formed a new confederacy, went to Westminster Hall in May 1258 in complete armour to attend another Parliament. When the king entered the hall there was a rattling of swords. His eye glanced timidly along the mailed ranks; and he asked: 'What means this? Am I a prisoner?' 'Not so,' answered Roger Bigod; 'but your foreign favourites and your own extravagences have involved this realm in great wretchedness; wherefore we demand that the powers of government be entrusted and made over to a committee of bishops and barons, that the same may root up abuses and exact good laws.' The king was obliged to accept the demands of the barons, and Parliament was dissolved, to meet again on the eleventh of the following month at Oxford. Here a committee of government was appointed, and it was enacted 'that four knights should be chosen by the votes of the freeholders of each country, to lay before the Parliament all breaches of law and justice that might occur; that a new sheriff should be annually chosen by the freeholders in each county; and that three sessions of Parliament should be held regularly every year.'

In 1264, at the instance of the Earl of Leicester (Simon de Montfort), writs of summons were issued for the first time on citizens and burgesses to attend a Parliament.

Though this was the only occasion during the reign of
Henry the Third when representatives of the people
gathered at Westminster, it formed a precedent and was
renewed under Edward the First. The assembly met in
January 1265 in the Great Hall, and the writs are still
in existence directing the sheriffs to elect and return
two knights for each county, two citizens for each city,
and two burgesses for every borough or burgh in the
country.

The two Houses, of course, sat together; and this appears
to have been the case until the reign of Edward the Third.
The first division of the Parliament into two Houses is then
marked by the fact that the House of Commons elected a
permanent Speaker, as at the present day. He was Sir
Thomas Hungerford, and he was elected in 1377. During
the latter part of the reign of Edward the Third, the
Commons held their debates in the Painted Chamber.
After this they assembled in the chapter-house of the
abbot of Westminster, where they continued to hold their
Parliaments till 1547, when the chapel of St. Stephen
in the Palace of Westminster was granted to them by
Edward the Sixth.

Another important innovation was made by Henry the
Third: the seats of justice, or courts of common law,
which before and after the Norman Conquest followed
the sovereign, were now made stationary, and appointed to
be held in Westminster Hall. Just before his marriage,
he sat in person in the King's Court, and later in the Court
of Exchequer. The law courts remained at Westminster
until 1882, when they were removed to the Strand.

The last of our kings who kept his court at Westminster
was Henry the Eighth. As a young and popular monarch,
accompanied by his first wife Catherine of Aragon, he had
gone in solemn procession to the abbey and to the palace,
on his accession to the throne. Londoners gave him an
enormous welcome. Westminster had now for centuries
been the seat of the royal palace, of the High Court

of Parliament, and of our legal tribunals; most of our sovereigns, since the Conquest, had been crowned and buried in the monastery of St. Peter.

For a short time the palace was the constant scene of masques and pageantry of every description, culminating in a truly magnificent tournament to celebrate the queen's delivery of a son—the king, on this occasion, riding forth on horseback from under a gorgeous pavilion of cloth of gold and purple velvet embroidered, powdered with fine gold.

Only a year later the palace was partially burnt, and though for a time Henry the Eighth appears to have used what was left of it, together with the grounds, he began to turn envious eyes on the princely possessions of Cardinal Wolsey.

There lay, just then, between the half-ruined Palace of Westminster and Charing Cross, on the bank of the river, the very magnificent York House, belonging to the see of York, in which Cardinal Wolsey, as Cardinal Archbishop of York, kept a state of splendour which rivalled, if it did not surpass, that of his royal master. Hubert de Burgh, Lord Chief Justice of England in the reign of Henry the Third, had a mansion on this site, having purchased it from the Dean and Chapter of Westminster, to whom it had been bequeathed. He left his house, about the year 1240, to the monastery of Black Friars, who sold it to Walter de Grey, Archbishop of York, who settled it not on his family, but on his successors in that see. Wolsey had undoubtedly increased its importance and beauty in the style of Hampton Court, and here Henry the Eighth first set eyes on Anne Boleyn, during a glittering masque presented by the cardinal.

Upon the fall of Wolsey, Henry the Eighth seized York House, upon which he was to build the palace of Whitehall, and two years later he built St. James's Palace on the site of an ancient leper hospital 'founded before the time of man's memory.'

From this period, therefore, the old palace of the Confessor ceased to be associated with the domestic history of the kings of England. Henry the Eighth, however, continued to take a close interest in Westminster. On 16th January 1538, the abbey of St. Peter was surrendered to him by Abbot Boston and twenty-four of the monks, and the monastery was dissolved. He converted it into a bishopric, with a dean and twelve prebendaries, and appointed the whole county of Middlesex, except Fulham, which was to remain with the bishopric of London, to be its diocese. Its new career was, however, to be short, for on the accession of Queen Mary the monastery was again restored to the order of St. Benedict, which was one of the most wealthy and learned in England before the Reformation, and did not again return to the status of a bishopric.

The fire of 1512 did not destroy by any means all the palace of Westminster. Most important of all to be saved was the Great Hall, or Westminster Hall, which William Rufus had intended to form part of a new palace, and which Richard the Second, patron of lovely things whatever his faults as king, had caused to be covered with the magnificent double hammer-beam roof, moulded and carved, which survived the shower of incendiary bombs. St. Stephen's Chapel, in which the Norman kings offered up their devotions, founded by King Stephen, but afterwards twice rebuilt, was also saved. Made in the purest style of Gothic architecture, the walls were covered with oil paintings of extreme beauty and the windows were gorgeously illuminated, but when this chapel was eventually converted into the House of Commons Chamber, its roof was concealed by a false ceiling and its mural decorations hidden by wainscoting. Beneath it was a wonderful crypt.

The celebrated Painted Chamber in which Edward the Confessor died was also saved. At the east end of this chamber was the ancient Parliament Chamber, beneath which was the vault, known as Guy Fawkes's Cellar, in which the

*C

conspirators in the Gunpowder Plot concealed the barrels of powder. Here, too, was to take place the memorable scene of the regicides affixing their signatures to the death-warrant of Charles the First.

In New Palace Yard stood the old building of the Exchequer and the ill-famed Star Chamber, a court of justice in the reigns of Henry the Seventh, Henry the Eighth, and Elizabeth. Every punishment, except death, was assumed to be within the power of the Star Chamber Court, and pillory, fine and imprisonment, whipping and letters seared in the face with hot irons, were ordinary punishments inflicted by this court.

Westminster Hall, therefore, continued after the palace fire to be the place adjacent to Parliament where the most important state trials took place, none more poignant than that of Charles the First, who was brought to judgment there. The king entered the hall under the guard of Colonel Hacker and thirty-two officers, and seated himself, covered, in a chair of velvet provided for him, and with a stern countenance surveyed the commissioners for the mock trial, amidst a total hush.

In the gatehouse built by Edward the Third at the end of what is now Tothill Street, Richard Lovelace, suffering imprisonment for his loyalty to his unfortunate master, composed one of the most beautiful songs in our language:

> Stone walls do not a prison make,
>   Nor iron bars a cage;
> Minds innocent and quiet take
>   That for an hermitage.

On the 8th May 1660, Charles the Second was proclaimed king at the gate of Westminster Hall. James the Second, after his coronation at the abbey with his consort, the beautiful Mary of Modena, partook of a most sumptuous and magnificent banquet in the hall, and so did William the Third and Queen Mary, Dymoke, the champion, making the customary challenge; Queen Anne and Prince

George of Denmark banqueted there, and two years later the grey walls were hung with trophies won by Marlborough at the battle of Blenheim. George the First and Second were crowned and feasted at Westminster, by which time the raising of the western towers of the abbey, begun by Sir Christopher Wren, had altogether changed the aspect of the edifice, though not quite in the way that Wren had expected—for he had planned to make as his principal feature a spire rising from the centre. If the Palace of Westminster was no longer a royal abode, the two Houses of Parliament had firmly established themselves there, and Edward the Confessor's church of St. Margaret, now twice rebuilt, was the scene where three times a year—on the anniversaries of King Charles's martyrdom, the Gunpowder Plot, and the Restoration of Charles the Second—the Speaker and the House of Commons attended to hear a sermon by the Speaker's chaplain.

The law courts were still at Westminster—no longer in the hall but in a building adjacent to it—when on 16th October 1834 a great fire destroyed the Palace of Westminster, all but the Great Hall and the crypt under St. Stephen's. Both Houses of Parliament were entirely burned down. 'There may be something ominous in such a catastrophe,' wrote a contemporary chronicler, 'at such a moment; the two contending bodies of the State, just arrayed in dire opposition to each other—the one insolent and overbearing in aggression, the other strict and obstinate in defence of its privileges—both buried in one common ruin!'

Great was the loss inflicted by this fire. The House of Lords was part of an ancient building known as the Court of Requests, and on the walls hung a tapestry representing the Spanish Armada, the gift of the States of Holland to Queen Elizabeth. The ancient Parliament Chamber, so often mentioned in the annals of the palace, had been destroyed earlier.

The House of Commons Chamber was originally the

chapel of St. Stephen, where the Norman kings had prayed. As a debating chamber it had echoed to the voices of Chatham, and Pitt, and Fox, and Burke, and Canning. The present St. Stephen's Hall occupies the same space as St. Stephen's Chapel of the ancient palace. Its beautiful crypt, or under-chapel, remains.

Between the House of Lords and the House of Commons was the Painted Chamber. This, also destroyed by the fire, was often used as a place of meeting for the Lords and Commons when they held a conference. When, earlier, the tapestry and wainscoting were taken down, the walls were found to be illuminated with ancient paintings which dated from at least 1322 and, amongst other subjects, depicted the canonization of the royal saint.

The Star Chamber had, since the suppression of the court which sat in it, been used as a depository for rubbish, and after the fire one side of it was found to be full of old 'tallies' used down to the end of the Georgian era, to keep the national accounts.

The new Palace of Westminster rose on the site of the old one. The first stone of the great modern Gothic structure was laid in April 1840 and the new House of Commons Chamber was first used in 1850, so that this magnificent room was only ninety years old when it was entirely destroyed during the great nocturnal raid of 10th May 1941.

This tremendous air attack, the final desperate fling in its series, the culmination of the battle which had lasted almost without interruption since 7th September 1940, had aimed, amongst its many objectives, to wipe out the historic glories of Westminster. Three hundred bombers had passed over the moonlit Thames in sickening waves. From the British Museum, from the Law Courts in the Strand— that other Gothic edifice opened with much pomp by Queen Victoria in 1882 when the courts had removed from the Palace of Westminster; from the War Office, from the Mint, from the Mansion House, from the Tower and from

Mayfair—that fair granted by Edward the First to raise revenue for the Leper Hospital in St. James's upon which Henry the Eighth was to build his fair palace—from all these places and many others, frantic calls had come for fire-fighting apparatus. Through it all, lit by distant flames, Big Ben was chiming the hours in the great clock tower 320 feet high, on the site of another erected by Edward the First when the palace was the home of our kings. All through these fateful weeks and months, the booming of Big Ben's nine strokes before the evening news bulletin carried a message that London was still there. It continued to strike the quarters while the Commons Chamber was being devoured by flames, and while all the streets between the Houses of Parliament and the abbey were filled with firemen's hoses, bringing water from the Thames. As had happened before in history—notably in 1299— the Palace of Westminster and the abbey church of St. Peter were burning at the same time, though the abbey was saved by divine providence. So also was the House of Lords Chamber. The bomb which crashed through its roof, piercing one of the front benches, buried itself harmlessly in the floor without exploding. Westminster Hall, the Great Hall of William Rufus the Norman, saved from the fire of 1512 which caused Henry the Eighth to forsake the palace, and saved from the fire of 1834 which had consumed the Painted Chamber, the Star Chamber, the Court of Requests, and St. Stephen's Chapel, was once again granted an extension of its life, so that we should picture more easily all the pomp and magnificence, all the joys and tragedies that had taken place within its grey and solemn walls since the Norman Conquest.

One of the bombs that fell on the Palace of Westminster was so powerful that it shook the shrine of Edward the Confessor in the abbey, and blew out all the windows of the chapel which Henry the Seventh had put up on the site of Henry the Third's Lady Chapel. A basket of incendiaries fell through the Lantern Tower upon which Sir

Christopher Wren had planned to build a noble spire, which, if it had existed, would have crashed in flames upon the oldest and most venerable part of the abbey.

Just as in the days of Edward the Third the Commons sought the hospitality of the Abbot of Westminster to assemble in the chapter-house, so, after the great nocturnal raid of 1941, this august body, without a chamber of its own, sought an episcopal roof within the abbey precincts. For a time it met in Church House, Westminster, a modern concrete and steel building used normally for church assemblies. Long before the destruction of the chamber, Mr. Winston Churchill had foreseen such a possibility and he insisted that everything should be made ready for a rapid move; that the House should indeed meet once or twice in Church House to accustom itself to new surroundings. Eventually the Commons were invited to use the chamber of the House of Lords, which had suffered no other damage than the loss of the stained-glass portraits of the kings and queens of England and the royal line of Scotland. The woolsack, where the Lord Chancellor sat as Speaker of the House of Lords, was removed and a temporary Speaker's chair placed at the opposite end of the chamber. The Lords sat in the king's robing room, where the king dons his robes of state before going to the House of Lords for the opening of Parliament. In order to equip it for its new function, two state chairs and a replica of the wool-sack were placed in their appropriate positions as well as three tiers of benches upholstered in red. Opaque glass replaced the stained windows.

Though part of the roof and rafters of Westminster Hall were destroyed, this venerable building has suffered too often from such mishaps for it not to emerge triumphantly from the ordeal.

When, the following Christmas Eve, Big Ben boomed midnight, the stone pillars of the abbey echoed, by the dim light of candles, to the solemn chanting of high offices. Not since monastic times had there been such a sight as this, necessitated on this occasion by the black-out. The service was held in the nave, and the communion table was in front of the rood screen above which is the organ loft.

The seats stretching right back to within a few feet of the grave of the Unknown Warrior were already filled. One sensed this by the fact that a few people were standing behind the last row of chairs. It was too dark to see anything clearly, for the only illumination came from two candles on the Communion table and two others in high candlesticks standing a short distance in front. Four flickering candles to light the whole nave with its delicate stone pillars disappearing aloft to merge with the tenebrous vaulting of the roof. The solemnity of this medieval setting had descended on human figures whose dress it was impossible to distinguish as they moved silently to their places. Soon one's eyes, more accustomed to the darkness, were able to appreciate the magnificence of the scene. The stained glass windows below the triforium became visible in a blue haze, while aloft the clerestory windows, being uncoloured, let in shafts of filtered moonlight. A bitter wind blew past the pillars, coldest where it ran along the stone floor waving the heads of the poppies round the warrior's tomb, and there was a faint smell of straw from the Nativity scene illuminated by a night-light. Big Ben boomed midnight, and from Jericho Parlour came a procession led by the choir, followed by the Canons, and lastly the Dean wearing the gorgeous cape made for the coronation of the present king. As this procession, chanting moved nearer to the Communion table the warm orange candle light fell on the rich vestments.—*The Incredible City*.

Already plans were being prepared to set up a Battle of Britain chapel in that of Henry the Seventh, with a window to each of the fifty-four squadrons; thus adding greater glory to the one-time monastery of St. Peter's. The memorial was unveiled by the king on 10th July 1947. A hole through the stone-work under the fine window, in the north corner, was allowed to remain, filled in with a few square inches of plain glass. Mr. Winston Churchill, not sufficiently recovered from an operation to attend, was represented by Mrs. Churchill. She doubtless recalled her husband's glorious words: 'These young men going forth every morning to guard their native land and all that we stand for, holding in their hands these instruments of colossal and shattering power.'

Big Ben, a lurid but magnificent sight during the great raid, was struck by a small bomb which destroyed some of the ornamental iron-work, damaged the stone, and broke the glass in the south face.   As it continued to chime, it sang:

> Lord, through this hour,
>   Be Thou our guide,
> That by Thy power,
>   No foot shall slide.

THE PALACE OF WHITEHALL

THERE IS NO better fun than trying to reconstruct a lost city.

The great Palace of Whitehall has disappeared like Atlantis. It once stretched from the abbey church of Westminster, the old palace of the Confessor and the church of St. Margaret, to Charing Cross; and from the banks of the Thames to St. James's Park—a glorious city of rose-tinted Tudor brick, green lawns, and shining marble statues. The most picturesque monarchs in our history feasted there and attended gay tournaments.

Henry the Eighth, wearing his befeathered and be-jewelled velvet pancake hat, first came here when York House was still the abode of Cardinal Wolsey, who gave the beautiful masque in his honour in the course of which the king first set eyes on Anne Boleyn, with whom he fell in love. Soon the cardinal was obliged to cede Hampton Court to his monarch, and immediately after Wolsey's death on his way to take trial for high treason in 1530, the king seized York House from the see of York and began to turn it into all the splendour of what was to be Whitehall Palace.

Henry the Eighth, inspired by Wolsey's passion for building, was determined to surpass him. He laid the foundations of St. James's Palace, and in order to join his new Palace of Whitehall with St. James's, situated in the sweet country air just south of the 'way to Readinge,' despoiled the Abbot of Westminster, whom he had not yet thought of turning out, of all the land west of the road leading from Charing Cross to Westminster. This land included what is now St. James's Park, which was to serve indifferently to the Palace of St. James and Whitehall.

As soon as the king took possession of York House he

began to plan and to build. He extended York House and built a waterside gallery overhanging the Thames, which was then much wider than it is now, with the result that his gallery was west of where the trams now run along the Embankment.

He added to the grounds of the see of York, making orchards and smooth bowling greens, and between the palace and the road from Charing Cross to the abbey he made a privy garden with a low wall against the road.

The king then turned his attention to the ground between the road and St. James's Park, on which he built a tilt-yard where the Horse Guards now stand, a cockpit, near the garden of what is now No. 10 Downing Street, and a tennis court behind the present Treasury buildings. He also put up some pretty red-brick houses for his courtiers, and in order to connect the two portions of his palace, he built two superb gates athwart the public road—one called the Cockpit Gate, where the Haig statue now faces porticoed Dover House, and the other called the King Street Gate, more or less where the Cenotaph stands.

The part of the road between the two gates became known as The Streete.

The Streete was very narrow and countrified, and one can imagine how pretty it must have looked with the gardens of his palace to the left as one went towards the abbey, and with the little red houses round the cockpit and the covered tennis court on the right.

The Cockpit Gate had an overhead passage in which the nobility could stand or sit, and behold from the windows the joustings and other military exercises taking place in the tilt-yard. Under the gate passed the rumbling traffic between the City and Westminster, and Henry the Eighth, offended by the number of funerals which passed between the two portions of his palace on their way from Charing Cross to the church of St. Margaret, erected a new cemetery on the other side of Whitehall in the new parish of

St. Martin-in-the-Fields. The parish of St. Martin-in-the-Fields was carved out of the old parish of St. Margaret, Westminster.

Never had there been such a pretty gate as the Cockpit Gate. There was a family likeness between it and the gateway of St. James's Palace, which was then rising so rapidly. Indeed, like Aeneas, Henry the Eighth could watch a new city rising before his eyes.

The Cockpit Gate and the King's Gate were built the same year—in 1532. The King's Gate made the connecting link between The Streete and King Street, a busy, built-up, narrow, cobbled thoroughfare, bordered at the abbey end by the courtyard of the Antelope Inn which had existed since 1443, and by the 'Blue Boare.'

While the gardeners were laying out the lawns and pruning the trees, while architects were planning the fountains and the bricklayers putting up the lovely extensions of the palace, Henry made love to Anne Boleyn, whom he married here at midnight on 25th January 1533, with a magnificence that had nothing to suggest her cruel end. In July he took her to Hampton Court.

Some years earlier, towards the end of 1526, the king had made the acquaintance of Holbein the younger, when the great painter had come from Basle to stay with Sir Thomas More, who was then in high favour with the king. Holbein brought with him a letter of introduction from Erasmus, who has left us a description of More's Chelsea residence, where the king first saw Holbein's paintings displayed on the walls.

More [writes Erasmus] has built near London, upon the Thames, a modest yet commodious mansion. There he lives surrounded by his numerous family, including his wife, his son and his son's wife, his three daughters and their husbands, with eleven grandchildren. There is not any man living so affectionate to his children as he, and he loveth his old wife as if she were a girl of fifteen. In More's house you would see that Plato's Academy has revived again, only whereas in the Academy, the discussions turned about geometry and the power of numbers, the house at Chelsea is a veritable school of Christian religion.

Very soon after Holbein had met the king at More's house at Chelsea he returned to Basle, and almost as quickly More fell out of favour. He was executed on 7th July 1535, and his head fixed on London Bridge.

For a short time Anne Boleyn returned to enjoy the delights of the Palace of Whitehall. The new city was now a paradise. Hentzner, who saw Whitehall, though somewhat later, yet gives us a picture of what it must already have looked like:

The Palace is truly Royal; enclosed on one side by the Thames, on the other by the Park which connects it with St. James's, another Royal Palace. Near are seen an immense number of swans who wander up and down the river for some miles in great security. In the park is great plenty of deer. In a garden adjoining the Palace is a *jet d'eau* which, while strangers are looking at it, a quantity of water forced by a wheel, which the gardener turns at a distance, through a number of little pipes, plentifully sprinkles those that are standing round.

Holbein returned to London in 1536, by which time the unhappy Anne Boleyn was being condemned to death by her wife-slaying monarch, who was turning his eyes towards Jane Seymour.

Holbein was lodged at Whitehall, and it is supposed that he occupied apartments in the Cockpit Gate because that gate has become so much associated with his name that a great number of historians suggest he was the builder of it, which cannot be the case. Nevertheless the gateway is now currently called the Holbein Gateway.

The lovely gate was constructed of small square stones and knapped flint, the two distinct colours—the white stone and the shining black of the flints—giving a chess-board effect. On either side of the archway were lofty embattled octagonal turrets.

Holbein painted a portrait of Jane Seymour in state, and executed many other beautiful pictures.

If Holbein's lodgings in the Cockpit Gate faced Charing Cross, he would have looked out on what was more of a square than a street. It was called The Green. To the west was the tilt-yard; to the east possibly a banqueting hall on the site of the present one, and the great gates of the palace. The entrance to the palace was in the form of a Tudor gateway, not unlike but less ornate than the Cockpit Gateway in which he lived, which ran due east athwart the street and thence, under the name of the Privy Gallery, joined up with the Waterside Apartments in which the king had his royal rooms.

The Green, in the direction of Charing Cross, narrowed considerably, and Holbein could probably see the cross from his windows.

When Henry the Eighth first arrived at Whitehall he found the cardinal's mansion at York Place facing the water, as was the custom, because the Thames was still the highway for traffic. Between the Green and this mansion there would already have been a garden and a courtyard. The mansion was decidedly princely. Was it not said by contemporaries that the banquets given by the Cardinal Archbishop of York were far more sumptuous than those of Cleopatra and Caligula? In the course of excavations made in 1938–9 by the ancient monuments branch of the Office of Works, the foundations of the Cardinal's Great Hall built by Thomas Rotherham (1480–1500), a former archbishop; the medieval chapel built just after the occupancy of Hubert de Burgh; a suite of apartments leading south of the Great Hall; an extraordinary undercroft, afterwards Henry the Eighth's privy wine-cellar; and the river wall, were discovered in very perfect state. Complete records were made before the land was churned up by the bulldozer.

As Henry the Eighth's views were even more sumptuous than those of the cardinal, he went on building.

He started by reclaiming the foreshore of the Thames to a depth of about 100 feet at its greatest, and to an ultimate length of 550 feet. Upon this he built his Waterside

Gallery, whose windows overhung the placid Thames, dammed to some extent by the piers of Old London Bridge.

He then built the Privy Gallery running up from the Waterside Gallery, past the Privy Gardens, to the Cockpit Gate which was athwart The Streete, and went even beyond it to the stairs leading down to St. James's Park.

Of the Waterside Gallery little was discovered except the river wall of fine ashlar (wrought stone); of the Privy Gallery, the huge hard chalk foundations of the eastern end were found in good condition. The chief interest of these discoveries was that they were the first confirmation of the ground plans engraved in 1747 by Vertue.

The king then built the Stone Gallery more or less parallel to the Waterside Gallery but nearer the garden, and in between these two galleries he built suites of apartments surrounding courtyards. It is reasonably certain that Holbein painted in rich plaster the ceilings of the Stone Gallery.

The western windows of this Stone Gallery looked across the Privy Gardens full of straight walks, clipped box, and patterned beds, to the low wall bounding The Streete.

While all this was going on, Henry the Eighth reorientated the medieval chapel of York Place to accommodate the court; and in 1938–9 the foundations of this chapel were found for the first time, as well as many of the superb medieval floor-tiles now in store, but the excavation came to a stop because the foundations continued under the roadway of Horse Guards Avenue.

The offices of the royal household lay beyond the courtyard entrance of York Place, and stretched right up to what is now Craig's Court, which is practically at Charing Cross.

Henry the Eighth built for his little son, the future Edward the Sixth, a magnificent block known as the Prince's Lodgings. They were at the extreme south end of the Water Gallery. This block was three storeys high, whereas the Water Gallery, in the time of Henry the Eighth, was one storey with a terrace roof. The king's three

children—the future Edward the Sixth, the future Queen
Mary, and the future Queen Elizabeth—doubtless played
in the Privy Garden, but each of these royal children had
a private establishment, and whereas Edward the Sixth, as
a child, had these apartments, in Whitehall (as well as at
Hampton Court), the future queens were not always in the
good graces of their royal father.

Henry the Eighth died at Whitehall while he was still
building and beautifying this superb palace. The chapel,
the cloister, the hall, and the king's chamber were hung
with black, and a fortnight later, on a cold February day,
the funeral procession, four miles long, started mournfully
for Windsor.

What a pretty picture Queen Elizabeth must have made
dancing to a fiddle in the Stone Gallery on a rainy day!
Masques were performed also at her command, and the
tilt-yard was her delight. Sometimes she would order
outdoor dancing, and at other times bear-baiting, but
most of all she loved the displays of her faithful and
devoted knight, Sir Henry Lee, who had made a vow to
present himself on 27th November of each year at the
tilt-yard. Finally, disabled by age, with much form and
in the true spirit of chivalry and romance, he armed the
new champion, the Earl of Cumberland, with his own
hands, in the presence of the queen. He then doffed his
armour at the foot of a pillar near Her Majesty's feet.

By the time James the First came to the throne the Tudor
buildings were probably not in perfect state of repair, but
chiefly they had gone out of fashion, the taste of the Stuarts
no longer being that of the Tudors.

The Streete was still pretty and countrified, as it was
within the precincts of the palace, but King Street, leading
from the King Street Gate to the abbey, was becoming
more and more of a narrow, dirty, hustling thoroughfare.

Nevertheless it must have been extremely picturesque,

and it was heavy with history. The old city of Westminster with its venerable abbey; the prison gatehouse built in the reign of Edward the Third; the Sanctuary with the church belonging to it which stood in the form of a cross and was of great antiquity; Westminster School where Ben Jonson had been a scholar; the Parliaments and the Law Courts over-flowed to some extent into King Street. The inn yards and the houses with their quaint signs made a strange con-trast with the well-paved road between the two royal gates, scented with the flowers from the Privy Garden.

In King Street during the reign of Elizabeth had lived the divine poet Edmund Spenser, who arrived there, ruined and broken-hearted, from Ireland, where his political oppo-nents had set fire to his house, in the flames of which an infant child, whom he had been compelled to leave behind, unhappily perished. According to Drummond of Haw-thornden, whose informant was Ben Jonson: 'The Irish, having robbed Spenser's goods, and burnt his house and a little child new born, he and his wife escaped, and after, he died for lack of bread in King Street, and refused twenty pieces sent to him by my Lord of Essex, and said, he was sorry he had no time to spend them.' 'Such,' comments Jesse, 'was the end of that great poet of whom Dryden said: "No man was ever born with a greater genius or had more knowledge to support it"—whom Thomson, the author of *The Seasons*, confessedly took as his model—whom Milton himself was not ashamed to confess as his original —by reading whom Cowley tells us that he was "made a poet"—and, lastly, whose *Fairy Queen* Pope tells us he had not only read "with a vast deal of delight" when he was only twelve years old, but read with no less pleasure after the lapse of nearly half a century.'

Anne of Denmark, James the First's queen, was given a separate establishment at Somerset House in the Strand, and Henry, Prince of Wales, was given St. James's Palace, though he did not occupy it until 1610. Whereupon he started to entertain in a more lavish way than his father, his household consisting of more than four hundred persons, amongst whom was Inigo Jones. The prince died at the age of nineteen at St. James's Palace, after which his brother, the future Charles the First, took up residence there.

Inigo Jones went to Italy to study architecture, but a few years later he was organizing masques for James the First at Whitehall and had become surveyor to the king. In 1619 the old banqueting hall of the palace was destroyed by fire, and Inigo Jones then drew up plans for its rebuilding.

A new scheme on a vast scale was also made to rebuild the palace completely, but the drawings that have survived were almost certainly made by Inigo Jones's nephew, John Webb, and may, or may not, have been taken seriously by Charles the First.

The palace was to have consisted of four fronts, each with an entrance between two towers. Within these there were to have been one large central court and five smaller ones. This great royal city would have eclipsed the Vatican, Versailles, and the Louvre, and Horace Walpole, speaking of it in later days, wrote: 'The intended Palace of Whitehall, if it had been carried out, would have been the most truly magnificent and beautiful fabric of any of the kind in Europe.'

This dream never materialized. We know that the design followed the lines of Inigo Jones's Banqueting House, which still stands opposite the Horse Guards, in our modern Whitehall, all that is left of the splendour of bygone days. Begun in 1619, it was finished within two years and is known as the Banqueting Hall because it was placed on the site of apartments that previously bore that name. The immense amount of money that any of the larger schemes would have cost was not available to Charles the First, and, even if seriously entertained, they were eventually dropped because of the Civil War.

Charles the First's reign is perhaps most intimately connected with Whitehall because he not only commissioned Rubens to paint the ceiling of Inigo Jones's Banqueting Hall, but he suffered his martyrdom on a scaffold erected in front of it.

Charles the First was at St. James's Palace on the morning of his execution. Colonel Hacker, having knocked at the door of the king's room, told him that it was time to depart. Charles took Bishop Juxon by the hand, and bidding his faithful attendant Herbert to bring with him his silver clock, intimated to Hacker, with a cheerful contenance, that he was ready to accompany him. On each side of the king marched a line of soldiers, while before him and behind him were a guard of halberdiers, their drums beating and colours flying. On his right hand was Bishop Juxon, and on his left hand Colonel Tomlinson, both bareheaded.

The procession passed through St. James's Park and entered Whitehall by the stairs up to the Privy Gallery, and passing over the Holbein Gate, went along the gallery to his bed-chamber in the palace overlooking the river, where he remained until summoned to the scaffold erected in front of the two windows of the Banqueting Hall nearest Charing Cross. As the windows had been filled up with masonry a hole was knocked through the wall to give access to it by planks. Charles gave his hat and cloak to Bishop Juxon, and having prayed, walked round the scaffold. In front of him he would have seen the tiltyard, to his left the Holbein Gate, and to his right, where the Admiralty now stands, Wallingford House, on the roof of which Archbishop Usher was lifting up his eyes to heaven. Then the king held out his hands to his people, and pulling off his doublet, kneeled down to the block.

Cromwell entertained the House of Commons to dinner in the Banqueting Hall on two occasions, and died at Whitehall. Charles the Second, on his restoration in 1660, arrived at Whitehall by way of the Strand, and very gay was the court there, and the grounds of St. James's Park, where the monarch exercised his dogs and fed his ducks. Evelyn has told us of the luxury and profaneness, the gaming and dissoluteness of the last days of Charles the Second's reign:

> The king sitting and toying with his concubines, Portsmouth, Cleaveland, and Mazarine, etc.; a French boy singing love songs in that glorious gallery; whilst about twenty of the great courtiers and other dissolute persons were at basset round a large table, a bank of at least £2,000 in gold before them.

But on the morning of his death, according to Macaulay, the light began to peep through the windows of White-hall, and Charles desired the attendants to pull aside the curtains, that he might have one more look at the day.

> He remarked that it was time to wind up a clock which stood near his bed. . . . He apologized to those who had stood round him all night for the trouble which he had caused. He had been, he said, a most unconscionable time dying, but he hoped they would excuse it. This was the last glimpse of that exquisite urbanity so often potent to charm away the resentment of a justly incensed nation.

At the time of James the Second's abdication the palace was in process of complete reconstruction under the guidance of Wren. These alterations obliterated the Henry the Eighth Privy Gallery range, and were to have extended to the river front. William and Mary came to Whitehall on their accession, but the king disliked the place, believing that it increased his asthma, and he acquired Kensington Palace, with which he is chiefly associated. Not only did he desert Whitehall—a Dutch laundress in 1698 was responsible for its end, destroying both the Tudor remains and what James the Second had started to build. The laundress had lighted a charcoal fire and placed some linen round it. The linen caught fire and blazed furiously. The tapestry, the bedding, the wainscots were soon ablaze and the woman herself perished. According to the *Post Man* of the time:

On Thursday between three and four in the afternoon, a dreadful fire broke out at White Hall, which soon reduced the noble palace to ruinous heaps and before twelve at night had consumed the king and queen's apartments, the Standing Wardrobe, with all the old and new buildings of the Palace to the Waterside. At about two yesterday morning, the fire broke out in the Guard Chamber, with such vehemence, that the Banqueting House was judged to be in danger, and most of the low gallery between there was blown up to secure it.

The fire left Whitehall in such a ruined state that from that time it ceased to be a royal residence. King William, from Kensington, had sent message after message to save the Banqueting Hall, but though the Banqueting Hall and the two old gates at each end of The Streete were saved, Whitehall suffered nearly as much by subsequent neglect as by the fire. Buildings near the cockpit were allowed to decay; and the Holbein Gate and the King Street Gate were pulled down during the reign of George the Second, the superb materials of the Holbein Gate being sold to repair the high roads.

MODERN WHITEHALL

TO-DAY one wide avenue leads from Trafalgar Square to Parliament Square.

Most Londoners are content to call the entire length of it Whitehall, but in reality it is only Whitehall to a few yards beyond the Cenotaph, whereafter it becomes Parliament Street; and until 1931 the part from Trafalgar Square to the Horse Guards was known as Charing Cross. In olden days it formed the Green, with the Banqueting Hall and the Palace Gate to the east, the tilt-yard to the west, and the Privy Gallery and the Holbein Gate to the south.

From here to just beyond Downing Street, Whitehall follows The Streete, beginning at the Holbein Gate and ending at the King's Street Gate. This is where Parliament Street begins, parallel but slightly east of the ancient King Street which was demolished to make way for the Foreign Office block and the Home Office block.

As you go up Whitehall from Trafalgar Square you will find Inigo Jones's Banqueting Hall on your left, opposite the Horse Guards. The Banqueting Hall was not at all damaged by the Battle of London. It looks almost like a modern building, and far more people stop to look at the Horse Guards, with the clock tower and the 1753 archway leading through to the parade ground in St. James's Park.

You may, however, visit the Banqueting Hall for a shilling, for it has become the Royal United Service Institution, and under the roof which Rubens painted (cut away and hidden safely during the air raids) are military trophies which red-coated Chelsea pensioners explain to soldiers from overseas and little boys. Behind the Banqueting Hall, towards the river, is the waste ground where already, before the war, the bulldozer was at work preparing the erection of modern government buildings. Twelve big houses, formerly owned by the nobility, but latterly used as temporary government offices, had been pulled down between 1937 and 1939, the most interesting of them being Cromwell House, built above the privy cellars of York Palace. There was a doorway with spandrels bearing the ancient arms of the see of York impaling Wolsey.

Three successive embankment walls were found before and during the war in perfect state—one wall built before Wolsey's time, one during Wolsey's occupancy, and one made by Henry the Eighth. Each wall was a little nearer the present embankment. Henry the Eighth's river wall ran past the east of Montague House.

Continuing your walk along Whitehall, pause for a moment after the Banqueting Hall and the Horse Guards (the tilt-yard) and imagine that in the old days you would have been obliged to pass under the Holbein Gateway, leading into The Street, with the gardens of the palace on your left and the cockpit buildings and tennis courts on your right, where now stands the Treasury with its façade built first by Sir John Soane (1824-8) and then by Sir Charles Barry (1846–7). These two architects built the present Treasury façade in two parts on either side of the old passage leading from The Streete to the cockpit, which was slightly to the east of the garden of No. 10 Downing Street. The original passage still exists though it is not a public thoroughfare, and you enter it through the door of the Treasury marked 'Privy Council Office.' It is a kind of lower storey to the main modern corridor leading from Whitehall to the Treasury, and the walls are of brick, with stone dressings.

The Soane-Barry façade of the Treasury in Whitehall is to-day much pockmarked and scarred by bomb damage. At a few minutes after ten on the night of 9th February

1944, a policeman on duty in Downing Street walked past the wartime barricade cutting off this street from Whitehall, and reported for duty to another policeman near the Foreign Office. The spring raids had begun and bombs were falling. Suddenly the two policemen heard a bomb screeching in their direction, and, running to a steel shelter, they stood back to back to prevent themselves from being blown over. The bomb fell in the middle of Whitehall, facing the Treasury, and they quickly ran out to inspect the damage. They found that the explosion had decapitated a young woman whose body lay on the pavement, but of whose head there was no sign. Search was made for it all through the night, but it was only late the next morning that it was discovered—on the *roof* of the Treasury building, severed as with a knife, blown up five storeys from the street, and turned towards the spot where Charles the First's scaffold had been erected three centuries earlier!

After Downing Street had been reopened to the public, the senior of these two policemen took me to the back of the Treasury, where a plane-tree grows between the Privy Council Room and the side of No. 10, shading the ivy-covered passage which leads into Horse Guards Parade. This passage was built by Kent under *his* Treasury building which he put up in 1733, and which is at right angles to the one in Whitehall. The Kent passage must not be confused with the Tudor one leading from The Streete, but curiously enough it begins more or less where the other one ends—that is to say on the site of the cockpit.

You might think that the Treasury building made by Kent in 1733, which faces Horse Guards Parade and has all sorts of crowns and monograms carved on the outside, was the oldest part of the Treasury, but in fact, though Soane and Barry occupied themselves with making modern façades to their building in Whitehall, they were less particular about modernizing the back, which incorporated much more of the Tudor apartments than even the Office of Works believed, until the war. Though Whitehall Palace proper was on the other side of The Streete, there were apartments round the cockpit and the tennis courts for courtiers and ladies-in-waiting, and traces of these are continually coming to light, as, for instance, when an air-raid shelter was dug at the south end of the Treasury, revealing a fine Tudor doorway.

These apartments on the St. James's Park side had been little damaged by the fire. They were known as the Cockpit Lodgings, and Cromwell had rooms here before the execution of Charles the First. After becoming Protector he moved to state apartments on the other side of the road. Shortly before the restoration of Charles the Second, Cockpit apartments were assigned by Parliament to General George Monck, Duke of Albemarle, and later to George Villiers, second Duke of Buckingham.

The first official statement of the Treasury moving there after the fire is an entry in the records of the Office of Works:

His Majesty [William the Third] having given command for the immediate fitting up the Vollary Lodgings at Whitehall for himself, the Cockpitt lodging for the Treasury Secretary's Office, Privy Council and Council of Trade, besides an apartment for himself there, and that some of the ruined offices should be repaired for the Board of Greencloth, and that the ground should be enclosed, and ruins that seemed dangerous, taken down.

It would appear that the Treasury moved into a building just north of the Cockpit Passage, the door of the present Treasury in Whitehall marked Privy Council Office. It was a brick, one-storey battlemented structure, which was later divided by floors into three storeys. Mr. Spiers, in the *Gentlemen's Magazine* for 1816, suggested that it was actually the covered tennis court built by Henry the Eighth, and he inferred this from certain records connecting the building called the Duke of Monmouth's lodgings with the old tennis court, and that it had been divided into three floors for the duke's use.

This, then, in spite of the Soane - Barry façade on

Whitehall, was admitted even before the war to be the oldest part of the Treasury.

The policeman who was talking to me under the plane-tree between the back of the Treasury and the side of No. 10 Downing Street, recalled the stick of five bombs which straddled Downing Street before Christmas 1940. The last of these bombs entirely destroyed a portion of the Treasury behind the Whitehall façade, and the damage was then cleaned up and the site used for storing coke. But the curious thing was that, whereas one might have expected the bomb to have made the doll's-house effect which generally happens when a building is sliced in half, it uncovered a beautiful rose-tinted wall which the experts quickly identified as one belonging to Henry the Eighth's tennis court, and this was one of the very few occasions when enemy action actually made a priceless discovery! Mr. Spiers had been proved right.

The destruction of the Treasury building which revealed this lovely wall cost a number of lives, and digging was made very difficult by the mass of masonry. The rescue work was watched from windows of his official residence by one of the greatest captains of all time, whose name will add new splendour to this historic ground. Winston Churchill, while directing the Battle of London, repeatedly called for quicker action in clearing the debris to rescue those trapped beneath these Treasury bricks. The policeman, who had seen him at that time pause here to give his order, spoke in the hushed voice of a man who had witnessed a scene even more inspiring than Henry the Eighth watching the bricklayers build his tennis court. This modest London bobby had seen great events in his day, for he had been on duty on this spot since the First World War was declared in 1914, and there was no need to remind him of the pictures which Downing Street had superimposed on those of Stuart and Tudor times.

He led me through the passage under Kent's Treasury building, and when in the Horse Guards Parade, pointed

D

to the door in the garden wall of No. 10 with the warm red roof of the Prime Minister's house caught by the sunshine. 'He used to pass through this door, his cigar in his mouth,' said the policeman, 'and, during the Battle of Britain, madam, he would bid me good evening.'

Yes, through that same door used by Sir Robert Walpole, Lord North, William Pitt, Lord Grey, represented by R. B. Haydon pondering by his fireside after a great debate on the Reform Bill, and, in the last war by Lloyd George, now slumbering amongst his native Welsh hills.

The King's Gate, standing at the southern end of The Streete, was a few yards beyond the Cenotaph where to-day Whitehall merges into Parliament Street. But it was slightly nearer to St. James's Park, for in the days of Whitehall Palace the land on which Parliament Street has been cut was part of the palace gardens and the bowling greens. King Street disappeared to make those two tremendous islands of government buildings—the Foreign Office and the Home Office, and, beyond Charles Street, the Ministry of Health and the Board of Trade.

Parliament Street was created after the burning of Whitehall Palace to provide a wider street to Westminster Abbey. It displaced the terraces, the sun-dials, and the statues about 1732. The narrow, muddy, and ill-paved King Street, to which it ran parallel, was superseded but not abolished. Not until 1868 was the first part of this ancient highway between the Court of Whitehall and Westminster Abbey effaced to make way for the new Foreign Office, Home Office, Colonial Office, and India Office. The remaining part of King Street, between Charles Street and Great George Street, was wiped out in 1898 when the second and larger government block was built to house the Board of Trade, the Ministry of Health, and the Education Department. The portion of this immense island site facing Parliament Street was completed by 1907, and the extension to St. James's Park in 1915.

The two modern piles, one in the Italian style and the

other in the Renaissance style, are magnificent successors
to the glory of Whitehall, and to appreciate their beauty
one needs to see them from St. James's Park as the sun
sets on a winter's evening. Together with the Horse
Guards Parade and the War Office buildings in the rear,
they form across the lake, framed by the trees, a sparkling
city of white domes and towers which is oriental in
splendour. Though Whitehall has changed, and will change
still more as soon as the new government buildings go up
by the water-side where the ancient palace stood, it is no
less beautiful than Inigo Jones's fabulous dream of which
only the Banqueting Hall remains. Rich and proud history
has been added to it. The Great George Street–St. James's
Park end of Renaissance island site became the War Cabinet
offices, and Mr. Winston Churchill had an office there
whose windows overlooked the old elms and Duck Island
where Charles the Second fed his pelicans. Though we
pull down our old buildings, we hold jealously to our
traditions.

*B*ehind us are the Cenotaph and Big Ben.   We are looking towards Trafalgar Square.   Modern Whitehall faithfully follows The Streete, a narrow thoroughfare surmounted by the Holbein Gate which divided the grounds of the ancient palace.

To the left is Downing Street, and beyond is the Treasury, scarred by high explosives but now refaced and, when this picture was painted, bright with geraniums in window-boxes.   During the February–March raids of 1944, a human head was cut off in Whitehall and hurled to the top of the Treasury building, where it was discovered by a policeman.   At almost the same time a wall of Henry the Eighth's tennis court was brought to light.

To the right, distantly, is Inigo Jones's Banqueting Hall, now a museum, outside which Charles the First was beheaded.

BUCKINGHAM PALACE

VICTORIANS used to say that Buckingham Palace was solid and comfortable, but that with the exception of St. James's Palace, it was the ugliest royal residence in Europe.

It is very difficult to judge the effectiveness of a famous landmark. Horace Walpole wrote some unkind words about the portico which Inigo Jones put up at the back of St. Paul's, Covent Garden, but to the Londoners of to-day that portico is as picturesque as what is left of the Piazza. George the Second pulled down the magnificent Holbein Gateway, rich in association with our kings since the days of Henry the Eighth, to widen the approaches to Westminster, and the glazed bricks were sold to repair the high roads. Think what tears we could have shed if St. James's Palace, the most glorious structure in the West End, had been demolished, as it nearly was, during the spring raids of 1944! Who would wish to pull it down to repair the Great West Road?

Let us not, therefore, pass any hasty judgment on Buckingham Palace.

The night that Londoners celebrated the end of the war with Germany—that May evening in 1945—Buckingham Palace was floodlit in a rosy hue and the king and queen and the princesses came out on the balcony to wave to the crowds, and possibly there had never been a more lovely picture in the history of our land. No other country could have staged such a scene because, to begin with, there was no other king in a combatant country.

By that time, of course, Buckingham Palace had its honourable scars.

The former pilot of the London-Berlin air service who, having donned Luftwaffe uniform, dived through the clouds before lunch-time one Saturday morning during the Battle of London to single out Buckingham Palace for attack, only helped to increase our affection for the building and the family who lived in it. On moonlight nights, when one crossed the suspension bridge over the lake in St. James's Park the palace looked more beautiful than it had ever done, bathed in milky white, with the rich foliage and the ducks in the foreground.

Buckingham Palace stands on the mulberry garden which James the First planted to encourage the production of silk in England. Thousands of young trees were brought from the Continent, and in due course John Dryden ate mulberry tarts in St. James's Park. There is only one mulberry-tree to be seen there now; you will find it opposite Queen Anne's Gate—and the day the allies invaded Normandy the gardeners picked the fruit, as they pick it every year, to sell at market.

The house was first called Goring House, then Arlington House.

Such it was when Henry Jermyn was being granted his parcel of land opposite St. James's Palace. Just then there was an invasion of ants in London and the Great Plague was beginning. But the important thing about Arlington House is that during that year the Earl of Arlington brought over from Holland a pound of tea for which he paid sixty shillings (much less than it would cost in Paris just after the last war), and it is commonly believed that the first cup of tea to be made in England was drunk where Buckingham Palace now stands.

Arlington House was demolished in 1703, by which time the West End was beginning to take shape. Then it was that John Sheffield, Duke of Buckingham, built a mansion of red brick upon the site which he called Buckingham House, wherein he gave an annual dinner to his friends at which he proposed this toast: 'May as many of us as remain unhanged till next spring meet here again!'

During the first half of the eighteenth century St. James's Palace had its most splendid years, for the palace was not only the main royal residence but it overlooked and dominated the new St. James's Street, which turned itself into an aristocratic lounge where only the privileged classes were to be seen. The St. James's Coffee-House, which has become immortal from the frequent references to it in the *Spectator* and the *Tatler*, was at the corner of Pall Mall. Of it Addison wrote: 'I first of all called in at the St. James's, where I found the whole outward room in a buzz of politics.' Here Swift received his letters from Stella.

And so we think of the palace and the street as synonymous—Queen Anne, George the First, George the Second, White's Chocolate House which Steele described as the centre of pleasure, gallantry, and entertainment, the sumtuous equipages, the sedan chairs, the drawing-rooms of Queen Caroline, the memoirs of Lord Hervey, and White's with its low window which now stands at the top of the street, but which used to be at the bottom, in which days Gay in his *Trivia* sang:

> At White's the harness'd chairman idly stands
> And swings around his waist his tingling hands.

Two years after his accession, George the Third bought Buckingham House for £21,000 and moved there from St. James's Palace. With the exception of the future George the Fourth, all his children were born at the new residence, and St. James's Palace was merely used for court days and other official ceremonies, but by that time St. James's Street was too well established and too full of atmosphere for it to suffer.

Curiously enough, George the Third is more often associated with Kew Gardens than with Buckingham House, but it was here that Dr. Johnson used to visit

Mr. Barnard the librarian, and here that, one day in February 1767, he had the private conversation with His Majesty which is recorded by Boswell.

His Majesty having been informed of his occasional visits, was pleased to signify a desire that he should be told when Dr. Johnson came next to the library. Accordingly, the next time that Johnson did come, as soon as he was fairly engaged with a book, on which, while he sat by the fire, he seemed quite intent, Mr. Barnard stole round to the apartment where the king was, and, in obedience to his Majesty's commands, mentioned that Dr. Johnson was then in the library. His Majesty said he was at leisure, and would go to him; upon which Mr. Barnard took one of the candles that stood on the king's table, and lighted his Majesty through a suite of rooms, till they came into a private door into the library, of which his Majesty had the key. Being entered, Mr Barnard stepped forward hastily to Dr. Johnson, who was still in a profound study, and whispered him, 'Sir, here is the king.' Johnson started up, and stood still. His Majesty approached him, and at once was courteously easy.

If you wish to carry away one other picture of Buckingham House, consider that either here or at Kew Palace was always a brightly decorated tree at Christmas in the room of Queen Charlotte's German attendant.

You will probably recall also that George the Third, just before he went finally mad, built on the towing-path at Kew an enormous castellated edifice which was never finished and was pulled down by George the Fourth.

George the Fourth then commanded the building of the present Buckingham Palace from the designs of John Nash, whom we shall ever associate with Regent Street. The palace was not finished until 1847, and so Queen Victoria was the first sovereign to live in it. Should you frequent old print-shops you will probably find pictures of the palace with the Marble Arch standing in front of it, which fact puzzles many people. When it stood where you will now find Queen Victoria's statue, the royal banner was displayed to show that the queen was in residence, just as now you will see it flying above Buckingham Palace when the king is there. The Marble Arch went to its present site in 1851.

Between the wars Queen Mary, just before the Jubilee, was visiting a sick child in hospital and said to her:

'Where do you live?'

The little girl answered: 'Near Harrods, ma'am. And where do *you* live?'

'I live near Gorringe's,' answered the queen.

*D

PICCADILLY CIRCUS

PICCADILLY CIRCUS is the heart of the empire. Many of us still think of it as a link with the nineties, when Kipling was singing of steel ships and distant conquests, the Nile and the burning sand, and when the Piccadilly Circus fountain had just been put up to commemorate the philanthropic Lord Shaftesbury, whose avenue was new and glittering.

The Circus, not very round, full of awkward corners, had grown out of the cutting of Piccadilly at right angles seventy years earlier by Nash, to make that triumphal way for the great Prince Regent between Carlton House and Regent's Park. Then it was called Regent's Circus, Piccadilly.

But, in truth, all this had merely happened because of a meeting of ways as old as London itself, a tiny bit farther east—to be exact, where to-day Haymarket meets Coventry Street.

That part of London we now call the West End grew out of these cross-roads.

When in 1660 Charles the Second returned to England to take possession of his throne, London finished at Charing Cross, where the Royal Mews stood on the site of Trafalgar Square. On warm summer evenings the people of Charing Cross must have walked as far as the top of Haymarket to enjoy the country air. Our great arteries of to-day are built out of the country lanes of yesterday. Pall Mall led to the almost isolated St. James's Palace built by Henry the Eighth. The Haymarket meandered up to the 'way to Readinge,' the arterial road out to the west, muddy, dangerous, but in springtime sweet with the blossom of the orchards. In the ditches grew the little wild bugloss which Gerarde, the Master in Chirurgerie, writes about in his *Herbal*.

Sometimes one comes upon a copy of this delightful book in the sale-rooms. I had the pleasure of turning the pages of one the other day at Sotheby's. It was the edition of 1633. I found the famous reference to the bugloss in Chapter 283. Here it it as I copied it out in pencil:

THE PLACE

The little wilde Buglosse growes upon the drie ditch bankes about Pickadilla, and almost everywhere.

THE TIME

They floure from May, or June, even to the end of Sommer. The leaves perish in Winter, and new come up in the Spring.

THE VERTUES

The root mixed with oile cureth green wounds, and adding thereto a little barley, it is a remedie against Saint Anthonies fire. It causes sweat in the Agues, as Plinie saith, if the juice be mixed with a little *aqua vitae*, and the bodie rubbed therewith.

The cross-roads formed by the junction of Haymarket and the 'way to Readinge' had a name. They were known as Piccadilly.

This word Piccadilly was spelt in a dozen different ways, but let us understand distinctly that it was the cross-roads which bore this name, not any part of the 'way to Readinge.'

A few houses clung to these cross-roads. The most important of them had a pretty garden and a cowshed in a lane running north towards a windmill. The small domain had been known since the beginning of the century as Piccadilly Hall. It had been acquired in 1612 by one Robert Baker, who had become rich in the tailoring business. His domain was called Piccadilly Hall not, one may take it, from any choice of his own, but in allusion to his former trade and to the fortune he had made by selling the laced collars called pickadills, which were then much in fashion.

Soon it was applied to the locality as well as to the house.

He died in 1623 but his widow went on living there, and
from time to time even built additional houses for which
she got into trouble—because they were said to foul the
springs of water which served the Palace of Whitehall.
From her home she could see the windmill, and adjoining
her property were two taverns, one of them, the 'Feathers,'
and the other, the 'Crowne,' which consisted of a cellar
divided into a kitchen and a buttery and above which
were the drinking rooms.

After Piccadilly Hall, the most important building was
the gaming house at the north-east corner of the Haymarket. Established in the summer of 1635 under the
control of the Lord Chamberlain, the Earl of Pembroke,
this powerful court official appointed his barber to run it.
Simon Osbaldeston was the barber's name, and the establishment became known as Shaver's Hall, not because
Osbaldeston was a barber, but because my Lord Dunbar
lost £3,000 there at one sitting, 'whereon they said a
northern lord was shaved there.'

The bowling green was very famous, and one of its
earliest frequenters was Sir John Suckling, the poet, the
greatest gallant of his time and the greatest gamester. His
sisters were obliged to make a scene at the bowling green
to prevent him from gambling away their dowries.

There were balconies, tennis courts, a fine bowling alley,
and an orchard planted with the choicest fruit trees. There
was also a banqueting house, having a pleasant room known
as the Green Room.

In 1644 a certain Colonel Thomas Panton, having made
an enormous fortune out of gambling, decided never to
gamble again. Instead he thought he would speculate in
land, so he bought Shaver's Hall to build on.

In due course his proposals were shown to Christopher
Wren, the surveyor-general, who said that he was strongly
in favour of them because they would open up a new street
from the Haymarket to Leicester Fields.

Henry Coventry, Charles the Second's Secretary of State,

bought part of the property and lived there. When the new street was built, because it ran past Henry Coventry's house, it was called Coventry Street.

The Great Fire and the memory of the Plague caused a rush of wealthy people to the fresher air of the undeveloped west, which Charles the Second had generously begun to parcel out on either side of 'the way to Readinge.'

Then began a building boom which, within a matter of a lifetime, was to create all that delightful part of London which now runs from the Haymarket to Devonshire House —that gay, wealthy, fashionable chess-board of famous streets—Piccadilly (as it was soon to be called), St. James's Street, Jermyn Street, Ryder Street, Sackville Street, Bond Street, and so many others which seem to bask in the history of St. James's Palace, and to retain the lingering romance of the Augustan age with its wits, its clubs, its dandies, and sedan chairs.

Charles the Second had given nearly all the land south of 'the way to Readinge' to the great Henry Jermyn, Earl of St. Albans. Nearly everything north of the highway went to his Lord Chancellor, Edward Hyde, Earl of Clarendon.

The two men developed their land differently. Henry Jermyn built squares and streets—Jermyn Street, St. James's Square, and Ryder Street. Lord Chancellor Hyde built himself, between the present Bond Street and Dover Street, the most superb palace. He was about as near to royalty as it is possible for a commoner to be. He owned Worcester House (itself a palace), in the Strand, where his daughter Anne Hyde had been secretly married to the Duke of York, the future James the Second.

The Duke and Duchess of York were now resident at St. James's Palace, and the Lord Chancellor was one of those who believed the air in this part of London to be sweeter than in the Strand. His new palace was to be called Clarendon House, and while it was building he went to live at Berkshire House, which stood at the bottom of

St. James's Street, next to St. James's Palace, and was at
that time about the only other building of importance in
the neighbourhood. Afterwards, Charles the Second gave
it to his mistress, Lady Castlemaine, Duchess of Cleveland.

As the Lord Chancellor Hyde had more land than he
knew what to do with, even for so great a palace, he sold
a parcel west of his grounds to Lord Berkeley of Stratton,
a Royalist commander in the Civil War, who built himself
a mansion called Berkeley House, whose gardens were so
large that they extended to the present Berkeley Square.
To the east of Lord Clarendon's palace, Richard Boyle,
recently created Earl of Burlington for his part in promoting
the Restoration, was to have a mansion on the site of
which now stands Burlington House.

So you see that the north part of the 'way to Readinge,'
which by now we may call Piccadilly, was rich in palatial
mansions, whereas to the south of it there were more
streets, more houses, but all very pretty and full of character.

At any rate all the orchards and the bugloss in the ditches
were disappearing. What a lot of planning and building
and hammering there must have been from now onwards,
and while the new town was rising from the green fields
the giants of the Augustan age were being born.

Swift was born the year Jermyn Street was built, Addison
a few years later. The wits and poets whose names are
linked with these picturesque thoroughfares may be said to
have grown up with them.

Lord Clarendon's sudden fall from favour and the pulling
down of his mighty palace almost as soon as it was built is
a little sad. One feels sorry for him, as one sympathizes
with Wolsey when he lost Whitehall and Hampton Court,
and saw too late the fickleness of fortunes rapidly acquired.
Londoners, wearied by the plague, the fire, and an un-
successful war, were incensed against the Lord Chancellor
for his display of luxury. He was accused, probably un-
justly, of having accepted bribes from Louis the Sun King
for the sale to France of the city of Dunkirk, which Oliver

Cromwell had seized from the Spaniards. He had also gone into what we would call the black market to buy stones which had been intended for the repair of old St. Paul's Cathedral, and that was not a popular thing to do.

Almost as soon as Clarendon House was finished the Lord Chancellor was deprived of the Great Seal, and on 29th November 1667 was forced to fly the kingdom. Evelyn, the diarist, has left us a melancholy picture of the once powerful statesman on the eve of his departure: 'To visit the late Lord Chancellor. I found him in his garden at his new-built palace, sitting in his gowte wheel-chaire, and seeing the gates setting up towards the north and the fields. He looked and spake very disconsolately. . . . Next morning I heard he was gone.'

And here is how the same diarist, on 18th September 1683, describes the passing of the noble mansion: 'After dinner I walked to survey the sad demolition of Clarendon House, that costly and only sumptuous palace of the late Lord Chancellor Hyde, where I have often been so cheerful with him, and sometimes so sad.'

Sir Thomas Bond, of Peckham, and other speculators bought the site and built four new streets on it—Dover Street, Albermarle Street, Stafford Street, and Bond Street.

By now a church was needed for this part of the town, and it was decided to build one on the ground belonging to Henry Jermyn. Sir Christopher Wren, who was to rebuild St. Paul's Cathedral and so many famous City churches destroyed in the Great Fire, as well as to put up the two western towers of Westminster Abbey, accordingly built St. James's, Piccadilly, at a cost of £12,000, but before it was finished Charles the Second was dead, and his brother, James the Second, was on the throne.

The church was made to face Jermyn Street, which at that time was more aristocratic than Piccadilly. No altar anywhere in England was more handsomely adorned. And as this part of London became increasingly fashionable, the congregation of St. James's mirrored it. Johnny Gay was singing in his *Town Eclogue of the Tea Table*:

> Saint James's noon-day bell for prayers had toll'd,
> And coaches to the Patron's levee roll'd,
> When Doris rose.

Some years later a rather austere writer, after stating in his *History and Present State of the British Islands* that 'there is no church in town to which so many of the nobility and people of quality resort as this,' makes this statement: 'The ladies show surprising memories on this occasions, being able to relate at their return what cloathes every woman of figure had from head to foot, the fineness of the lace, and the colour of every ribbon worn in the assembly.'

The cross-roads at the top of Haymarket remained the important junction.

They were still so during the Napoleonic wars. We shall examine in the next chapter how Regent Street cut Piccadilly a hundred yards from its terminus, and then swept round to form the Quadrant, thus making a new and more important junction than the old one. Regent Circus, Piccadilly, was the name. Booking offices for coaches, and later for the first railways, were much in evidence. Now we come again to the nineties, when Piccadilly Circus really became the heart of the empire.

Shaftesbury Avenue was a new thoroughfare. The old Pavilion Music Hall had been pulled down and its successor built within six months. The whole of the circus had, in fact, been enlarged to make a fitting approach to the new arm stretching through Soho to the new Cambridge Circus.

Lord Shaftesbury, after whom the avenue was being named, had been a great philanthropist. Shortly after his death Alfred Gilbert, a young sculptor, perhaps the most brilliant this country has produced, for whom Rodin had immense admiration, was in the studio of Boehm, the queen's sculptor, when he was asked to make a statue of Lord Shaftesbury to stand in the Circus. He answered that he could not undertake a statue which was mostly frock-coat and trousers, but he would try to find something to symbolize Lord Shaftesbury's work. He went back to his own studio, and within four hours had fashioned an idea in clay which made the good Boehm exclaim: 'Gott in Himmel! Don't touch it! Don't touch it!'

When the model was finished it was cast in bronze. The night before the unveiling, 27th June 1893, Alfred Gilbert was dining at the Garrick Club with a merry and dignified gathering, who were all looking forward to seeing the Piccadilly Circus fountain the next day. Midnight came, one o'clock, two o'clock, and soon only Irving the actor, Toole the comedian, and Gilbert remained. Irving lived against Bond Street, and Toole, near to Gilbert, in Maida Vale. Just as dawn was breaking they decided to go to the Circus. Gilbert himself, in Isobel McAllister's admirable biography, has told how touching was that pilgrimage while a new day broke. The poor sculptor tried so hard not to show his nervousness; his friends were so sympathetically tactful. The suspicious workmen, guarding the fountain hidden all round by a canvas, would not let the three men in evening dress even peep at a corner.

Londoners were cruel to this great genius. They broke and stole the delicate drinking cups, wrenching them from the hand-made chains. The fountain was not finished because it would have cost too much. Gilbert was only paid half the money it had cost him, and it proved one of a series of disappointments which early in the century made him flee to Bruges.

Thus the nineties were as cruel as they were picturesque. The flower girls, in their shawls and straw boaters, began to sit round the fountain under coloured parasols, their wicker baskets full of blooms. Piccadilly Circus became splashed with colour—soldiers, Kipling's soldiers, in red tunics, hansom cabs, the second London Pavilion with its electric lighting, shoeblacks in red uniforms and pill-box hats, the Criterion Restaurant, the smartest place in town, where confidence men and flashily dressed crooks gathered at the Long Bar. The London Pavilion advertised its electricity, which then was so very new. The great Macdermott sang there. The butcher-boy and the messenger lad whistled his ditties, as an earlier generation of errand boys had sung one of his most famous songs during the Russo-Turkish war in 1878.

We don't want to fight, but by jingo if we do,
We've got the ships, we've got the men, we've got the money too.

The jubilee in 1887 had given new glory to the age.

The day I took my missus to the jubilee.

The empire was a mighty fact, and this was the heart of it.

Coventry Street led into Leicester Square, the home of the Alhambra, the Empire music-hall, and the naughty ladies. Both halls were famous for their promenades, which were done away with in 1914, thereby ending an era.

But in the nineties the promenade of the Empire was known as the best club in Europe. Empire builders back from the wilds of Africa were sure to meet their friends there, as well as the ladies they had dreamt of under the burning sun.

There was a barrier which divided the circle from the promenade. Winston Churchill, in his Sandhurst days, removed the barrier and burnt it publicly in the middle of Leicester Square.

When the theatres emptied, the patrons, including the naughty ladies, flocked to the night restaurants—the Globe in Coventry Street, which stood on the site of the future Café de Paris blown up by a bomb during the Battle of London. The Globe had private rooms where the Piccadilly Johnnies entertained the ladies of the Empire promenade. Others went to the Continental Hotel in Lower Regent Street, which was a respectable county hotel by day and a place of revelry and naughtiness by night. Yet

When Charles the Second returned to England in 1660 to take possession of his throne, the ground you are looking at was a small agglomeration of dwellings where four country roads met. Violets grew beneath its hedges and in the spring the air was sweet with apple blossom.

Because of a private house called Piccadilly Hall, the cross-roads were known as Piccadilly. The wide but muddy thoroughfare straight ahead was the 'way to Readinge.' The Haymarket led to Charing Cross and Windmill Lane to a real windmill.

The Piccadilly Circus of to-day took shape during the Napoleonic wars, when Nash planned Lower Regent Street and Regent Street to link up the palace of the great Prince Regent with Regent's Park. First it was known as Regent Circus, Piccadilly.

Piccadilly Circus came only gradually into the language. The jubilee of 1887 gave new glory to the age. The empire was a mighty fact, and Piccadilly Circus became the heart of it. Shaftesbury Avenue was built and the old Pavilion music-hall put up on its present site. Then came the little god whom Londoners of their own accord christened Eros.

Memories of the nineties still cling round Piccadilly Circus, but the last of the flower girls are disappearing. Why are they not replaced by sweet seventeens?

No bomb, during the Battle of London, fell on this beloved ground, which is the essence of London to us all.

others went to the St. James's Restaurant, which stood on the site of the present Piccadilly Hotel. It was the rendez-vous of sportsmen and crooks.

The Café Royal was attracting the gourmets, the artists, and bohemians. The ladies who had been unable to find some top-hatted aristocrat to take them out went into Regent Street. Four-wheelers ambled gently along, waiting for fares to St. John's Wood, where most of the girls lived. When St. John's Wood was rebuilt, the music-halls echoed with the ditty:

> What will the poor little birds do now?
> They 'll flap their wings and away they 'll go
> And fly to the wilds of Pimlico.

At the corner of Lower Regent Street, and facing the London Pavilion, stood, as it still stands, the Criterion Restaurant and Theatre.

This beautiful building, whose elegance is never quite appreciated, was put up in 1873 on the site of the White Bear Inn which, with its picturesque cobbled yard, had probably been there since the days of the Lord Chancellor Hyde. It had splendid beams, galleries open to the wind, fashioned windows of blown glass. The Criterion was designed to put under one roof an extremely large res-taurant, reading, billiard, hairdressing rooms, cigar divan, concert hall, ball-room, and theatre. Perhaps this is the best proof of the appeal which the circus was making at that time. The theatre opened on 21st March 1874 with *An American Lady*, by H. J. Byron, and *Topsyturveydom*, by W. S. Gilbert. The whole theatre is below ground, which would probably not be allowed under present regulations.

The first underground tube station in Piccadilly Circus came in 1906, and in 1925 the fountain was removed to facilitate the station's rebuilding. Gilbert had not designed his figure to represent Eros, or indeed, any classical per-sonage. Faithful to his promise, he wanted to picture charity (the Earl of Shaftesbury's charity) flying swift as an arrow, bright and glowing charity, running to succour the needy.

But Londoners, knowing perhaps how many rendezvous by lovers were kept beneath its bow, christened it Eros, and in this guise the little god became dearer to them, more in keeping with the slight naughtiness of the Circus. In 1925, when it was taken away, Londoners suddenly discovered how much they loved it. Their instinct told them that it was, with the statue of Charles the First, the finest piece of work in all London.

Eros was not removed again until the outbreak of the Second World War.

By then the new underground station was dealing with thirty-two million passengers a year, and the Circus at night had begun to look like New York's Broadway, with lights running across a dozen façades.

Now it was plunged into darkness, and a few nights after the beginning of the Battle of London all sorts and conditions of people, with their mattresses, their blankets, their coats, bags, rugs, pillows, their most precious belongings, and their fortunes, descended into the underground, where they lay like refugees in the passages, on the escalators, and on the platforms from dusk to dawn. The trains came in and out bringing more hot air with them, but here Londoners felt safe, and soon, with the help of the authorities, Piccadilly Circus station dealt with four thousand on a busy night.

Above, during the day, traffic dried up to a trickle. Sometimes the Circus at midday was empty, but it became cosmopolitan as never before. By the third Christmas the cocktail bars in Piccadilly were crowded with soldiers, sailors, and airmen, not only of the home country but of the Dominions and the free allied nations. Norwegians and Dutch, French and Poles in their respective uniforms crowded the hotel foyers. Some airmen and a few technicians back from Murmansk and Leningrad told stories of the Russian campaign fought in temperatures of twenty to thirty degrees below zero. A young officer, wearing a picturesque headgear with the wide brim turned up on one side and decorated with a bunch of bright green feathers, was just back from Gambia where the temperature of the day of his departure registered one hundred in the shade. His talk was of a brother officer mauled by a panther, of others bitten by pythons or eaten alive by white ants. . . . Merchant sailors, who only a day or two earlier had been swimming in icy waters while watching their stricken vessels take a final plunge, passed through the streets with clothes too big or too small for them, and modest, almost shy faces. Pilot officers, who a few hours earlier had been looking down from their bombers over Bremen or Cologne, commandos just back from a secret raid on enemy-occupied territory, Frenchmen just released from Russian prison camps passed unnoticed through Piccadilly Circus.

The following Easter I watched the throb of the Circus a moment from the steps of Swan & Edgar's. There were fourteen other women besides myself waiting for something or somebody on these steps. They had probably said to fourteen men that morning: 'Meet me at the Eros entrance of Swan & Edgar's.' On the other side of the Circus, between Etam and Shaftesbury Avenue and below the huge Guinness clock, the empty shop, where the preceding month collections were made for warship week, was now taken over by the Ministry of Food to teach housewives how to make the best of the new national flour.

Soon the Americans came; the most welcome invasion London has ever known.

Jeeps replaced the growlers of the nineties. Adele Astaire worked at the Rainbow Corner in Coventry Street, which was the largest and most important of the American Red Cross clubs; her brother Fred was appearing in a film at the Empire in Leicester Square, which picture-house stood on the site of the music-hall from which Winston

Churchill, as a cadet, ripped the barrier which he burned in the middle of Leicester Square. The former undergraduate had become the symbol of the British Empire, and was guiding the country to victory through the greatest trial in her history. German bombers were making mighty, fantastic bonfires in Leicester Square, where on occasion the sky was red with the flames which destroyed great buildings in it, and high explosives chipped the statue of Shakespeare put up by the financier Grant in 1874.

Coventry Street, leading from Piccadilly Circus to Leicester Square, had become known as the Half Mile and was crowded with fresh waves of American troops. It was not only the favourite beat of the Londoner on a Sunday afternoon. War workers from the provinces thronged the pavements, seeking the glamour of London. Troops from the empire, and Americans from the forty-eight states described its varying phases in letters to home. Hundreds of thousands of them will keep to the end of their days memories of this—the most famous half mile on the face of the globe.

No bomb ever dropped in Piccadilly Circus proper during the entire course of the war. This is a strange fact to record, because it shows that the Luftwaffe never obtained a bull's-eye. You could have spent the whole war seated on the Eros plinth without suffering a scratch.

Before we come back to the Circus and to the return of Eros we must consider what had happened to St. James's, Piccadilly, which Wren had put up to serve all the people who had gone to live in the new part of the town.

Just after seven on the night of 14th October 1940, all the force and fury of the raid fell on this historic stretch of Piccadilly. Wren's roof quivered, and from the tower came tongues of fire. The outdoor pulpit was shattered, and the spire, which had never looked quite straight, like the tower of Pisa, lay in pieces on the tombstones of the courtyard. A bell dated 1686 fell ringing sepulchrally to earth, and the Victorian rectory collapsed, imprisoning the verger and his wife below the stone slabs.

A huge crater was made in the middle of Piccadilly, and on the opposite side of the street the Fifty-Shilling Tailor's building had broken out into a sheet of fire, and as the heat became more intense, a number of dummies were catapulted into Piccadilly, looking in the fearsome light like corpses. Bentley's oyster bar and El Vino in Piccadilly Place were severely blasted, but it was from Bentley's that the first rescuers went to the rectory of St. James's Church. The verger and his wife were trapped in the kitchen behind a six-foot wall, and while the bombs continued to fall some volunteers, under the guidance of a soldier, commandeered a compressor used for mending the road and started to drill the stone. Not till the next morning did they reach the kitchen. The verger's wife was dead and the verger died later.

After the raid services were held on Sundays in the south aisle, which had been turned into a little church in itself. The windows which were against Jermyn Street were filled with board, which did not prevent the cold winds from whistling in to beat against the shivering worshippers. At Easter there were spring flowers on the altar and next to the harmonium. It was impressive and pathetic.

All the history of Piccadilly lay in the ruined church and its courtyard—almost since the days when the bugloss grew upon the dry ditch banks along the 'way to Readinge.' The courtyard remained very desolate till one morning some gardeners arrived and a notice was put up to say that Viscount Southwood had endowed a garden to commemorate the courage of the people of London. Paths were laid out, beds planted, and soon there arrived rhododendrons splashing their bright colours against the burnt beams of Wren's stricken roof. In May 1946 Queen Mary opened this garden of remembrance, which continued thereafter to become more beautiful until it seemed that the scars were hidden in a resurrection of flowers and green leaves, shaded paths and seats for passers-by. Lord Southwood did not live to see his garden finished, but Londoners are grateful to him for it.

The war had been over two years before Eros was brought back to the Piccadilly Circus fountain. Everything seemed to drag just then. Tattered blinds hung from many bombed houses whose cracked façades and boarded-up doors hid vile dumps of old cans and charred wreckage. The heat of summer hung like a haze over these sores in the famous, beloved streets built on Henry Jermyn's parcel of land. Where my Lord Chancellor Hyde's noble palace had stood, weeds grew here and there for the second time. In Piccadilly Circus, the lights that used to run up and down the Bovril sign, the Guinness clock, and the front of the London Pavilion had not come back because the miners were not digging out enough coal to light the heart of the empire.

Londoners, who at various times had treated Gilbert's fountain so cruelly, now yearned for the return of this shining figure they had christened Eros. He was a symbol of themselves and the freedom they had fought for. He reminded them of the days when Piccadilly Circus was as gay, as bright, and as noisy as Broadway, and with its return they could hope that life would become a little less grim.

Until the day before Eros was due to come back there had been a heat wave, but it had been broken by a thunder-peal which roared and growled, and quivered and spat so very like an exploding rocket that many people that lunch-time had looked up, expecting to see the 'plume' rising above some stricken building. But instead of dust and brick, there came down such torrential rain that in many streets the road blocks were thrust up. Buildings, like the London Library, not yet properly mended, though it was so long after the bombing, were slightly flooded.

The storm had upset the weather, and the sun, therefore,

which the next afternoon should have welcomed the little
god, was quite hidden by cloud after a short appearance
in the morning. People passing through the Circus at
about midday stopped to look at the workmen preparing
the hoists inside the steel scaffolding. Loud-speakers
had been placed round the hoarding to relay the official
speeches at half-past three. There was a white awning
for the important personages, some chairs, an orange
ladder, and the arms of the L.C.C. with gold lion and
red cross.

Eros was coming by lorry from Southfields, where he
had been cleaned and given a new bow, and the newspapers claimed that his journey would be triumphal. Some
even printed the route which his lorry would take. He
was supposed to arrive at half-past two.

At about this time I began to walk slowly along Piccadilly
in the direction of the ceremony. There was no air. One
felt that any moment the heavens would burst as they had
done the day before. The police were beginning to divert
traffic. The crowd was to have the place all to itself.

Eros had arrived and was being gently hoisted. There
were movie cameras at almost every window, and others
on cars—the only vehicles allowed—which from time to
time crawled round the fountain.

It was a curious crowd, not very thick, not quite the sort
of crowd I had expected, for it was strangely cosmopolitan
—Americans and French, South Americans, and some
Indian women, very beautiful, wearing saris, and having
precious stones embedded in their foreheads, but chewing
gum, which somehow seemed not right. How long would
India remain in this empire whose centre we now still
proudly trod? A middle-aged woman passed with a
younger one who looked like her daughter. The daughter
wanted to stay. The mother grew angry, and said: 'You
see, there's nothing to wait for! Anyway, who ever
thought of making so much fuss about a statue?' The
daughter was obliged to follow, but she kept on looking

back almost tragically.   Two terribly good-looking American boys in civilian clothes which were only half so and
proclaimed they were on leave, had struck up a conversation with a young English officer in a beret who said:
'I 've just come all round the Cape.'   The American boys
asked: 'How do you get to the White City?   We want
to see the dogs.'

The rain started, and the crowd thinned out.   Only those
who really intended to remain now braved a bath from
heaven.   But for these there was one enormous advantage.
We could saunter round and round the plinth, listening to
the music being broadcast for our benefit, looking at the
people, enjoying a tea-party atmosphere without jostle or
traffic.   I took from my bag a scarf to protect my hair, and
a copy of the previous night's *Evening Standard*, in which
Eileen Ascroft had written a page of exciting details about
the Circus.   She told us that the Monico had just been sold
and that the London Pavilion was scheduled to be pulled
down in 1956 under town planning so that the Circus
could be enlarged.

The rain was fine and persistent, and after a time one
forget it.   Two young Frenchwomen with tall umbrellas
and cork shoes met in front of Swan & Edgar's, and the
one who had just arrived said: 'I hope I haven't kept you
waiting?'   How many times is that thought expressed
each day in front of the famous store?   Swan & Edgar's
has been a meeting-place for more than a century.   Not
long after the shop opened, one of its assistants, called
Charles Frederick Worth, thought he would go and design
dresses in Paris.   He began to attract notice during the
Crimean War, found favour with the superb Countess of
Pourtalès, and was introduced by her to the Empress
Eugénie, for whom he invented a new form of the crinoline.
When our present queen went with the king in state to
Paris before the outbreak of the war of 1939, Her Majesty
wore a number of particularly pretty crinolines which
charmed the French.

The London Pavilion was being repainted cream, but the work was only half finished, and it seemed to be sorry for itself not being ready in time to welcome Eros. Hedy Lamar was playing in the film, *The Dishonoured Lady*. If I am still alive in 1956 I shall be terribly sorry to see the Pavilion taken down. All the windows everywhere were open, and people were sitting at them as if waiting for a royal procession. Nothing at all was happening under the awning of the plinth. Three workmen were leaning over the girders, and the two flower girls, who were young when the fountain was unveiled fifty-four years ago this very day, were seated below, silently, stoically, becoming drenched. This was said to be a great day for them, but I am a little tired of hearing these wrinkled faces sung. Is the new, or at least, a newer generation, never to smile behind the flowers of Eros?

The Criterion Restaurant was freshly painted cream with bright green verandas. Unlike the Pavilion, the Criterion was quite finished. Unless you have already noticed that this is the prettiest, most delicate building, look at it more carefully next time you pass. The customers, the cooks, the waiters, the maids, and the managers were all sitting or standing at open windows between the graceful statuary made to represent the four seasons. There was a swarthy individual with a fez who must have served Turkish coffee at lunch. Just above him beamed a dark face with a mouth like a melon, wearing a tall white chef's hat.

Because there was no traffic anywhere near us, and because the rain deadened a multitude of other city sounds, one had the impression of having been wafted back against the current of time—to when the Cri advertised its cigar divan and elegant newly constructed dining-room. Suddenly from behind me came the sound of a cavalcade, and, turning quickly, I saw a dozen police officers, some on splendid white horses, others on sleek chestnuts, arriving along Glasshouse Street. It was strangely moving. Then from somewhere else the important personages ran across

This view is from the steps of Swan & Edgar, where we so often wait for our friends. This is one of the oldest stores in London and produced the great dressmaker Worth, who went to the court of Napoleon III, to dress the elegant Empress Eugénie.

On the right is the graceful building of the Criterion, freshly painted in cream, with green balconies, to welcome Eros back to town after the Second World War. The London Pavilion, once a music-hall, and afterwards the home of many glamorous revues, is a cinema. To the left of it is Shaftesbury Avenue, where the American G.I.s had their Rainbow Club. To the right, straight in front of us, is Coventry Street, the glittering 'half-mile' leading to Leicester Square.

to their awning, protected during their short journey by officials carrying open umbrellas. Lady Nathan, chairman of the L.C.C., made a little, feminine speech, exactly what was needed, and then came Sir Alfred Munnings, president of the Royal Academy, whose voice through the megaphones was simply stupendous. He will go down in history as a great painter of racehorses.

SHAFTESBURY AVENUE

LET US CONSIDER Shaftesbury Avenue as it appeared to Londoners on the eve of the first Christmas after the war.

The weather was bitterly cold—that sudden, biting, numbing cold which comes upon us unawares, though at heart we are always longing for a return of those Dickensian Yuletides when the Thames froze over and snow covered the ground, making a picturesque background for holly and ale and mince-pies. But on this occasion the cold was accompanied by something that was half mist and half fog, something that clogged one's make-up and brought tears to one's eyes, and made the gas lamps at the far end of the street appear like oranges against the grimy buildings.

There was nothing in particular to show that Christmas was only a fortnight off except the newly opened wine-shop, which was freshly painted and ablaze with electric light, with the labels hardly dry upon the bottles and cotton wool hanging on wire against the window to represent snow. It was the newest and gayest shop in the whole avenue, and seemed to have sprung up specially for the occasion to meet the demand of Christmas shoppers, who had just been informed in Parliament that though beer would be fairly plentiful in public-houses, many of which would remain open later at Christmas, supplies of spirits and wines would only be slightly better than a year earlier. Wine-shops with anything to sell, and many, like this one, were opening all over the West End, found that intending customers were willing to form docile queues to obtain something more congenial than the coloured, flavoured, and fortified liquid which was being openly sold by less honest establishments.

Eros had not yet returned from the country and his

plinth was still boxed up with sand-bags and wood and advertisements exhorting Londoners to save the money they had made during the plentiful war years, but already traffic was streaming round Piccadilly Circus at a rate which recalled the days before the war, and the lights were going up modestly, though not with sufficient brilliance to lift Shaftesbury Avenue out of its semi-obscurity.

The ochre-tinted, columned and porticoed side of the London Pavilion, decorated with immense posters in colour to advertise the film of *Captain Kidd*, grimly faced that portion of the Monico and Lyons' which since the entry of America into the war had been the Rainbow Corner Red Cross centre for enlisted men, and though so many Americans were each week leaving Europe to return home there were sufficient here to form two or three idle rows drawn up haphazardly along the pavement between the news-reel theatre in the Circus and Denman Street.

Here then was the start of the new avenue which was hewn out of Tichborne Street and the squalid approaches to Soho, to enlarge Piccadilly Circus and give it a new arm, in the late eighties when Queen Victoria was celebrating her jubilee. We unwittingly tread amongst the shades of the old Pavilion with its marble-top table across which the chairman looked when he was ready to announce a new turn. The ochre-tinted theatre which replaced it came with the dawn of electricity, and was constructed by night as well as by day to finish it within six months. Dead and almost forgotten is the great Macdermott, and we find it almost difficult to recall the brilliant nights between the two wars when Sir Charles Cochran staged some of his most lavish pieces in this tremendous London landmark from which the paint is peeling and whose roof is covered with soot. The one or two remaining flower girls who sat under Eros when he first shot his arrows through the heart of the town drew their worn shawls over their wrinkled foreheads, treasuring up memories which they will take with them to the grave. Eros was breathing the clear air of the country, like the life-size white bear which for so many years stood outside the historic pre-cursor of the Criterion and now decorates the little garden of the White Bear Tavern at Fairchildes, amongst the hop-fields of Kent.

The American G.I.s were making new history in Shaftesbury Avenue, for they set up there a commerce which was amongst the strangest the street has known, selling the fountain-pens, the watches, the cameras, the diamond rings, the binoculars, and the cigarette cases which they had bought, plundered, or pillaged during their con-quest and occupation of Germany. Little bowler-hatted men relieved them of these things for cash which would help to while away their remaining weeks of exile.

Windmill Street, which with hedgerows and sweet cottages led from Mrs. Robert Baker's Piccadilly Hall to the 'way to Paddington,' now only runs a few yards beyond the Windmill Theatre which never missed a performance during the whole of the war. But in Charles the Second's time the windmill—the real one, in the field behind Mrs. Baker's garden—flapped its wide arms to the *left* of the road, and where it once ground corn a flying bomb ex-ploded on a roof-top before lunch one summer day in 1944, when all the costers were in the busy street market.

Shaftesbury Avenue is a human, lovable hotch-potch which has grown up untended during the last sixty years. Many people would have liked it to have been born a few years later, for the L.C.C. to have built a wide, imposing thoroughfare like the new Regent Street with its granite façades and cold, impersonal carriage-way; but Shaftesbury Avenue was a Cinderella from the start, when all the planners did was to cut through the houses lining that part of the Circus and then enlarge the road which already divided Soho from Coventry Street, as in the very old days a country lane here divided the fields of St. Giles from those of St. Martin. Yes, from the very day the avenue was opened there were empty sites and hoardings amongst

E

the new buildings, and then fashion swung this way and that, until it was half a street of theatres and half a street of Victorian chambers and buildings which still have the gift of conjuring up the London of Sherlock Holmes. Now all this is begrimed by war, gladdened by brightly lit windows of cheap and glamorous lingerie, enlivened by the sound of tinned music, made rather mysterious by the narrow nocturnal-living streets which flow into it from Soho, and deafened by the never-ceasing roar of the crowds tramping along Coventry Street on their way to and from the tinsel gaiety of Leicester Square.

As evening falls, so come the theatre crowds to the Lyric to see *Duet for Two Hands*, just as after the last war they went there to applaud Doris Keane in *Romance*; to the Apollo to see Noel Coward's *Private Lives*, and to the Globe to see *While the Sun Shines* by an author who once had so many plays running here at so many theatres that the avenue became known as Rattigan Alley. But while the sun, when there is any, shines upon the solid Edwardian façade of the Globe, death has touched the Queen's, born a year later (1907). Through the curved stone entrance lie, dark and damp, the charred beams where during four reigns famous actresses trod the stage.

As if to mock its gloomy misery, the noise and light of Wardour Street permeates its icy stillness, rising from little shops and fair booths which stretch with Hogarthian picturesque to the Half Mile of Coventry Street.

This little stretch of Wardour Street stands exactly on that part of Colman Hedge Lane which, in the days of Mrs. Baker, skirted the wall of the Military Yard. It is full of life and light, and has dark mysterious alley-ways. Noisy, colourful, and full of surprises, its oldest shops took their roots here more than a century ago, and its oldest craftsmen have watched it change and yet remain much the same for seventy years and more, for many were born here, and, now that they near the grave, pass slowly up and down the same staircases that heard their childish laughter when they were learning to walk. Others are absolute newcomers, bringing with them the distorting mirrors and the tinned music of the fun fairs dear to these American G.I.s homesick for Coney Island, who come over from Rainbow Corner, through which so many millions of their compatriots passed from its opening on Armistice Day, 1942 until this Christmas, when it was about to close its doors.

It has famous public-houses like the 'George and the Dragon' at the north-east corner of Shaftesbury Avenue, and the 'Falcon' at the corner of Lisle Street, and perhaps the 'Falcon' took its name from the mews in Charing Cross before Edward the Sixth rebuilt them to form stabling. There are little restaurants like Chez Victor, where French officers and newspaper correspondents dined during the phoney war, when their country was still considered to have a matchless army. These men, proud of their heritage, stumbled out into the first London black-out from this tiny restaurant talking about the future war about which they understood, alas, so little, remembering Foch, pinning their faith on Gamelin, on Daladier, and on white-haired Marshal Pétain, then biding his time in Spain. When France fell, some of these *habitués* of Chez Victor hurried back on the last ships to their own country; others formed themselves into the little band who nightly broadcast to their enslaved compatriots through the B.B.C.; others joined de Gaulle and added the Cross of Lorraine to their uniforms. Some were parachuted over France and died.

Willy Clarkson, the theatrical wig-maker, has left his mark upon this street where, since the days of Sarah Bernhardt who laid the foundation stone in 1904, of Henry Irving who laid the coping stone in 1905 of Clarkson's famous shop, that magical name appeared on every theatre programme until the bearded wig-maker's death just before the Second World War. Those premises, charred by a fire much talked of at the time, were more weird to visit during the 'phoney' war than even Mme Tussaud's waxworks. There were labyrinths under the shop with thousands of wigs from thousands of tragedies, comedies, and musicals, all slightly damp from the firemen's hoses and smelling of burn and make-up, which you could visit by candle light, taking care not to stumble into deep wells that seemed bottomless. The wigs disappeared, the shop was cleaned, and eventually became the home of theatrical designers of a new order of things. It is divided from an old print-shop by a merchant of talking parrots, singing canaries, Persian kittens, finger-tame budgies, and monkeys, and in the old print-shop you may still come across many of Willy Clarkson's costume designs which its owner, Mr. Bayly, has collected during the past few years, some of them reminding the older generation of shows they had almost forgotten, but which in their youth proved memorable—milestones—the *Quaker Girl*, the *Country Girl*, and other successes reminiscent of the Adelphi and Daly's. You will find also in this print-shop models of hansom cabs which our grandparents played with when they were children in the nineties, and other things dear to the Londoner. Mr. Bayly was preparing to move to the arcade between Piccadilly and Jermyn Street. There are shoe shops, some of which cater especially for the theatrical profession—heels so high that they make one giddy at the thought of wearing them, and signed photographs of our best-loved actresses. There is Pinoli's restaurant which Charles B. Cochran remembers in the days of its eight-course dinners for two shillings, back in the eighties, when Shaftesbury Avenue was newly cut. In her office on the second floor you will still find Charles Pinoli's daughter, Mme Branchini, who with her son and daughter run the place as a family business, little changed since her father founded it in 1880, having come there from the Hyde Park Restaurant which stood on the site of Selfridges. This famous restaurant in Wardour Street had been an eating-house before even Pinoli took it over—it was the Rome and Venice, and before that, long ago, a coaching inn.

The Rome and Venice had tried to stage a fire in order to obtain the insurance money, but the fire was put out by the wine which burst from its bottles in the cellars. In Pinoli's day it became a rendezvous—not, strange to say, for the theatrical world—but for barristers, doctors, and the curators of our national museums. Mme Branchini still owns the original menus for the one-and-sixpenny lunch—hors-d'œuvre, soup, sole colbert, tournedos, chicken sauté, roast partridge, Neapolitan ice, dessert, and cheese; and for the two-shilling dinner—whitebait, mutton cutlets, pheasant, and four other dishes, all washed down with Chianti wine!

Like the Windmill Theatre, Pinoli's never closed throughout the war.

On three nights—14th October, 11th November, and 18th November 1940—not a single client walked into the long restaurant. The receipts show the word NIL. On 6th November there was one client who dined in stately glory while the bombs fell, shaking his plate and spilling his Chianti!

Across the way Mr. Douglas Withers lives amongst his violins in the shop over which he first saw the light of day in the year 1879. At the age of three he sat in his baby chair, watching the cavalcade in Wardour Street upon which he has looked ever since. Twenty years before that, his father, Edward Withers, had moved his business here from Coventry Street, making violins, as his father had made them before him, copying exclusively the Stradivarius and Guarnerius models, using old and carefully selected wood.

Mr. Douglas Withers is to-day the doyen of his craft and among the last of the great violin makers. In all London only three ancient and famous firms remain, and two of them are in Wardour Street.

Mr. Withers, fingering an old fiddle, will recall his memories of the street of his birth for your pleasure. He will tell you, for instance, that when he was a baby, opposite his nursery window there was a bird shop outside which the owner's wife, Mrs. Isaacs, sat in her bonnet and

shawl, taking the air, and that this firm is still in existence,
though it has moved to Upper St. Martin's Lane. Then
came Henry Godfrey, a jeweller, who in turn moved to the
corner of Panton Street and Whitcomb Street, where, at the
age of ninety, he is still to be found, having grown up with
his shop.

Who now remembers Marie Lloyd's public-house, known
to every enthusiast of the music-hall, and to all the cabbies
of town in the nineties? There is a place where they sell
perfumes across the way from Mr. Withers which hides
behind its facia the gilded sign of this joyous establishment.
Willy Clarkson sold his wigs on the site of a jam factory;
next to Bravington's there was a railing behind which, one
day a man, either because he was drunk or for a wager,
took off all his clothes, hanging them up on the spikes,
after which he sauntered towards Piccadilly. Police whistles
were for ever shrieking, for these were the times when the
Champagne Charleys were kicked down the stairs of the
Leicester Lounge, where now is Stagg & Russell's.

'Where the Black and White Milk Bar stands in Coventry
Street was a ladies' bag-maker—one of the finest craftsmen
of his day who, like my father, lived over his shop. For
craftsmen flourished then, and had time to make what
pleased them.'

He plucked a string of the instrument he was nursing in
his hand, and said:

'My father took as long as four or five years to varnish
an instrument, for if each coat did not dry (and this needs
the warmest of summer days), the work was spoilt. He
did this at his mansion in the old Clapham Park, where
regular chamber-music parties were held. It was largely a
family quartet, as they played what was considered to be
the finest English set of instruments (two violins, a viola,
and a violoncello), all made by my grandfather from maple
wood of great age and rare beauty which was discovered
by accident in the attic in the old Coventry Street shop at
the beginning of the last century. To-day, I have too much

repair work to make any more violins, and of course the
skilled craft is rapidly becoming a thing of the past.   It is,
however, a family business, and my nephew has now been
with me for some twenty-five years and will, no doubt,
carry on the traditional name.

'Mr. Hart, another famous violin-maker, retired some
time ago from his century-old business in Wardour Street,
three doors away from me, and I was fortunately able to
engage his leading workmen.   Yes, this is a traditional
craft.'

The last of the G.I.s thronged Shaftesbury Avenue,
mingling with the early theatre queues and the typists
halting a moment on their way home to blink at the lighted
lingerie and blouse shops between Wardour Street and
Dean Street, where the charm was lessened by the knowledge that the quarter's supply of coupons was running
low.   The jeweller had become the modern stockbroker.
'We buy for cash old gold, silver, antique and modern
plate, coins and rings, second-hand jewellery, diamonds,
and precious and semi-precious stones.   Sovereigns, forty
shillings and threepence.'   Who would bring a sovereign
to the jeweller for this price when the black market offered
twelve pounds each for them?   But the watch and the ring,
the precious and semi-precious stone, were commodities
the soldier back from the Continent could always resell at
a profit.   He wandered from shop to shop, offering wares
he was unwilling to dispose of on the kerb in front of
Rainbow Corner.

From Dean Street and Frith Street come the noise, the
light, and the nocturnal effervescence of Soho, its restaurants—Chinese, Italian, Greek, and French—its café bars,
and its laundries which work late into the night.   The
atmosphere of the continental village seeps round the
hoardings of the dimmer part of the avenue and gives an
air of mystery and romance to it.   But the strangest of all
sights is the façade of the oldest theatre in this part of the
town—the Shaftesbury, through whose windows and doors,

open to the wind and the rain, you may see the auditorium
and the stage, set out on the ground in tiers and cavities
like a Roman ruin over which the lava of Vesuvius might
have passed.   There is something eerie about this ochre-
tinged façade on the avenue which still has the entrances
through which playgoers, since Forbes Robertson first
played Orlando in *As You Like It* on the theatre's opening
night on 20th October 1888, have passed.   One is almost
tempted to pay one's money at the box office and walk
through the doors marked dress circle or stalls, but like a
child's toy this façade is a pure mockery, leading merely
to a deserted arena which you may explore to your heart's
content by turning into Newport Place and climbing over
the low barrier.

Here, in the moonlight, you may dream of all those
plays, comedies and tragedies, which Londoners paid to
applaud or to boo during rather more than half a century.
One feels that same interest in reconstructing the past
glories of this theatre as an archaeologist must throb to
when coming across Egyptian remains.   It is astounding
how clearly a theatre may be visualized by its foundations.
Pit and stalls sweep gently down to where the orchestra
vibrated to the leader's baton, and across the footlights is
the dark, abysmal cavity beneath what was once the stage.
In Gerrard Street, where there is a piece of wall left, still
stands the stage door with its globular light under which
so many young actors and actresses must have felt a thrill
to pass, when on the threshold of making a name.   You
may imagine the doorkeeper's lodge and the dressing-rooms
once filled with flowers, but how small a space this little
world was confined to in actual square feet.   It represents
but a dark corner to the right of the stage, and all that is
left of human happiness and sorrow is a rusty safe against
which is affixed like a fungus the weather-beaten remains
of a blond wig.   The gangways between the stalls, and
parts of the stairs leading up to the circle and down to the
bar, in some cases with directions still written upon them,

allow one's imagination to people them with ghosts, those of the programme-sellers and the men and women in evening dress who came here to laugh and shudder at Edgar Wallace's *Squeaker* in 1928, and to applaud *The Middle Watch* and the many successes of Ian Hay, and to boo *Before Sunset*—that play which in 1933 caused a riot, compelling a director of the owning company, a former amateur wrestling champion, to pick up the rowdiest of the trouble-makers and throw him out into the avenue.

Indeed, this is the oldest theatre hereabout, opened two months before the Lyric, rather more than two years before that pock-marked, red-brick Royal English Opera House opposite, built by D'Oyly Carte for Sir Arthur Sullivan's grand opera *Ivanhoe*, which was so little a success that the house was sold to Sir Augustus Harris, who changed its name to the one you will immediately recognize it by—the Palace Theatre. The Apollo dates from 1901, the Globe from 1906, and the ill-fated Queen's from 1907. Thus you have the whole story of Shaftesbury Avenue's theatreland.

The destruction of the Shaftesbury is more than the passing of a theatre, for its ruined outline gleams in the moonlight beside a car park which hides the scars of death and sorrow. The land-mine which brought down the theatre fell in the street, demolishing also two blocks of Newport Dwellings, killing forty-eight and injuring eighty-three. Here lived the little people of Soho on the site of Newport Market, frequented two and a half centuries earlier by French emigrants who fled to London after the revocation of the Edict of Nantes. Against it, in Gerrard Street, 'fifth door on the left hand,' lived the poet Dryden. The emigrants whom Dryden saw plying their trades round the market gave Soho its foreign atmosphere.

These tenements, therefore, stood on famous ground, and many an Italian waiter and French cook, crowded out from Old Compton Street, found them comfortable and easy of access.

* E

The fire station facing the Palace Theatre had already been destroyed in an earlier raid—that of 5th October 1940—on which occasion the caretaker and his wife and two tame rabbits which they kept as pets slid down with the debris, from the top of the building to the first floor, which because of the fire engines underneath was built especially strong. At the end of their toboggan journey the man and woman, in their night attire, rubbed their eyes and wondered if they had been dreaming. Then one of the rabbits nibbled the caretaker's hand, and he saw that he was overhanging Shaftesbury Avenue. The firemen brought the family down in a chute. The second rabbit was dead; otherwise there was no casualty.

As soon as the war was over the fire station was patched up again, but the firemen who had lived through these appalling nights were dispersed. Once more the station had resumed its original importance, covering a district which stretches from Kingsway to the Ritz Hotel, and from Middlesex Hospital to the Thames. The fires they were called upon to attend were no longer the mighty conflagrations of the Battle of London—smoking chimneys and burning oil in Soho kitchens, but in some ways more difficult to deal with, because in peacetime the fireman must be careful not to make more damage by water than is strictly necessary.

Cambridge Circus cuts Shaftesbury Avenue in two. Henceforth the avenue sweeps north to New Oxford Street and the confines of Bloomsbury, leaving misty Seven Dials on its right. Charing Cross Road, connecting Trafalgar Square with Tottenham Court Road, was completed in 1877, so that this great piece of planning was done simultaneously, completely transforming this part of London—the most important scheme since Nash had built his Regent Street. The Palace Theatre, having passed from grand opera to theatre, from theatre to cinema, and back from cinema to musical comedy, is still, with its yellow brick and semi-eastern façade, the most imposing building in the

circus. Let us stand for a moment on the island site in
the centre of Cambridge Circus and consider the strange
diversity of interests and landmarks all round us—the
lingerie and theatres of Shaftesbury Avenue; W. & G.
Foyle with its stock of three million volumes in Charing
Cross Road; the St. Martin's and Ambassador's theatres,
built at the beginning of the last war, and the Ivy Restaurant,
dear to theatrical folk, in narrow West Street; the Marquis
of Granby public-house dividing West Street from Earlham
Street, famous for its jellied eels; Zaehnsdorf's, the master
bookbinders, the last of their craft in town, dividing
Earlham Street from the second half of Shaftesbury Avenue,
where music publishers and milk bars stretch their signs;
the northern arm of Charing Cross Road separated by
Mooney's Irish House from diminutive Moor Street which
leads into Old Compton Street, heart of Soho; another
public-house, dividing Moor Street from Romilly Street
—all these streets and houses and shops glittering with
electric signs.

REGENT STREET

THE PALL MALL, which in 1660 was bordered on the south by the low wall of St. James's Park and on the north by two rows of elm-trees, had a few houses at the corner of the Haymarket. When Henry the Eighth was building the palace from 1532 onwards, Erasmus had resided in one of these houses—that same Erasmus who gave Holbein a letter of introduction for Sir Thomas More, at whose house in Chelsea the painter was first introduced to the king.

Then it was a country lane, and so it remained until Henry Jermyn, Earl of St. Albans, received those orchards in St. James's Fields upon which he was to build St. James's Square, Jermyn Street, and those other streets between Pall Mall and Piccadilly. Nell Gwynn became a resident in Pall Mall, where she was close to Charles the Second's royal apartments in the Palace of Whitehall. We know little about her neighbours except that one of them was Dr. Sydenham, an eminent physician, who lived there from 1658 until his death in 1689. Nearer the palace were the pheasantry and the place where the game of pall mall was played. In 1660 Isabella, the daughter of Archibald Lumsden who furnished malls, bowls, and scoops here during the reign of Charles the First, petitioned Charles the Second for a tenement in St. James's Field as promised to her father, who had spent over £400 in keeping up the sport. A Mr. Samuel Morland, in the same year, petitioned for the return of his house, garden, and stables in Pall Mall, which had been taken away from him during the Commonwealth.

After this the street developed in tune with the great

building boom started by Henry Jermyn to the south of
Piccadilly and the Earl of Clarendon to the north of it.
A few coffee-houses even made their appearance, and there
is a delightful story about a woman in whose coffee-house,
during the reign of James the Second, the Earl of Peterborough saw a canary that piped twenty times which he
tried to buy for Lady Sandwich, but the owner would not
part with it and so the earl secretly changed it for another
which did not pipe. Some time later the earl went back
to the coffee-house and asked the woman whose canary no
longer piped if she was not sorry she had not parted with
it, whereupon she answered: 'No, no, if your lordship
will believe me, it has moped and moped, and never once
opened its pretty lips since the day that the poor king
went away.'

Defoe wrote:

I am lodged in the street called Pall Mall, the ordinary resi-
dence of all strangers, because of its vicinity to the Queen's
Palace, the Park, the Parliament House, the theatres, and the
Chocolate and Coffee Houses where the best company frequent.

Gay, in 1716, wrote his famous lines:

O bear me to the paths of fair Pell-mell.
Safe are thy pavements, grateful is thy smell!
At distance rolls along the gilded coach,
Nor sturdy carmen on thy walks encroach.

About this time two very important things happened in
Pall Mall.

On the site of the old pheasantry against the palace, Sir
Christopher Wren built Marlborough House for the
illustrious victor of Malplaquet and Blenheim, whose
duchess had obtained the land from her royal mistress.

At the other end of Pall Mall, Carlton House was built
by Henry Boyle, later Baron Carleton, successively Chancellor of the Exchequer, Secretary of State, and President
of the Council.

MARLBOROUGH HOUSE

These two mansions were to grow up together, eventually becoming royal palaces. One of them still exists; the other was pulled down, but not until it had made history and inspired Nash to build Regent Street and thereby form the circus at Piccadilly.

Marlborough House is of red brick ornamented with stone, and is seen at its best from the Mall in winter when the trees are bare. But when it was first built it stood amongst groves of chestnut-trees—to the west it opened on to the gardens of St. James's Palace, and to the south to the park, which was still private. On the death of Queen Anne, the Duke of Marlborough made a public entry into London, attended by more than two hundred gentlemen and a train of coaches. Eight years later he died, and an even grander procession took place on its way to Westminster Abbey. His widow, Sarah, continued to live at Marlborough House where she delighted to speak of 'neighbour George,' the Hanoverian king who lived in St. James's Palace. Long afterwards, for she lived till 1744, she was anxious to make a more noble entrance into Pall Mall, but Sir Robert Walpole, not being on good terms with her, bought up the houses and frustrated the scheme.

The mansion was bought by the Crown in 1817 for Princess Charlotte, daughter of the Prince Regent, who was living in Carlton House where a year earlier she had been married to Prince Leopold, but the princess died in childbirth before the purchase was completed, and her husband, afterwards King of the Belgians, lived in it for fourteen years.

On the accession of Queen Victoria, Marlborough House became the home of William the Fourth's widow, the Dowager Queen Adelaide, who died there, and later it was given to the Prince and Princess of Wales, the future Edward the Seventh and Alexandra. To-day it is the town house of Queen Mary, and it was here in January

1946 that the Duke of Windsor came during a visit to London, when he said: 'I am going to see the king, my brother. It was because he will be in London this week for the general assembly of the United Nations Organization that I arranged to come over. I also want to deal with various private business—and some personal matters, like getting a few shirts repaired.'

CARLTON HOUSE

The history of Carlton House, though shorter, was much more spectacular.

Lord Carleton bequeathed it to his nephew, the Earl of Burlington, who sold it in 1732 to Frederick, Prince of Wales, who was to live on such bad terms with his father George the Second at St. James's and at Kew. The lawns and parterres were immense—stretching from Spring Gardens in Whitehall to those of Marlborough House— and in summer Frederick breakfasted under a marquee on the lawn. After his death, the Dowager Princess of Wales divided her time between the White House at Kew, Leicester House, and Carlton House, and here, as at Kew, the Earl of Bute, who was reputed to be her lover, constantly visited her, arriving in the sedan chair of Miss Vansittart, the maid of honour, who lived in Sackville Street.

But most of all, Carlton House will be remembered as the home of George the Fourth when Prince of Wales, Regent, and King. The ceremony of conferring the regency on the prince was performed there with great pomp on 5th February 1811; and in the following June, the Prince Regent gave a supper to two thousand; a stream with gold and silver fish flowing through a marble channel down the central table. At one time he formed the idea of building a long gallery uniting Carlton House with Marlborough House and St. James's Palace.

From the moment the future regent and king was given

Carlton House to celebrate his twenty-first birthday, this Prince of Wales, most lovely to look on, flung the money an admiring country had granted him through the windows of this stately mansion. Fleeing from the dreadful dullness of his parents' court, its routine and dreary occupations, he occupied his endless hours of leisure changing from one uniform to another, from Scotch kilts to field marshal's clothes; inventing new styles of dress; carousing with his friends, playing practical jokes, drinking himself tipsy, borrowing money from his servants, driving from Brighton to Carlton House in four and a half hours, and intriguing the town with the stories of his amorous adventures. Whether he really married Mrs. Fitzherbert according to the rites of the Roman Catholic Church in Carlton House or not is really immaterial. It earned him the title of the great lover of his age, and many there were who supposed he would have been willing to forfeit his throne for her bewitching eyes. He inspired, or perhaps mirrored, the dissolute living of Arthur's, Almack's, Bootle's, and White's, which a later generation looked back upon with horror and condemnation—though the young men of fashion who, during the gay nineties, painted Piccadilly Circus and Leicester Square red and let rats loose in the night clubs of their day, were little better. If we compare their mode of living with that of the nineteen-twenties when another Prince of Wales was leading fashion, the Embassy Club and Quaglino's were tame places indeed, though another royal love-story was soon to rock the nation.

The forecourt of Carlton House was divided from Pall Mall by a range of columns which supported nothing. These gave rise to the lines:

'Dear little columns, all in a row,
What *do* you do there?' 'Indeed we don't know.'

Four years after the prince had taken up residence there it was modernized at great expense, and in 1815 important alterations were made inside.

THE TRIUMPHAL WAY

Meanwhile the prince had made the acquaintance of John Nash, who was appointed architect to the Board of Works. John Nash drew up designs which, with the help of his royal patron, changed the whole aspect of this part of London.

If you look at a plan of the town before Nash started to build you will see that Piccadilly, as in the days when it was bordered by green fields and orchards, ran all the way to its intersection by Great Windmill Street and Haymarket. In other words, the cross-roads effect of the sixteenth century was maintained.

Between the forecourt of Carlton House and Piccadilly, there were numerous small streets, and on the south of Piccadilly was St. James's Market.

Nash designed a large open space in front of the forecourt of his master's palace and a wide thoroughfare, as a grand vista, cutting Piccadilly at right angles at the point where it was to sweep west in a Quadrant, and then join up with Oxford Street by following the existing line of Swallow Street.

Originally the idea was for it to lead magnificently to Regent's Park.

A very small part of Swallow Street, not needed by Nash, remains to this day under its own name, connecting Piccadilly, opposite St. James's Church, with Regent Street. The rest of it, that which was swallowed up in the new avenue, was a narrow, picturesque, cobbled street, full of small inns and livery stables, which, not so long before, had been the haunt of highwaymen.

The making of Regent Street quite altered the eastern end of Piccadilly, which was cut at right angles, a hundred yards west of Windmill Street and the Haymarket. The sweep of the Quadrant also added an arm to this meeting of the ways. The old cross-roads therefore gave place to a circus which Nash called Regent Circus, Piccadilly.

At the Oxford Street end the architect designed the shop fronts with delicate curves to repeat the circus effect. This he called Regent Circus, Oxford Street.

The St. James's Market, which Nash was obliged to destroy to make the first part of his triumphal road, was as old as anything in this part of London, and Henry Jermyn, Earl of St. Albans, would have known it. Gay tells us in his *Trivia* that it was famous for veal, and you can imagine the stage-coaches clattering up past the vegetable and fruit stalls to the courtyard of the Mitre Tavern and that of the White Bear Inn, on the site of which the Criterion now stands.

The great Prince Regent had scarcely mounted the throne as George the Fourth when Carlton House, the inspiration of this great avenue, was pulled down. It was hardly surprising that to the Londoner of to-day, this palace, like Leicester House, is but a hazy name. Thackeray himself, who at least had caught a glimpse of it in his youth, wrote:

I remember peeping thrugh the colonnade at Carlton House, and seeing the abode of the great Prince Regent. I can see yet the guards pacing before the gates of the place. The place! What place? The palace exists no more than the palace of Nebuchadnezzar. It is but a name now. Where be the sentries who used to salute as the Royal chariots drove in and out? The chariots, with the kings inside, have driven to the realms of Pluto; the tall guards have marched into darkness, and the echoes of their drums are rolling in Hades. Where the palace once stood, a hundred little children are paddling up and down the steps to St. James's Park. A score of grave gentlemen are taking their tea at the Athenaeum Club.

The pillars of the screen were taken to Buckingham Palace; the columns of the portico form that of the National Gallery in Trafalgar Square. As for the tall granite column surmounting the steps leading to St. James's Park, it commemorates the Prince Regent's brother, the Duke of York, who did not live long enough to occupy his fine new house, which later became the London Museum.

In the years just preceding the advent of Queen Victoria, George Augustus Sala, who, later, with his white waist-coat, crimson nose (a colour brought about by the knuckles of a Haymarket night-house proprietor), and scarlet tie, was to become one of the most popular writers on London, lodged above those pretty colonnades of early Regent Street. In *Twice round the Clock*, he wrote:

I think I am qualified to speak of the place, for, walking down it the other day, I counted no less than eleven houses, between the two circuses, in which I had at one time dwelt. But they were all early, those remembrances, and connected with the time when the colonnade of the Quadrant existed.

He goes on to say that this colonnade afforded not only a convenient shelter beneath, but was a capital promenade for the dwellers in the first floors above.

The entresols certainly were slightly gloomy; and moustached foreigners, together with some gaily-dressed company still naughtier, could with difficulty be restrained from prowling backwards and forwards between Glasshouse Street and the County Fire Office. The first floor balconies above were in my childhood most glorious playgrounds.

He used to poach on the balconies of his neighbours, and in these escapades his aider and abettor was a tall, handsome man, with a crimson velvet under-waistcoat who used to carry a 'sabarcane,' half walking-stick, half pea-shooter, from which he would discharge clay pellets at the vagrant cats on the adjoining balconies. He also used to lean over the balcony and fish for people's hats with a salmon hook fixed to the extremity of a tandem whip. He would insist on winding up the new French clock with the snuffers.

It was he who made nocturnal excursions from parapet to parapet along the leads, returning with bewildering accounts of bearded men who were gambling with dice at No. 92; of the tenor of the Italian Opera, who, knife in hand, was pursuing his wife (in her night-dress) about the balcony at No. 74; and of Mademoiselle Follejambes, the *premier suiet* of the same establishment, who was practising pirouettes before a cheval glass at the open window of No. 86, while Mademoiselle Follejambes' mamma, with a red cotton pocket handkerchief tied round her old head, was drinking *anisette* out of a tea-cup.

The colonnades were also fruitful in memories.

There was a delightful bird-stuffer's shop at the corner of a court, with birds of paradise, parrots, and humming-birds of gorgeous plumage, and strange creatures with white bodies and long yellow beaks and legs that terrified while they pleasured us. Then there was the funeral monument shop, with the mural tablets, the obelisks, the broken columns, the extinguished torches, and the draped urns in the window, and some with the inscriptions into the bargain, all ready engraved in black and white. . . . There was Swan and Edgar's (with a real Mr. Swan and a real Mr. Edgar), splendid and radiant, then as now, with brave apparel (how many times have I listened to the enthusiastic cheers of Swan and Edgar's young men, on the occasion of the proprietors giving their annual banquet to their employees?), and even then replete with legends of dishonest fares, who caused a cab to halt at the Regent Street entrance, got out, said they would be back in a moment, and then darting through the crowded shop, knavishly escaped at the Piccadilly end.

Those were the days when Regent Street abounded in gambling houses with their regiments of rogues, called 'Greeks,' who decoyed strangers into these abominable dens.

The judases, the smoke-blackened ceilings, the dark-panelled walls, the guttering tallow candles shedding their light on the green tables—those grasping hands, those bloodshot eyes staring at the dice with incipient madness; these nightmares require an effort of the imagination. Those senseless nights when young men of allegedly good breeding woke honest citizens with their raucous cries shock our ideas of decency to-day.

From the very beginning the Regent Street shops were fashionable, and Jay's, like Swan & Edgar's, has grown with the street. Prints of Jay's show it as a 'Mourning Ware-house,' all hung with black, because it specialized in putting, not only aristocratic families, but every member,

from the gardener to the cook, of their vast households
into crêpe.

But when these shops we still frequent were young,
Regent Street was bohemian. At the time Sala wrote
about, there were bakers' shops, stationers, and opticians
who had models of steam engines in their windows. The
little grocers sold marmalade, brown sugar, and Durham
mustard. You could buy a penny cake of chocolate.
There were music shops, shawl shops, jewellers, French
glove shops, perfumery, and point lace shops, confectioners,
and milliners.

Soon the little shawl shop became a vast, palatial building
with marble pillars supporting the roof, mirrors lining the
walls, Turkey carpets covering the floor, and eastern vases
adorning the windows. Handsome chandeliers shed their
pearly light around, denoting the opulence of wealth and
the refined taste of the proprietors. The cashmere shawls
therein cost no less than three hundred guineas!

There were the makers of the parasol, that pretty adjunct
to mid-Victorian dress, of which the Sylphide was then
most popular, whose light and graceful form could be seen
in all the most fashionable drives and promenades in and
near London; and here in Regent Street, also, was the
house of Johnson, hatters to Queen Victoria.

We see, therefore, the beginnings of a Regent Street which
in due course was to become the home of great stores, but
still, at that period, it was encountering stiff opposition
from St. Paul's Churchyard, of all places, for the City clung
to its early importance as a shopping centre.

If you visit what is left of Paternoster Row since the
great fire of December 1940 you will see that the only
shops left are drapery establishments. The dim publishing
houses have been rolled away; so also has the hotel where
Charlotte Brontë put up when she came to town, very shy,
from Haworth Parsonage. Yes, everything but the drapery
stores has become open country with granite boulders and
chickweed.

On the shelves of the London Library there is a guide to London in 1851, in which your attention is drawn to the elegant and tastefully disposed shops near Paternoster Row where 'well-dressed women thronging every avenue, attract the visitor's attention, impelling her alike to wonder and admiration.' Here she could find the largest plate-glass windows in London, behind which were exhibited the rich silks of Lyons and Spitalfields, the superb velvets from Genoa, the ribbons from Paris and Coventry, and the delicate laces from Valenciennes, Honiton, and Buckinghamshire. Capricious, indeed, must have been our grandmothers, staying doubtless at the Belle Sauvage Inn on Ludgate Hill, who could not gratify in such stores their wishes.

But gradually the City lost the tussle, and Sir Arthur Liberty was to bring to Regent Street even more splendidly the wonders of China and the Indies. His plate-glass gradually became even more impressive than that in the avenues near Paternoster Row.

While the aesthetes 'walked down Piccadilly with a poppy or a lily' in their medieval hands, and while the *Mikado's* lilting tunes were charming theatre-goers at the new Savoy Theatre, this Arabian Nights store influenced the country homes of England.

When the new Regent Street was completed in 1927, King George and Queen Mary drove along it in state. It had become the widest and the noblest of the arms radiating from Piccadilly Circus, but for a number of years after that triumphant drive the street seemed too wide and too noble to have that warm friendly atmosphere which a street needs to claim a corner in our hearts. But all the stores were by now very fine, and two famous Paris houses, the Galeries Lafayette and the Louvre, had lately opened branches there, bringing the most lovely things from France at a time when fashion required us to wear beaded dresses, or short skirts, with cloche hats.

The grey cold morning of 18th September 1940 provided

the most grandiose spectacle of Regent Street's one hundred and twenty years of life. On that day, I stood as near Oxford Circus as one could get, with thousands of girls who worked in the great stores, watching the mighty fire which, begun during the night, was still consuming a million pounds' worth of rich silk in the house of John Lewis in Oxford Street. Such wealth of material would have appeared fabulous indeed to the early drapers of Paternoster Row whose first plate glass was the marvel of the town. The fire raid had filled the streets with shattered glass more than a foot deep. The first incendiaries had fallen on the island site of the great store, quickly burning it to the ground, and the strong wind drove the flames to the east block on the other side of Holles Street which, though burning furiously, remained structurally intact. Peter Robinson's, at the north-east corner of the circus, was opened up as with a knife.

So tenacious are early trends, not only in people but in streets, that the Quadrant remains in our London of to-day something of an amusement centre. Of course, tastes have changed. The modern cafés have replaced the gaming dens, while the New Gallery Cinema stands where Mademoiselle Follejambes of the Italian opera practised pirouettes before a cheval glass.

It was in the late eighteen-forties that the gambling hells and nocturnal high jinks of this part of Regent Street quite disappeared and a new era began.

As the London season of 1864 was drawing to a close, Daniel Nicolas Thévenon, a native of a Burgundian village, and his hard-working peasant wife, arrived in Regent Street from France with five pounds between them. Their grandson, Captain Nicols-Pigache, has told how they rented a vacant shop in Glasshouse Street, which they turned into a small café on condition that they allowed the owner free board and lodging until debt and interest were repaid. Every morning the peasant woman pushed her hand-cart to Covent Garden to buy the produce that her husband turned

into gold. The Café Restaurant Nicols became the rendez-
vous of kings, princes, artists, judges, sculptors, and men
of letters, who preferred this bohemian atmosphere, the
excellent food, good wines, and sparkling conversation of
this café, to the morose pleasures which another generation
had sought in the showy reflections of aristocratic Crock-
ford's. In due course the Restaurant Nicols was renamed
the Café Royal, and its bearded and portly owner made a
fortune which allowed him in the eighties to lay out a
country estate for his family at Surbiton which he named
Regent House. At this point a London solicitor named
Tyrrell Lewis approached the former French peasant
for capital to help an undertaking known as the Alcazar
in Leicester Square—a playhouse founded by Alexander
Henderson which was then in difficulties. Nicols soon
became owner of both freehold and building and in
1884 the place was renamed the Empire. Three years later
the playhouse became a music-hall whose name personifies
the nineties. The Café Royal in Regent Street and the
Empire in Leicester Square bring nostalgic memories back to
Londoners who believe that the nights of their youth had a
glamour that we shall never know. For many long years the
Nicols's family box at the Empire was placed at the disposal
of the evening's most distinguished client at the Café Royal.

Nicols died in 1897, after which a Mr. Oddenino was
appointed manager of the Café Royal, where he secured the
backing of one of his customers to build a restaurant of his
own. Thus the Imperial Restaurant was born immediately
next door to the Café Royal, which situation it still occupies.
The Quadrant, therefore, shared with Leicester Square the
hub of night life as it had done in the past. The story of
the Café Royal is one of the romances of the town, and the
subsequent tragedy whereby the Nicols family lost their
splendid inheritance, owing to the rebuilding of Regent
Street in the twenties, is one of those harrowing repetitions
of fortunes won and lost in a night which pave the streets
of London.

One likes to look upon that family group reproduced in Mr. Nicols's book and dream for a moment on the glory which was Nicholas Thévenon's. The Shah of Persia made him immense offers to purchase the entire *corps de ballet* of the Empire. Nicols smiled politely at the shah who, perhaps, was not as rich as he. Consider this man of immense girth, as fat as Henry the Eighth, as powerful as a Rothschild, his eyes half closed, an almost square bowler-hat resting comfortably on his white forehead, his ample beard, his massive watch-chain half hidden by the champagne bottle on the white-clothed table pressed forward by his ample belly. All who were famous and gifted in the nineties were proud to be greeted by this man who only a few years earlier had wondered where his next meal would come from, while his little wife, now bonneted and becaped, had sewed until her eyes ached.

He died too young, this Nicolas Thévenon, but already a whole era was passing with him. His widow, whose hand-cart was stored in the stables with the broughams and the landaus made obsolete by the petrol engine, lived to see the first years of the war of 1914–18, when the Café Royal was made turbulent by men on leave from the blood baths of the Somme, but the immense rebuilding scheme of the post-war years swallowed up the fortune which the peasant couple, now both laid to rest, had accumulated by hard work.

In the spring of 1948 I was introduced to Mr. Nicols, for whom the story of the Café Royal is now merely a terrible dream. He is happy in quite a different career, but he recalled for me some of his feelings a quarter of a century ago, during the last cruel months when, bewildered in a maze of intricate figures, he saw, through no fault of his own, the Café Royal slipping out of his hands. One day, finding the situation unbearable, he went to Paris, and it was there, he told me, that he heard in a casual conversation with an old customer, that the Bank of England had just put in a receiver. That was the end. It was not even worth while returning to London. He would have been a stranger in his gilded palace, so he took the night train for Cologne, where he had heard of some work, but when he arrived the post was filled. From Cologne he rushed to Berlin, where Louis Adlon had been looking for a director for his famous hotel, but again Mr. Nicols arrived too late. Somebody else had just been appointed!

Not many years after Mr. Nicols had travelled so dramatically to Berlin in the hope of finding some sort of employment to keep him alive, Hans Kempinski, then at the head of one of the greatest catering businesses in Europe, sat in his office in Berlin apprehending the moment when the mighty empire he reigned over would tumble about his shoulders. His name—Kempinski—glittered in immense letters by night over the famous Potzdamerplatz, from the dizzy heights of the Vaterland where once every hour an artificial thunderstorm broke over a huge tableau of the Rhineland, in front of which thousands of Berliners drank their beer and talked about the new Hitler movement. Kempinski was about sixty then. There were now many restaurants under the family control, but at this very moment when the business had become as important as the one which Nicolas Thévenon's former customer Joseph Lyons had founded in this country, Kempinski saw that his rich banking accounts, his stocks of wine and food, his great restaurants sturdily built of steel and cement, his name which had become famous throughout Central Europe, his pictures, his estates, and motor cars—all these were but tinsel which might slip through his hands in a single night while he and his family were led to torture and death.

Kempinski, his son Gerhard, and his daughter-in-law Mélanie therefore came to London, where, like the Thévenons seventy years earlier, they opened a restaurant off Regent Street. There is something immensely pathetic about Nicolas Thévenon's grandson walking out of Regent

Street into the unknown; and the still rich and powerful Kempinski, not even yet despoiled of his earthly treasures, beginning again, at sixty, like a penniless immigrant, in a strange country which he was too old to understand, thinking, as he must have done at night: 'Everything across the water is as I left it. Shall I, dare I, go back and take possession of what belongs to me by the labour of my hands?'

When war broke out, Hans Kempinski made a journey to America and died there almost immediately. His mighty restaurants in Berlin are shattered now, but in Swallow Street you will see his name glittering with electric light bulbs over the immensely popular restaurant which his daughter-in-law Mélanie Kempinski is carrying on. This Swallow Street, this remnant of the seventeenth-century street which ran from Piccadilly to Oxford Street, the remainder being swallowed up by Nash's Regent Street, has a character all of its own. There is something of Montmartre about it—a Montmartre which would have sprung up where Pope and Addison walked. Not quite English and yet not quite foreign, the mixture is a strange reminder of the days when the colonnades of the Quadrant attracted people of other lands. Perhaps it gains from not having the width of Regent Street proper or from the way it holds hands with Piccadilly—a link between the 'way to Readinge' and the drive in front of the palace of the great Prince Regent!

There were still noblemen's stables in this part of Swallow Street when Martinez, who was to become a personal friend of the late King Alfonso of Spain, built a restaurant there in 1923. Martinez is no ordinary restaurateur. Towards the end of the 1914–18 war he had founded a Spanish Club in Welles Street, Oxford Street, where the great fire raged in September 1940. His choice of Swallow Street for the setting up of his restaurant makes a strange story. He had been to visit premises in Piccadilly where a finely appointed restaurant was for sale. The interior was perfect, but upon leaving it he felt glad to find himself again in Piccadilly, for which reason he decided against the place, and it was while walking thoughtfully through Swallow Street that he saw the stables so reminiscent of an earlier age. By six o'clock the same evening he had taken possession of them, and within a few months opened the restaurant so frequently patronized by his monarch who, after losing his throne, visited Martinez at his private residence.

Swallow Street possesses two other restaurants of importance—Veeraswamy's India Restaurant, whose turbaned doorkeeper is a picturesque figure in the street; and Bentley's oyster bar, which moved to its present position from a site in Piccadilly Place next to El Vino. Piccadilly Place is a narrow passage leading from Piccadilly into Vine Street, where the West End's most famous police station stood since 1868 on the site of the old watch-house, home of the Bow Street runners. The police station, amalgamated with that of Great Marlborough Street, moved on 15th July 1940 to the dazzling new station in Savile Row, where less than two months afterwards it was damaged by a land mine which killed three men and injured thirty-three. One of the police on duty was bayoneted against the wall by a jagged piece of glass.

Both Bentley's oyster bar and El Vino in Piccadilly Place were blasted in the great raid which set St. James's Church, Piccadilly, on fire and destroyed the rectory.

Piccadilly Place has become deserted and in Vine Street the blue lamp of the old police station is cracked, and one thinks of the criminals and boat-race night revellers who were brought before sergeants on duty depicted by Edgar Wallace. Part of the station now serves as an aliens' office. Meanwhile the lights of Swallow Street burn more brightly than ever, as the London oyster man flourishes beside the Spaniard, the Indian, and the son of that Berlin refugee who lies buried across the Atlantic.

Bentley's were not the only ones to have anxious moments during the Battle of London. A delayed-action bomb having fallen in Regent Street, opposite the arch of Swallow Street, Martinez was obliged to send his customers away half through dinner and seek for himself and his wife, who was ill at the time, the hospitality of a nearby hotel, where for twenty hours they listened for the explosion which might utterly destroy their restaurant. Consider the feelings of this unfortunate man, moving from the suffering woman he loved to the window from whence he could glance at the business he had built up over so many years, knowing that everything therein was in perfect order, the wrought-iron embellishments he had brought over from Seville, the portrait of his monarch who had just died in exile, his cutlery and his wines which he could never replace; that all these things were as he knew them, but that at any moment they could disappear in a cloud of rubble! How small and mean now seemed those high jinks of regency days, when the bloods of the town passed through this same street to pillage, out of drunken fun, some milliner's establishment in the colonnaded Quadrant. Not till six o'clock the following evening did the bomb explode, but though the front of the Spanish restaurant was blasted and the restaurant damaged, Martinez made his way in by torchlight an hour later, and the following day served eighteen lunches in the sherry bar, after which date the restaurant remained open day and night.

In the Quadrant, night after night the great new buildings of the Café Royal and Oddenino's were packed with men and girls on leave, crowding the cocktail bars, queueing up for tables in the restaurant, and sitting on those red plush divans of the Glasshouse Street café which poor Mr. Nicols had designed before the financial tragedy which wrecked his dreams.

After the war of 1939-45 had been finished for some months, Regent Street began to take on quite a new aspect. The world's great air companies descended upon it, bringing palatial offices and bright lights. This wide street, which hitherto had worn a rather cold expression on its

features, suddenly seemed to find a soul. Its very dis-
advantages were being turned to account. While the
papers talked about a scheme to widen Piccadilly, Regent
Street suddenly seemed to have become just the right
width from pavement to pavement. This was obviously
going to be the street of to-morrow, and quite certainly
those who were responsible for rebuilding it twenty years
earlier had been proved intelligent.

Why had all these air companies chosen Regent Street?
They had come there logically borne on warm trade winds
blowing from the direction of Cockspur Street!

In the days when Kipling sang the empire and the throb
of steel ships, Cockspur Street, that appendage of Trafalgar
Square, became the West End home of such great companies as the Cunard, the White Star, the C.P.R., and the
P. & O. which sent our empire builders out east. All
these companies had charming little models, but at first
one did not meet them beyond Pall Mall, as if they were
a trifle frightened of stepping on the toes of the sahibs in
clubland.

Then, especially between the two great world wars, not
only shipping companies but also travel agencies sprang up
in both Haymarket and Lower Regent Street. In Haymarket one saw posters of American locomotives with
cow-catchers and clanging bells in the windows of the
American Express Company. On the opposite side of the
street one was fascinated by Dutch ships, German ships,
including the then proud *Bremen* and *Europa*, and French
aeroplanes, these last at the offices of Air France. Only
the Germans have gone.

Lower Regent Street had the Blue Star's West End
office with the fine model of the *Arandora Star*, which was
torpedoed with so many of our London *restaurateurs* on
board soon after Italy had declared war on us. The
Portuguese and the Swiss set up tourist bureaux here, and
the Irish came along too. In the spring of 1948 the
Cunard Line, having deserted Cockspur Street, set up in

magnificent offices, flying its flag high above the roofs of
Lower Regent Street.

The travel movement has therefore for some time been
creeping towards Piccadilly Circus, up the two parallel
avenues. Perhaps this is only right, because Piccadilly
Circus, when it was Regent Circus, Piccadilly, was, if you
remember, the chief booking centre for the last of the
stage-coaches and the first of the railways.

But whereas the shipping companies seemed to hesitate
about crossing Piccadilly Circus, a great number of air
lines, some of them quite new to London, circled, figura-
tively speaking, over Eros, and made elegant landings in
Regent Street proper. Regent Street had every reason to
welcome them. The street gained enormously.

A WALK ALONG REGENT STREET—CHRISTMAS 1947

For Regent Street, Christmas 1947 was more than just
another Christmas. The street with a new aspect wanted
to show itself off. Besides, this was its twentieth
anniversary.

Though things were becoming more expensive almost
every day, the stores were beginning to gather in the
advantages of peace. This was a Christmas of daffodils
and lilac, the most magnificent silks and satins from France,
longed-for perfumes and cosmetics in vast quantities, dolls
from Milan who opened and closed their ravishing eyes
and sweetly said 'Mama' in Italian, sugared fruit from
Cannes which, as a child, one read about in Mme de
Ségur's *Malheurs de Sophie*, and quite a lot of other things
which we had apparently been given in exchange for
machinery.

The Milanese dolls looked at the throngs passing along
Regent Street from almost all the stores, and their expres-
sions were so human, their real hair so beautifully curled,
and their straw hats so colourfully beribboned that one
smiled for the joy of seeing them. They stood in pairs

round tiny fir-trees in the windows of Swan & Edgar's. This great store had curving tubes of red, white, and blue fluorescent lighting which, in its various forms, could be seen all down the street, changing the entire aspect of nocturnal London. The mysterious yellows of a century and more were disappearing in favour of vivid whites and pinks and blues, a revolution of considerable magnitude, killing the more artistic shadows of London by gaslight and early electric lamp.

From the swing doors of the Piccadilly Hotel came a party of South Americans, who now hurried into B.O.A.C., whose 'Speedbirds cross land and sea.' The great office, banked with flowers, whose employees were dressed in smart blue uniforms with gold buttons, had over the door: 'It's a Small World by Speedbird.' Further on one saw clocks and watches from Switzerland which, according to Board of Trade regulations, must not cost more than a certain price so that as many of them might be imported as possible. Shops for the sale of Swiss watches appeared to have opened all over the town. Beyond Swallow Street one passed the New Gallery, where Charlie Chaplin was exchanging the role of clown for that of Bluebeard. A great new French bookshop in the modern style had just opened, and next to it was Gérard, the florist's from Bond Street, with its windows springlike with hyacinths, daffodils, violets, lilac, orchids, tulips, carnations, and mimosa.

Daylight at evening! Spring flowers before Christmas! It's a small world by Speedbird! Regent Street was the busy finger pointing to the future. Here the Belgian tourist centre had had tiny Christmas trees of cotton-wool, beautifully dressed medieval figurines, and posters inviting one to cross on a new Channel packet and bathe at Ostend. The Swedish Air Lines had built their façade of wood, the most magnificently polished teak, with their name laid across it in light blue. Here was modern architecture at its most effective, a symphony of pastel shades, and inside, what could be more enchanting than the climbing vines whose tendrils stretched against cream-coloured walls? What a delightful idea for the office of to-morrow where peaches will ripen in artificial sunlight warmed by beneficent rays! The enormous expanse of the more distant wall had a huge map painted on it, with air-lines stretching from Stockholm to Moscow, to Rio de Janiero and to Istanbul. A little farther on was Belgium's Sabena, with a light blue carpet and smart little arm-chairs with tubular cream frames on a parquet floor, cream walls with life-size photographs showing the loading of a machine and its subsequent take-off, and a great mass of flowers by the window. Lastly, I think, on this side of the street, came the Irish Air Lines with a bevy of pretty, dark-eyed Dublin girls behind an emerald-green counter, while the windows were simply covered in spring blooms. London–Dublin now in ninety minutes, said the poster with its shamrock leaf over white and yellow stripes.

Across the road the lights of Dickins & Jones glittered on the damp pavement of this warm drizzly evening, and beckoned one inside to admire the riches of this magnificent store with its high walls, half cedar wood, half cream, its huge Christmas-tree with the fairy waving her wand on the topmost branch, and its masses and masses of daffodils, which even decorated the smart little desks of the chief saleswomen. There was a delicious smell of fir-tree, spring flowers, and Lanvin's Arpège, which for some reason seemed to dominate all the other perfumes from the great French fashion houses. But most tempting and disturbing of all were the moirés with silver threads running through their rich texture, the satin brocades, the velvets, the pure silks, and the cotton zephyrs from Lyons which gleamed and shimmered and spread their enticing folds all round one, inviting one to turn them into dresses for every occasion.

The windows of Liberty's, where our grandmothers admired the treasures of the Indies, showed hand-made lingerie from Paris; Jaeger's had a Christmas tree, but,

F

alas, no knitting wool; Fuller's had big white boxes of sugar plums from Avignon, but 'not a chocolate left in the place, madame'; Hamley's had a bevy of koala bears, 'Australia's gift to the nursery'; and the Galeries Lafayette an orgy of perfumes, lingerie, house-coats, and adorable dolls in heavy brocades from Quimper in Brittany, so magnificently attired that our eyes blinked with surprise and wonderment. Here were Kodak's and Boots', and, where Revillon, the furrier, used to be, the American Overseas Air Lines! In the distance, the lights of the Café Royal.

What a glorious place, in spite of restrictions, was Regent Street on Christmas Eve!

ST. JAMES'S AND THE GREEN PARK

WHEN EDWARD THE CONFESSOR was living in his new Palace of Westminster, a branch of the Thames curved round the monastery of St. Peter forming an island which, from its being overgrown by thorns, was called Thorney Island.

The land now occupied by St. James's Park was low and marshy, with a pool in the centre known as Cowford, and when each spring the branch of the Thames overflowed its banks, St. James's Park was partly flooded. To the north of St. James's Park there were dense woods, in which a stream called the Tyburn had its source at Hampstead. The stream meandered across Oxford Street, watered the fields of the future Mayfair, ran over the 'way to Readinge,' through the hollow of the Green Park, and emptied itself into the Thames near Vauxhall Bridge. Somewhere in the neighbourhood of Buckingham Palace it connected with Cowford Pool.

The only habitation in St. James's Park was the Leper Hospital, which Stow tells us was founded before the time of any man's memory. Our earliest record of it dates from 1100. Grim and desolate indeed must have been this hospital for 'maidens that were leprous, living chastely,' on the fringe of its watery meadow.

The branch of the Thames which stretched its arm round the monastery of St. Peter disappeared a hundred years after the Conquest, and the rivulet connecting the Tyburn with Cowford Pool dried up. It is not very clear in what state Henry the Eighth found St. James's Park when he demolished the Leper Hospital and built St. James's Palace in its place, but he certainly drained the land, and we know that he built a wall round the park and ordained many commodious things within it for his pleasure and use.

135

In the charter from Abbot Islip to Henry the Eighth relative to this acquisition there appears the name of Rosamond's Land, a name which we find clearly marked as a pond near the present Buckingham Gate. In the pond were fishes, and beside it a mound with some pretty trees, while in the park were many deer.

James the First, who introduced the mulberry-trees in the park, also made a menagerie there in which he kept camels and an elephant he received from the King of Spain, hawks and live sables from the Czar of Muscovy, two antelopes from the Great Mogul, and a tame leopard from the King of Savoy. At the other end of the park, near the entrance to Spring Gardens, Whitehall, the young Prince of Wales—who was later to set up his own establishment at St. James's Palace, where he died at the age of nineteen—and his brother Charles, planted some young trees which many years later the unfortunate King Charles pointed out to Bishop Juxon on the morning he was led to his execution. For a brief moment, towards the end of the Commonwealth, we see Oliver Cromwell wandering through the empty rooms of Whitehall, the garden, and the park, a terror to all who beheld him; then, with the Restoration, began the brilliant days.

Even before Jermyn and Hyde were laying out the West End as we know it by building on those parcels of land north of St. James's Palace which Charles the Second granted them in 1664, the king was busy planning the park. His first idea was to approach the great French landscape gardener Le Nôtre, who had just laid out the gardens of the Tuileries for Louis the Fourteenth and who was drawing up the plans for the future Versailles, but Le Nôtre was of opinion that the natural simplicity of St. James's Park had more grandeur than even he could impart to it, and persuaded the king not to fashion it in the French way. Charles the Second accordingly altered his scheme and made a canal running much as it does now from the mulberry garden, where Dryden ate mulberry

This picture was painted from County Hall.

You will see Cleopatra's Needle and Charing Cross Bridge which Kipling sang when the continental boat trains used to pull out romantically across it, taking Londoners to the burning sands of Africa.

The great Shell-Mex building has replaced the old Hotel Cecil, but the Savoy still houses millionaires of many lands who gaze across the embankment gardens at the murky river, dreaming of the Neva, the Elbe, or the Seine.

Beyond the Savoy stands the insignificant building that after the First World War housed 2LO, forerunner of the B.B.C. The modern Waterloo Bridge is magnificent and catches every particle of sun. In the Middle Temple the plane-trees mourn their lost treasures. You can see the Elizabethan ball, gravely damaged, where Twelfth Night was first performed. Behind it you must imagine Fountain Court, which Dickens describes in Martin Chuzzlewit.

The tower on your right is the Shot Tower.

A V2 once plunged into the mud-bank here.

tarts, to Whitehall, nearly opposite the Cockpit Gate. Goring House, on the site of our Buckingham Palace, occupied during the Civil War by William Lenthall, the Speaker, was about to shelter the Earl of Arlington, and Rosamond's Pool was where to-day you will find the children's playground between Buckingham Palace and the Wellington Barracks. Birdcage Walk was planted with two lines of trees, and Duck Island, the breeding-place of the numerous waterfowl, instead of being in the centre of the lake as it is now, was at the side of it, a little nearer to Storey's Gate.

Pepys records how three hundred men were daily engaged in uniting the different pools and springs into one sheet of water to make the canal. A thicket of trees was planted round Rosamond's Pool, which became such a romantic spot that it was sung by all the poets of the age, and their successors, as the favourite place for lovers. Wycherley, Congreve, and Otway mention it in their plays.

Meanwhile, as Pall Mall was changing from a country lane to a residential street, the dust from the passing coaches annoyed the players of the game and they transferred their activities to a new mall within the park, on each side of which were planted goodly elms and sweet limes extending all the way from Goring House to Spring Gardens, past the pheasantry on the site of which, in the reign of Queen Anne, Marlborough House was to rise next to St. James's Palace.

General Monk, who had been responsible for the restoration, was made keeper of the park, which in the autumn of 1660 was opened to the public, and Sir John Flock, who had been a constant follower of Charles the Second in exile, was made governor of Duck Island, a picturesque sinecure afterwards given to the Chevalier de St. Evremond.

Charles the Second spent many of his happiest hours in St. James's Park, and through the eyes of the chroniclers of the time we have charming pictures of the gay, good-humoured monarch surrounded by a bevy of pretty women, sauntering through the alleys, watching the pelicans being fed, or examining the withy-pots or nests for the wild fowl to lay their eggs in, a little above the surface of the water, in the decoy round Duck Island.   Charles's love for his dogs was not the least lovable trait in his character, and when any one of them was lost he was not above composing an advertisement for it to be printed in the *Mercurius Politicus*:

We must call upon you again for a Black Dog, between a Greyhound and a Spaniel no white about him only a streak on his Breast and Tayl a little bobbed.   It is His Majesty's own Dog, and doubtless was stoln, for the Dog was not born nor bred in England and would never forsake his Master.   Whosoever findes him may acquaint any at Whitehall, for the Dog was better known at Court than those who stole him.

We find Pepys in the summer of 1663 hurrying along the Old Pall Mall on his way to the park, and there meeting that Earl of St. Albans who was to build St. James's Square, Jermyn Street, King Street, St. James's Church, Piccadilly, and all those other places we have learned to love, walking beside the remarkable Henrietta Maria, daughter of the great French king Henry the Fourth, and Marie de Médicis, and widow of the unfortunate Charles the First.   She was living at St. James's Palace with the Duke of York.   What a grand lady was the queen-mother!   Her eldest son was on the throne, her second son was to reign as James the Second, and her daughter, the beautiful Henrietta Anne, was married to Monsieur, brother of Louis the Fourteenth, the Sun King, then building his Palace of Versailles.   The French called Henrietta Anne Henriette d'Angleterre, and who can read Bossuet's oration upon her premature death without tears, for this great prelate's words are amongst the jewels of the French language?   With Pepys for our guide, Queen Henrietta Maria and the man who built St. James's Square and

Jermyn Street (they were supposed to have been secretly married) become real people, and we almost see them walking slowly towards the gate of the park where Pepys found a great many coaches and heard that the Duchess of York, the Earl of Clarendon's daughter, Anne Hyde, had just been confined of a son.

Charles the Second and Queen Catherine, with the ladies of honour, had gone on horseback to Hyde Park, and presently the cortège came in sight, the queen looking mighty pretty in her white-laced waistcoat. Then Pepys followed them to Whitehall, and into the queen's presence chamber, where all the ladies walked, talking and fiddling with their hats and feathers, and changing and trying them on one another's head, and laughing.

On warm summer evenings the Mall was crowded until the small hours of the morning for fresh air and flirtation, and here you would see the fashions piping hot from Paris —the beaux as fine as the ladies—Beau Hewitt with an equipage of six French footmen and a page behind him; the king, sauntering with his dogs, smiling at pretty faces under ribbons and feathers, or walking alone as far as Constitution Hill to see his brother returning from the chase at Hounslow.

Picture also that Sunday morning in 1666 when, the weather being mighty hot and Pepys weary, the good man lay down upon the grass by the canal and slept awhile.

And so the years go on, and we even see Dutch William, who was to forsake Whitehall for Kensington Palace, building himself a little summer-house on Duck Island.

Then to the Augustan age when St. James's Street saw Steele and Addison and Pope, and Dean Swift and John Gay, and when the Clarindas and the Belindas of the *Tatler*, patched and painted, swept along the Mall.

By 1770 St. James's Park had gone out of fashion, and both Duck Island and Rosamond's Pool were swept away. Buckingham House was now the property of

George the Third, who had bought it eight years earlier for £21,000.

His son, both as Prince of Wales and later as Prince Regent, used Carlton House as his town residence, but in 1814, when John Nash the architect, already very famous though he had not yet designed Regent Street, was appointed deputy surveyor-general, designs were drawn up for transforming Carlton House. Nash was also called upon to provide gay buildings of a temporary nature for peace celebrations. The Treaty of Paris had been signed in the spring and the Napoleonic menace appeared at an end. The Government felt that the national prestige would be all the better for a victorious flourish. Nash added some temporary accommodation at Carlton House for a fête in honour of the Duke of Wellington, but this was not enough, and 'displays of joy still more striking and appropriate to the occasion' were planned for August. John Summerson, in his admirable book on John Nash, says that they would have taken place earlier, but were so elaborate that they needed many weeks to prepare. There was some danger of anticlimax, for 'peace was now become a circumstance with which the public mind was familiarized.' Luckily the centenary of the accession of George the First, founder of the dynasty, coincided, so the inscriptions were changed and the new displays of joy directed to the occasion.

In St. James's Park there still existed Charles the Second's long canal, and over this Nash built a Chinese bridge, with a huge pagoda in the middle and pavilions at each end. The lawns were illuminated and the trees hung with Chinese lanterns.

In the midst of the celebrations the pagoda, which had been pouring forth showers of rockets, suddenly burst into flames. A man leapt from the tower into the water, cracking his skull on a floating stage. Most of the pagoda fell into the canal. The bridge was unharmed, and together with the stump of the pagoda was used by pedestrians for many years.

* F

St. James's Park looked a wreck after the peace celebrations, and it cost the Government a considerable sum to repair the damage.

When in 1820 the Prince Regent succeeded to the throne as George the Fourth, the plans for rebuilding Carlton House were dropped. The king was anxious to leave this residence 'at the top of a street,' and to erect a new palace suitable to his kingship. Nash, now even more famous for the building of Regent Street, was called upon to rebuild Buckingham House and, as the venture cost more and more money, Carlton House was pulled down to defray the expense.

At the same time Nash transformed St. James's Park, which, with its straight canal, had become a swampy tract. He made a long, curly lake with islands, removed the bridge of 1814, levelled Birdcage Walk, and placed iron railings all round the park.

Buckingham House became Buckingham Palace. A thousand workmen tried to complete it in time for the king's birthday in 1830. Many of them worked by candlelight till ten o'clock each night and more and more money was spent, but the king did not live to celebrate his birthday.

The palace, for which Nash and his royal master were so much blamed, is to-day one of the most glorious sights in London. The suspension bridge in St. James's Park, against which now grows the fig-tree whose hard unformed fruit cover the grassy shores in autumn, was put there by Queen Victoria in 1857, and the bed of the lake was raised and covered with concrete, the deepest part not exceeding four feet.

THE GREEN PARK

At the restoration of Charles the Second, the Green Park was a swampy meadow planted with willow-trees and intersected with ditches. On the north it was bordered by the 'way to Readinge,' our modern Piccadilly, and to

the east by St. James's Street. To the south, Pall Mall
was continued to the gardens of Goring House, whence
Constitution Hill branched off as it does now to the present
Hyde Park Corner.

Charles the Second added the Green Park to St. James's
Park, but he made few embellishments beyond building an
'ice house' in the centre where cool drinks were served in
the summer, and making a deer park at the western end.

In Faithorne's plan of 1658 only one house is shown
opposite the palace in St. James's Street, but that house
was nearly as large as the palace itself. The mansion and
grounds occupied the corner of St. James's Street and the
extension of Pall Mall towards Constitution Hill, and it
was called Berkshire House, after the Howards, Earls of
Berkshire.

For a very short time after the Restoration this mansion
was occupied by Lord Clarendon, and it was doubtless
from here that the Lord Chancellor and his lady carried
Evelyn in their coach to see their new palace rising on the
site of what is now Bond Street, Stafford Street, and
Albemarle Street. This was rather more than a year after
the Duchess of York, Clarendon's daughter, had been
confined of a son in St. James's Palace.

In 1668 (by which time Lord Clarendon had forsaken
both his new palace and the town), Charles the Second
gave Berkshire House to his mistress Lady Castlemaine,
created Duchess of Cleveland (she whom Pepys describes
with a yellow plume in her hat), but shortly afterwards
Lady Castlemaine disposed of the old house, sold the large
garden, and reserved only the south-west corner on which
stands to-day Bridgewater House, the property of the Earl
of Ellesmere and the largest private mansion in London.

Part of the gardens which Lady Castlemaine sold became
St. James's Place. We therefore see a line of houses
rising between St. James's Street and the Green Park.
Meanwhile Charles the Second had granted a strip of land
at the top end of the street to the Earl of Arlington, then

living at Goring House, and upon this strip was built Arlington Street.

Because the Green Park was rather desolate and marshy, we hear of a good many duels there right up to the time of George the Second. Lord Hervey, who had left us such vivid glimpses of Queen Caroline, George the Second's queen, fought a duel here on a January afternoon in 1730 with William Pulteney, whose sword might well have robbed us of those memoirs if his foot had not slipped at the precise moment he held the advantage. Queen Caroline, that same winter, instructed the Board of Works to prepare a private walk along the row of mansions between St. James's Street and the park, for the royal family to divert themselves in the spring. She also thought of building a residence in the park, but apart from putting up a small pavilion, called the Queen's Library, the scheme was not carried out. On her way to this pavilion on 9th November 1737 to breakfast there, she was taken ill of the rupture from which she died ten days later at St. James's Palace, a scene Lord Hervey has minutely described for us. Important modifications of the Green Park took place when George the Third bought Buckingham House, which thereafter became a royal residence. Several acres of the park were annexed to make the palace gardens a year later—the wall separating it from St. James's Park was taken down and a railing put up instead. There were then two lodges in the Green Park, one on the top of Constitution Hill and the other at the south-east corner of the park on ground now occupied by Lancaster House, the late home of the London Museum. Gradually the Green Park became as fashionable on warm evenings as had the Mall half a century earlier, and people looked down upon the gay promenade from the bow windows and balconies at the back of the houses in Arlington Street. Lady Mary Coke, returning from the country to the small house in the park belonging to Lady Bateman, wrote in 1766: 'The Park perfectly green and six and twenty cows feeding upon the rising ground; not one Deer in sight. Some fine people walking under my windows, which rather hurts than improves the view. Two Arabian jessamins in full bloom, blowing into my room, where they have lived three years.'

During the coronation festivities in 1821, while Londoners were admiring Nash's Quadrant in the new Regent Street, a balloon was let up in the Green Park and upon it were the words: 'George the Fourth, Royal Coronation Balloon.' It rose with a slight inclination to the north, and owing to the clearness of the atmosphere remained visible for nearly half an hour.

A few years later the Chelsea Waterworks Company constructed a large reservoir in the north-east corner of the park, opposite Stratton Street, Piccadilly, but it was removed in 1855, by which time the entire park had been drained and planted with trees.

There are more trees in the Green Park now than at any time since pre-Restoration days when Londoners went bird-nesting there. You will find the beech and the old English elm, the sweet-flowering lime, the London plane-tree, the oak, the hawthorn, the maple, the sycamore, and the beautiful mountain ash. There is something much more rural about the Green Park than its carefully tended neighbour on the other side of the Mall. The grass grows high; sometimes sheep feed upon it, and sometimes you will smell the newly mown hay. Its leafy trees in summer give a distinction to Piccadilly which in places retains a good deal of the Victorian skyline, and in winter the low white mist drifts across the bare boughs, while southwards the sun makes a big orange ball. At its western extremity, over the Hyde Park Corner entrance into Constitution Hill, is the Wellington Arch surmounted by the quadriga, or chariot of peace, erected in 1911. Constitution Hill, along which Charles the Second, while walking with the Duke of Leeds and my Lord Cromarty one day, met the Duke of

York returning in his coach from a morning's hunting on Hounslow Heath, was then a dusty footpath bordered by willows. The present motor road was made in 1907 by taking away a small slice of the Green Park. The Mall of Restoration days still exists, but as a riding track alongside the new Mall, made as a memorial to Queen Victoria at the beginning of the century, though its extension from the Duke of York's Steps to Charing Cross was not opened until 1911. Queen Caroline's Walk from the Mall to Piccadilly still skirts the gardens of the great mansions which are the descendants of Berkshire House, the most magnificent of which is Bridgewater House, built a century ago from the designs of Sir Charles Barry.

This palace in the Italian style, its windows blasted, its superb picture gallery burned and wrecked, its great saloon a mockery of those pre-war days when its receptions were princely, the gilt ceilings of the first-floor state room overlooking the park crumbling and falling, is yet one of the most gorgeous sights in London, and shimmers, exteriorly undamaged, in the morning sun beside the Grecian beauty of Spencer House. Many smaller houses, no less historic, have been burned to the ground, the undergrowth from their gardens, grown wild, stretching budding tentacles over shattered foundations. The ghosts of Addison and John Wilkes, Mr. Secretary Craggs and Perdita roam over the bricks and brambles between St. James's Palace and the Green Park, and from the narrow passage, once darkened by abodes of the rich and the famous, you may bend down to look at the remains of a kitchen range, walls darkened by the smoke of once merry fires crackling in the hearth, deep cupboards not so very long ago stored with sweet-scented linen, and sideboards in which hung delicate crockery whose pieces, crushed to fine dust, line the very path you walk along.

Where the little houses of Arlington Street once had gardens joyously meeting the park, stands, undamaged by the Battle of London, the gigantic block of flats which

bears the name of this famous street, in which Horace
Walpole wrote his witty, urbane letters, and at the corner
of Piccadilly, in the French style, towers the beautifully proportioned Ritz Hotel built in 1906, when its steel
girders caused as much wonderment to Londoners as the
luxury of its fittings.

The Munich crisis cast a shadow of uneasiness over the
Green Park, along which during the years of peace revellers
had walked home in the early hours, exchanging the smoky
atmosphere of restaurant and night club for the sweet air
scented with hay or flowering limes. In Piccadilly, between
Stratton Street and Bolton Street, a depot was set up for
the distribution of the first gas-masks, which brought us
up against the reality of war for which we were unpre-
pared, and almost overnight bands of men, armed with
picks and spades, passed through the gates opposite the
Green Park underground station, to make those trenches
between the gardens of Arlington House and the bunch
of Cornish elms whose dark green foliage gives shade to
nurses and children in summer. Towards the middle of
August one of the very first barrage balloons to be set up
in London made its appearance at the western extremity of
the park facing Hamilton Place, almost on the same piece
of grass from which one hundred and eighteen years earlier
had gone up George the Fourth's royal coronation balloon.
Few Londoners understood what role the barrage balloon
was to play, and large crowds watched its installation. At
first it was supposed that the cables were in some way to
be connected one with another to form a net, but by the
time war was declared on that famous Sunday morning in
September when the sirens first sounded, though for a
false alarm, the pattern of the barrage as we were to know
it for so many years had taken shape. The Green Park
had its own siren serving Piccadilly, the great new buildings
in Park Lane, and the aristocratic squares of Mayfair, from
which their owners were making preparations to depart.
This siren was hidden between the wheels of the great

chariot of winged peace on the summit of the Wellington Arch, and at first was operated by the sergeant in charge of the little-known police station at the foot of the arch, where hangs the giant key which opens the central gate when royalty passes that way.

Now the lights went out in those delicately fashioned lamp-posts which border the gravel walks of the Green Park, and Piccadilly was no longer a ribbon of scintillating diamonds. Fear stalked through the town and a Bren-gun carrier and a red double-decker omnibus collided in the darkness of Hyde Park Corner, where there was not even the glimmer granted six months later from lamp-post and vehicle. Soldiers arrived to lay circles of barbed wire all across the grass, which had turned yellow after the heat of a torrid summer, but on moonlit nights in Green Park the balloon in all its silver beauty rode gently at anchor above the trees which were shedding their curly brown leaves amongst the barbed netting.

A year later, when the grass was again tired and brown after a summer which had been as hot as it had been disastrous, holiday-makers sitting in the deck-chairs of the park one Saturday afternoon watched silver specks in the blue sky, hardly visible when they came against the strong sun. The Battle of London had started, and in the evening when the sirens wailed, the fierce fires in dockland glowed above the roof of the Ritz and its gigantic neighbour, Arlington House. The first bomb which fell in the Green Park killed a soldier and a girl, flirting on a park bench, just within the railings along Piccadilly—romantic lovers too careless of death falling from the dark sky, so entirely engrossed in what Wycherley would have called their assignation, that they departed this world together, happy until the very end.

These were the times when Londoners thought their silver balloons so beautiful that many said: 'We never want to lose them.' They certainly looked lovely against the moon, but on rough nights the taut cable howled, and at the height of a nocturnal raid the Green Park balloon broke from its moorings, and its steel whip knocked down the chimney stacks of Piccadilly and Clarges Street with the rapid sound of machine-gun fire.

From time to time so many delayed-action bombs fell in the park that the gates were closed to the public for three or four days in succession, but for the most part the gravel walks gave the illusion of country surroundings to Londoners, whose bloodshot eyes revealed that they were short of sleep. The children, all but two or three whose names were known to all the *habitués*, had been evacuated with their nurses, but at Easter the deck-chairs were arranged under the Cornish elms and the chair-man waited with his roll of buff tickets for his customers to brave the chill winds.

Towards four o'clock one morning the Green Park witnessed a sight so magnificently terrible that it is strange to think how few people gathered to gaze upon it. The dark night had suddenly become deathly still, except for the distant crackling of burning timber. The air was thick with smoke, and in the middle of Piccadilly workmen from the gas company were gathered round a flaming leak. Otherwise the wide road was absolutely empty. The gates into the park opposite Half-Moon Street were open, and a dozen, perhaps two dozen people, were hurrying in the direction of St. James's Palace, which appeared to be in the centre of an immense brazier which stretched all the way from the bottom of Arlington Street to Lancaster House, the huge building at the corner of the Mall designed by Benjamin Wyatt for the Duke of York, George the Fourth's brother, who did not live to see it finished. Yes, the flames stretched along Queen Caroline's Walk almost from one end to the other, and, there being no water to extinguish them, the fires grew redder and brighter at every moment, throwing into impressive relief the white Grecian façade of Spencer House whose marble figure surmounting the apex stood out like a goddess poised above the inferno.

The stables behind Spencer House had set fire to the roof
of the immense picture gallery of Bridgewater House,
Barry's square Italian palace, in which the eight largest
pictures, the only ones to be left behind, were disintegrating
in thick smoke which poured out of the wide northern
windows.   Half a dozen smaller mansions were collapsing
in flames where once the gardens of mighty pretty Lady
Castlemaine's queenly residence heard the laughter of her
royal lover.   By what miracle did the red-brick palace of
St. James's escape destruction that night?   Lurid was the
gateway outside which Pepys and Evelyn had gossiped and
through which a good hundred years earlier Henry the
Eighth, attired in white and silver, used to ride out on May
mornings to pick fragrant boughs in the woods about
Kensington.

This spectacle, as gorgeous as it was heart-breaking,
passed almost unnoticed in the multiplicity of events, and
as the weather grew warmer the chair-man in the Green
Park would pick the mushrooms which flourished in the
long grass under the barbed-wire entanglements of a
morning, and at nine o'clock he would take them in a
basket to a greengrocer's in Shepherd Market, where they
were sold at a good profit both to him and to the shop-
keeper, for who would guess that mushrooms grew along
the banks of Piccadilly, once famous for the small bugloss
or ox-tongue?   This chair-man was an out-of-doors man,
and in the winter varied his occupation by delivering cables
for the wireless company, and he took as much pleasure
in exploring our London streets during the cold season as
in summer he took in searching for herbs and mushrooms
in the park.

During the following winter, when the first snows fell,
men arrived with acetylene blow-lamps to cut down the
iron railings dividing the park from Piccadilly, and suddenly it seemed as if the town was fringed with the country.
As new vistas were opened, Londoners suddenly realized
the tremendous beauty of the tree-lined avenue leading

from opposite Half-Moon Street to the golden-winged
figure above the distant Queen Victoria Memorial—an
avenue as noble as those which so often grace old French
châteaux, straight as the flight of a bird, long enough for
the boughs at the end to encircle their objective, so deserted
in these days of war that one had the impression of having
the most beautiful vistas of London all to oneself.   Here,
if it was needed, was proof that the beauty of the Green
Park is almost of our own generation, for this avenue is
Edwardian, while the beautiful wrought-iron gates leading
to it, which stood in front of the old Devonshire House,
were put here between the wars.   These wrought-iron
gates, like the railings, were taken away so that the grass
and the trees merged with the pavement.

Soon a new encampment made an appearance in the Green
Park between the bandstand and the Mall.   At first it consisted of a circular steel hut with a crazy chimney, a gravel
and sea-shell path framed by two magnificent catalpas, and
a narrow sentry-box above which were the words: 'The
Bombers' Moon.'   In the evening wisps of white smoke
curled up from the chimney, and the hut looked just like
the shoe of the old lady in the nursery rhyme who had so
many children she didn't know what to do.   To the north
of it the R.A.F. boys built a fort with earth and silver birch
trunks, Red Indian style, in the middle of which they put
one of those very modern searchlights that turn round
automatically by wireless control, and then they set about
making a garden for vegetables and another for flowers,
and the gravel walks were lined with white stones.   A
small white terrier, bombed out by the raids, attached itself
to the encampment where it was known by the name of
Spike, and at dinner-time you could smell the soup made
from the vegetables in the garden.

The Green Park therefore had two charming residences,
and the inhabitants of the Bombers' Moon vied with those
of the balloon site in growing those giant marrows which
in peacetime one used to see exhibited at flower and

vegetable shows organized by the vicar. The silver balloon rode serenely above the houses in Piccadilly, illuminated by the gleam of the searchlight which bathed the darkened streets of the town in a soft white light, which made them look even more romantic than they really were.

One day, again, a bulldozer was brought to the park where, between the Cornish elms and the avenue leading from Piccadilly to the Queen Victoria Memorial, a great hole was dug, from which the earth was piled in a miniature mountain all along the avenue. For many weeks Londoners speculated about its meaning, until it took the shape of a very pretty lake of considerable depth and lined with cement. By day as by night it was guarded by a curious old man who lived like a hermit in a shack beside it. He spoke English with a very quaint accent—he was probably Maltese—and he took his functions so seriously that when the dogs of the neighbourhood bounced into the lake just beginning to fill with water, he would rush out from behind his coke brazier with bare feet and shout angrily at any of us who happened to be near: 'Keep avay dose animals, madam, I tell you dis is drinking vater!'

But unlike the reservoir of the Chelsea waterworks which was built in the days of George the Fourth, whose coronation balloon made such a stir, the water was not to drink but to supply the fire service, who had no intention of again being caught with empty hoses as on that famous occasion when the mansions facing Queen Caroline's Walk had burned themselves out. Of all the sumps in London, this was perhaps the most ornamental, as befits that of a royal park, and, though never put to use, it made a pretty sight for the people who in summer sat in their deck-chairs under the shade of the Cornish elms. Children sailed their boats in it and dogs romped on its lapping sides, and for thousands and thousands of nocturnal lovers it had the same attraction as Rosamond's Pool three centuries earlier.

The chair-man who gathered mushrooms on dew-decked mornings had been temporarily replaced by a colleague who was formerly a famous pastry-cook and whose son was a captain in Malta; and the Munich trenches, now beautifully lined with cement walls and oak props, had become the domain of a gentlewoman who was very jealous of her functions, for any child who sought to enter her domain was promptly shooed off. The deserted gardens of the noble mansions along Queen Caroline's Walk flowered with sweet lilac and tulips pushed their delicate heads above the rubble, for nature triumphs over everything, and soon the Green Park was to live through its most glorious days, for the American army was marching into the town.

The 787th United States Military Police Battalion, having taken up its headquarters in a once-famous club at the corner of Piccadilly and Whitehorse Street, began to hold its Saturday morning parades on the beautiful green lawns to the west of the avenue leading to the Queen Victoria Memorial. Here was unfurled the Stars and Stripes. The flowering may-trees heard the music of their martial bands, and never had there been a prettier sight than when these fine men with their white helmets and white gaiters wheeled and formed fours or stood so smartly at attention while their national anthem was being played, the sounds echoing over the two catalpas guarding the entrance to the Bombers' Moon and mixing faintly in the distance with the music of the changing of the Guard in the courtyard of Buckingham Palace.

Now on bright afternoons our American allies played baseball, a new game to Londoners, beside the long mountain of earth thrown up from the ornamental lake, on which earth, grass was beginning to grow, making it a pleasant place to lie or sit, and idly watch the prowess of these players. And on warm evenings new assignations were made between man and girl beside the pond.

The paths and lawns of the two parks link the club houses of Piccadilly with the government buildings of modern Whitehall, and three times a day during the war, in the morning, at lunch-time, and in the evening, the gold-bedecked admirals, the red-tabbed generals, and senior officers of the R.A.F. and the civil servants of important rank, bowler-hatted, black coated, and carrying rolled umbrella and brief-case, walked briskly along a route which experience taught them to be the shortest. These distinguished persons were the despair of the gardeners, who in spite of the bombs which uprooted the trees and scattered the tulip bulbs, sought to keep the parks as neat and as pretty as they could. The fact is that the gardeners were up against that trait in human nature which delights in making a short cut—even if it is to the detriment of the lawns. Not only the railings but also the curved borders of the grass had been taken away, with the result that if one of these gentlemen noticed that by crossing a grassy mound the road could be shortened, he led the way, and soon, his example being followed, the lawn was cut by a a muddy track.

One sympathized to some extent with these august offenders. What joy in spring to watch the trees burst into bud, brush against boughs heavy with lilac blossom, and tarry on the suspension bridge to throw bread to the ducks! They were, in fact, enjoying the same idle pleasures which Charles the Second found so much to his taste. The man from the sea with twenty minutes to spare before his conference in Queen Anne's Mansions, his colleague from Bomber Command with a dispatch-case full of plans for loosing new terrors on the Ruhr, and the Cabinet Minister's P.P.S. during his lunch-hour, leaned over the steel bridge with a paper bag full of crumbs. The Merry Monarch had bequeathed them a gentle pastime.

In the morning the towers and spires of modern White-hall take on the aspect of an oriental city; in the evening the sun sets over Buckingham Palace, which appears to rise from the willows on the water's edge. At the bridge the workers of Whitehall divide, some going towards Queen Anne's Gate, where before leaving the park they

glance at the thermometer which stands opposite the
only mulberry-tree left in St. James's, a descendant of the
trees planted by James the First in his mulberry garden.
The luscious fruit is gathered every year in punnets, and
this rite was even observed during the historic invasion
of Normandy.   Other people take the path along the lake,
shaded in summer by poplars and the finest of oak-trees,
and across the lawns on which Charles the Second's Duck
Island stood, now rolling grass and old elms, upon which
Winston Churchill looked from the window of his office
in the War Cabinet offices in the Renaissance block
finished in 1915.

On the grass plots round Duck Island in the old days
grazed cows, which at noon and in the evening were driven
to the approaches of Whitehall, where they were tied to
posts and milked for the benefit of passers-by who paid a
penny a mug, and so strong was this tradition that until
1904 a small kiosk stood where the Mall now extends to
Admiralty Arch, and here cows were kept and fresh milk
sold.   Charles the Second's Mall, of course, only ran from
what is now Buckingham Palace to the Duke of York's
steps.   The extension of the new Mall to Admiralty Arch
is as recent as 1911, for before then traffic used Pall Mall.

The Horse Guards Parade was closed to Londoners
during the war, and people looked with interest at the
ochre-tinted fort built at the western end of the Admiralty,
a windowless monstrosity which hid the great secrets of
world communication.   So secret were its functions that
Londoners hardly dared to speak about the building, above
which flourished, in summer, a pleasant roof garden.

It is a little strange that the Duke of York's granite
column, standing on the site of the Prince Regent's Carlton
House, was never demolished by high explosives, which
were equally powerless to knock down Nelson in Trafalgar
Square.   One thinks, in this connection, of a workman
calmly seated on the summit of the lofty wireless mast
above the Admiralty one June morning in 1944, when

flying bombs were roaring past him at the rate of one a minute.

In Carlton House Terrace, that row of stucco houses in which the great and wealthy lived in Victorian days, there was a corner building where the Nazi ambassador, Ribbentrop, as he looked out in Munich days across the trees of the park at Buckingham Palace shining on one side, and Big Ben and the towers of the abbey rising on the other, dreamed of reducing this great and powerful city to dust and ashes. To no purpose did the scene before him unfold the history of this country since Canute sat at Westminster and the monks of the monastery of St. Peter walked along the banks of Cowford Pool. How pitiful did that embassy become, deprived of its swastika trappings, its heavy Teutonic furniture, and its ridiculous paintings of Hitler.

On winter evenings during the black-out, the walk from Whitehall's Storey Gate to Piccadilly was a strange adventure. Sometimes it was pitch dark, but long experience taught the Londoner each path, each shrub, each tree. When the moon rose the lake looked ethereally beautiful, and the traveller, having crossed the deserted Mall, saw a shaded light behind gay cretonne windows in the house shaped like a shoe, which looked more than ever as if it were a picture from a fairy-tale book. The lilac bloomed again, and during the invasion spring the Americans, growing each month in numbers, swarmed over the park, drilling, playing baseball, lying on the grassy lawns, courting the girls, offering cigarettes and candy to Londoners, taking photographs of each other against the sky-line of Piccadilly, and watching our Home Guards jumping in and out of the trenches that proved such pitfalls for the unwary. The Dutch, the French, the Belgians, and the Poles joined the crowds basking in the sun in the Green Park drawing-room between the Cornish elms and the ornamental lake—the Dutch from their offices in Stratton Street and Arlington House, the French from the modern block of offices in

Carlton House Terrace where the tricolour with its Cross
of Lorraine flew high above the parks, and the Belgians
and the Poles from Belgravia.   Even when the first flying
bombs roared through the sky the chair-man continued
quietly to collect his pennies, and nobody even thought to
scurry into the cement labyrinths built during Munich days.
Suddenly the Green Park balloon disappeared and the silver
fleet which had ridden at anchor above the roofs of London
for nearly five years like a gleaming canopy was no more,
and those people who had said 'They must never go,'
hardly noticed the change.   But now on sunny days, if
you had looked southwards down the avenue which leads
to the Queen Victoria Memorial, you would have seen,
far, far away, the great curtain protecting the town from
these low-flying missiles.   One of them landed on the
deserted hutments of the Green Park balloon, denuding
the plane-trees of their rich foliage.   Another knocked
down the wall of the king's garden.   The vegetables on
the balloon site grew to maturity in the absence of the
owners who had planted and reared them so lovingly, and
the inhabitants of Piccadilly gathered the rich booty on
warm evenings.   Towards the end of August the stricken
plane-trees broke into bud as if it had been spring, and by
September they were in full foliage for the second time that
year.   The searchlight crew now lit red flares towards midnight all round their encampment to give our bombers
above the illusion of a city on fire, and the whole of the
park was painted crimson, which increased the fairy-like
atmosphere of this enchanted wood.   Then girls replaced
the men at Bombers' Moon, and the following spring you
would see them knitting on stools at their front door,
while Spike the mascot and a she-cat with her young
occupied the sentry-box.

Our Green Park witnessed the most picturesque and the
most moving of the nation's peace celebrations at the close
of the long war with Germany.   For the first time since
darkness had covered the town Buckingham Palace was

bathed in rosy light, and the king and queen with the young
princesses appeared on the balcony, facing both the new
Mall, made as a tribute to Queen Victoria, and the old Mall
under whose shady trees Charles the Second had played,
along which Pepys and Evelyn had sauntered and Lady
Castlemaine, back from the royal chase, had ridden with
a yellow plume in her hat. The ghosts of Addison and
Steele, of Pope and Gay and Dr. Swift, of Lady Mary
Wortley Montagu, and of old Sir Robert Walpole must
have risen to acclaim this moment when a new and glorious
lease of life was being given to the island of their greatness.
The girls of the Bombers' Moon gave their last party in the
grounds of their pretty domain. Soon the searchlight was
taken away and the shutters put up. Spike, the mascot,
haunted the deserted site and barked pitifully at the moon
until, during the rowdy celebrations at the close of the
Japanese war, marauders tore down the encampment,
burning all they could find, trampled the gardens and cut
down the boughs of the trees, desecrated the lawn of the
Green Park drawing-room, setting fire to deck-chairs and
benches, leaving the parks in such a sad state of disorder
that it took months to repair the damage.

Gradually the lights of London went on again and Piccadilly shimmered against the bare trees, whilst the lake in
St. James's Park reflected the warmth of great buildings
backing on to Birdcage Walk. The barbed-wire entanglements were rolled away, revealing strong shoots which
had grown from acorns and poplar seed-vessels; and everywhere the gardeners gathered the dead leaves to make
bonfires whose good smell filled the crisp wintry air. The
Americans deserted the town, and the military police from
Whitehorse Street no longer paraded in the Green Park
on Saturday mornings. The last G.I.s photographed their
sweethearts on the gravel paths before sailing home across
the Atlantic, and R.A.F. men pulled down the sweet
house of Bombers' Moon, leaving only, for some reason
unexplained, one wall which marred the landscape because

it was the lavatory wall. The ornamental pond, which had never been used by the fire service, was drained, and children and dogs romped on the cement bottom.

January brought the United Nations Conference to London, and the Horse Guards Parade, with the barbed wire swept away, became a car park for the delegates meeting in Central Hall, Westminster, the headquarters of the Methodist Church, built in 1912—the dream of Sir Robert Perks, a London lawyer—and just as Rainbow Corner in Shaftesbury Avenue was being closed by Franklin Roosevelt's widow, a delegate to the conference, work began on the removal of an unexploded bomb which, during the battle of London, had crashed through the suspension bridge in St. James's Park, burying itself deeply below the concrete bed of the lake.

To facilitate this work, the lake which had not been cleaned for eight years was drained, and the water poured through the outlet opposite the Horse Guards Parade, leading finally to the Thames at Barking. A few weeks before Christmas, Londoners had seen the first Italian prisoners in the park. These men, clothed in their green uniforms, had been relaying the grass near the bird sanctuary, and as soon as the lake was empty they started to pile up in neat little rows the mud and slime which was to be buried in an immense pit dug by bulldozers on a lawn facing the Queen Victoria Memorial. The weather turned extremely cold and on the 19th January snow fell. A small sheet of water to the south of Mr. Hinton's island cottage had been left for the wild fowl, and the two pelicans waddled on the ice amongst the widgeons, the shovellers, the gadwalls, the shelduck, and the mallard. Suddenly there appeared in this crowded space three red-breasted geese and a snow goose—possibly from the Serpentine. 'Feathers,' the strange bearded tramp, who had a generous heart, fed the colony with bread with which he was not over well supplied for his own needs. There had been some speculation as to the number of fish that the retreating waters in

These are the tender colours of the Green Park in early summer. We are walking from the direction of Buckingham Palace towards the mansions which stretch from the Mall to the Ritz Hotel at the corner of Piccadilly. One night, during the Battle of Britain, these noble mansions appeared to be on fire almost from end to end, and there was no water to put out the flames.

The house with the Grecian figures belongs to Earl Spencer and bears the name of his distinguished family. He has lent it to Messrs. Christie the auctioneers, whose premises in King Street were entirely destroyed. Thus pictures, tapestries, jewels, and silver are displayed in this glorious setting every week. On this side of Spencer House, but almost hidden, is Bridgewater House, until recently town house of the Earl of Ellesmere and famous for its picture gallery.

Consider the pretty sweep of Lord Beaverbrook's former home, Stornaway House, wrecked by a land-mine but externally still beautiful. Warwick House, adjoining the passage, has again become the home of the young Lord Rothermere, who lent it to the Red Cross during the war.

The passage is Milkmaid Passage and leads through Stable Yard to St. James's Palace. The notice in the foreground reads: 'St. James's and the Green Park: Regulations of 1872 and 1926.'

One can almost hear the band playing in the bandstand just out of this picture. This is where we take our children on summer evenings.

the rest of the lake would leave high and dry, but except for a few bream the catch was disappointing. Most of the little fish were carried away to the Thames in the sewer. Winston Churchill, the great artificer of the peace, had just landed in the United States, and as one glanced up at the window of the War Cabinet offices from which during the anxious years he must so often have looked out on the park, it was curious to hear the songs and accents of these Italians taken prisoners during the desert campaign of 1942, when the war had not yet turned in our favour.

All the time the loud-speakers on the Horse Guards Parade were calling cars needed by the delegates of the conference at Central Hall—this parade ground on which during the reign of George the Third soldiers were flogged in public, and the unfortunate individuals caught by the press-gangs were drilled for the first time.

Back in the Green Park, Irish labourers were removing the oak beams from the Munich shelters. They made splendid bonfires to keep themselves warm, and the Dublin brogue floated across the frosted grass which made a white carpet under the Cornish elms. These men, who lived in hostels, were provided with sandwiches before leaving for work, and we, the small band of women who all through the war had frequented the park, sat with them round their fire while our children skated on the ice puddles at the bottom of the sump.

Meanwhile a van of immense size drew up at the entrance to Bridgewater House to take away from the damaged palace the furniture which had not been removed in 1940. The fourth Earl of Ellesmere had died at the age of seventy-one on 24th August 1944, and his successor, the fifth earl, had just returned from Germany where he had been a prisoner of war for five years, having been captured with members of the Highland Division just before Dunkirk. The young owner, having tried unsuccessfully to obtain a permit to restore the mansion, was now stripping it.

Spencer House, that elegant Grecian palace adjoining

Bridgewater House, was still owned by Earl Spencer, for whose forbears it was designed in 1756 by John Vardy, the architect of the Horse Guards, and General Gray, the amateur designer, secretary of the Society of the Dilettanti. Earl Spencer vacated it at the end of 1926 when he let it to the Ladies' Army and Navy Club, who were there until it was damaged by fire. A land-mine falling to the south-west of the house brought down the ceiling of the famous Painted Room decorated by James (Athenian) Stuart, but the paintings upon canvas were saved. The beautiful iron gates were removed without any warning for salvage, and towards the end of the war the mansion was requisitioned by the Ministry of Labour, whose uniformed messengers sat in the great entrance hall which once saw powdered footmen.

Meanwhile, the gardens of these great mansions grew wild and forlorn.

The draining of the lake in St. James's Park, and the removal of the Bomber's Moon and the Munich shelters in the Green Park, proved to be only the beginning of a vast scheme to make the two parks ready for the peace celebrations in June.

Bulldozers in driving rain and sleet churned up the Green Park, driving the cement of the shelters into the damp ground, knocking down the last wall of the search-light station, and finally attacking the fire service pond until nothing was left but a ploughed field upon which gradually the grass began to sprout. This stretch of flat ground suddenly appeared very large. The cosiness had gone out of the Green Park drawing-room, which was no longer sheltered by a wicker railing and tall weeds. Children had no water upon which to sail their boats.

Meanwhile Londoners were suddenly told that a 1,000-lb. bomb lay under the bed of the lake in St. James's Park at the northern end of the suspension bridge on which they had crossed so often, sometimes leaning over the parapet to feed the ducks. Now that the lake was drained, the large hole which the bomb had made was visible. Sappers prepared to remove this bomb which they nicknamed Baby Blobs, and on 7th February, traffic through the park having been diverted, civilians kept at a safe distance, and windows at Buckingham Palace and Marlborough House opened to prevent damage in case of an accident, the bomb was made harmless after five and a half hours' 'cooking.' Queen Mary, who had spent the previous evening at home, went to the cinema.

The suspension bridge had been saved, but it was now decided to paint it and to renew the floor-boards, with the result that the next morning, Londoners began to cross the cement bed of the lake, which for a time became the playground of all the children in the parks.

A second unexploded bomb, weighing 500 lb., had cut through the bed of the lake forty yards nearer the palace, and this one was rendered harmless on 21st February, but there remained a third, a few paces away, as large as the first, and more difficult to deal with. It was under a gravel walk near the Cornish elm which stands guard over the shrubbery. This bomb, which the sappers called Annie, lay fifty-two feet below ground, and the experts, unable to remove the fuse, decided to detonate it at 7 p.m. on 26th April. The detonation of Annie brought quite a crowd of people to distant parts of the park, whence they were eager to watch the great explosion. Princess Elizabeth was at Buckingham Palace and Queen Mary at Marlborough House, and once again all the windows were left open.

Falling earth hampered the sappers and the bomb went off twelve minutes late, rocking the houses as far as Piccadilly, but no window was broken. Queen Mary visited the scene immediately after the explosion, and half an hour later Londoners were allowed past the barriers.

KENSINGTON PALACE

ON CHRISTMAS EVE, 1689, Dutch King William the Third and Queen Mary drove up in the royal coach to take up residence at the former home of the Earl of Nottingham at Kensington, which henceforward was to be known as Kensington House.

If at the same period of the year one walks through Kensington Gardens in the direction of the Round Pond, one can easily imagine the scene with the trees shrouded in a white mist, and in the distance a farm-cart, filled with logs, the axles creaking, will probably make its leisurely way, as many a cart has done before, along the smooth, deserted path leading eastwards to Hyde Park. The holly-trees will be full of berries, and now and again one will hear a dog barking.

From the time of Henry the Eighth the legal family of the Finches had been connected with Kensington. Then, during the first year of the Restoration, when Charles the Second was laying out St. James's Park, Sir Heneage Finch bought the Kensington property from a younger brother. This Sir Heneage became successively Solicitor-General, Lord Keeper, Lord Chancellor, and Earl of Nottingham. He built a house which he called Nottingham House, leaving it in due course to Daniel, the second earl, an up-right politician, lugubrious of aspect, who, being leader of the anti-Jacobite Tories, was approached by William the Third when the little Dutch king was anxious to find a royal residence out of the smoke of the town, but nearer than Hampton Court.

William the Third paid the earl 18,000 guineas for his house, and decided to spend the winter there. Though he had resided for some time at the Palace of Whitehall, the close proximity of the Thames had increased his asthma, and the smoke from what a merchant in Haymarket called 'the newly discovered sea-coal' made St. James's equally distasteful to him.

History has left us some pretty glimpses of the sickly, taciturn, but self-willed Dutchman in what Evelyn calls his 'very sweete villa, having to it the Park, and a straight new way through this Park.' While his amiable and loving queen was planning the gardens in the Dutch style to please her husband, discussing the red-brick enlargements of the house with Sir Christopher Wren and Grinling Gibbons, the incomparable carver, or gossiping with Congreve, whose plays she so much admired, we see William, a great man in a little crazy body, 'no godhead, but the first of men,' as Prior sang, bending over the fire-place, drinking gin and brandy with the cunning, uncouth Peter the Great whom the king had lodged in York Buildings and who, after spending his morning studying the art of ship-building, would join his royal host at Kensington. In the King's Gallery you will yet see over the chimney-piece a curious map of north-west Europe, surrounded by the points of the compass, and a dial hand moved by a rod connected with a vane on the roof, to enable William to know, while sitting at the fireside, whether the wind was of a nature to allow him, safely, because of his asthma, to venture outdoors. Peter the Great was more fascinated by this contrivance, copied later by the tea merchants of Mincing Lane, than by anything else he saw at the palace. Yes, these two sovereigns must have got on well together, the one sipping his gin, the other his brandy, hunched over the fire, the Russian adding pepper to his drink. Both had queer ideas, born of their shyness. The barbarous czar, being taken to the House of Lords by William, but unwilling to meet these gentlemen, peeped at them from a window on the roof, and at a ball on the Princess Anne's birthday, contrived to be invisibly present in a closet prepared in advance for him, whence he could see without being seen.

G

Wraxall gives us a charming picture of the Dutchman unbending to amuse a child. This scene also took place in the gallery, so narrow, so unpretentious, that it is almost strange to reflect what historic events have taken place in it. At one end of the gallery William was in his closet, engaged in business; at the other end of the gallery the queen, by his desire, had made tea. With Queen Mary was the Dowager Countess of Northampton who had brought her little grandson, Lord Buckhurst, not quite four years old, who was playing with a child's cart in the gallery. The tea was made and the queen was becoming impatient, whereupon the child, dragging his cart behind him, went to knock at the closet door.

'Who is there?' asked the King.

'Lord Buck,' answered he.

'And what does Lord Buck want with me?' replied His Majesty.

'You must come to tea directly,' said he, 'the queen is waiting for you.'

King William immediately laid down his pen, and opened the door; then, taking the child in his arms, placed him in the cart, and seizing the pole, drew it along the gallery, quite to the room in which were seated the queen, Lady Northampton, and the company. But no sooner had he entered the apartment than, exhausted with the effort, which had forced the blood upon his lungs, and being naturally asthmatic, he threw himself into a chair, and for some minutes was incapable of uttering a word, breathing with the utmost difficulty. The Countess of Northampton, shocked at the consequences of her grandson's behaviour, which threw the whole circle into great consternation, would have punished him; but the king interposed on his behalf.

On Saturdays William spent the day at Hampton Court; at other times he would drive to St. James's Palace, and as His Majesty often returned home from St. James's after dark by way of Constitution Hill and Hyde Park, he ordered three hundred lamps to be placed along the road.

These illuminations were described as 'very grand and inconceivably magnificent.' The way through Hyde Park was full of ruts and it swarmed with highwaymen, and so common had robberies become, that William ordered his guards to patrol the park till eleven o'clock each night, and when he held his basset table at Kensington Palace the patrols were doubled, marching to and fro all night, so that the guests might carry home their winnings unmolested.

In the summer the lamps were taken down and stored in the wood-yard at Kensington Palace. The Ring at Hyde Park was not what it was in the days of Charles the Second, when the Duchess of Cleveland sometimes rode there on a white palfrey, with a red velvet saddle and bridle covered with gold lace. This ring, a circle, not very large, enclosed by rails in an open field, was where fashion used to ride and drive. When the coaches had turned for some time round one way, they would face about, and 'turn t'other.' It was the dream of Pepys, or rather, the dream of his wife, to have a coach, instead of driving round in a hackney, with so many people knowing them, and you will recall his delightful description of what happened on that April day in 1669: 'Thence to the Park, my wife and I, and here Sir William Coventry did first see me and my wife in a coach of our own, and so did also this night the Duke of York, who did eye my wife mightily.' You will remember also how the Chevalier de Grammont sent over to Paris for the most elegant and magnificent *calèche* that had ever been seen, as a present for Charles the Second, who was quite delighted with it. The queen, imagining that this splendid carriage might bring her luck, wished to be seen in it first, with the Duchess of York, whereupon Lady Castlemaine, having seen them in it, told his Sacred Majesty just what would happen if her rival La Belle Stewart rode in it before she did. 'Whereat the King was very much perplexed.'

King William was no man to continue this pretty nonsense. He was not particularly fond of his new subjects and preferred his Dutch friends, clipped hedges, and military reviews, to periwig, ribbon, and feather. The Ring, deprived of the royal presence, lost its glamour, but the town of Kensington certainly benefited by the presence of the court, and though the gardens attached to the palace were not large, London and Wise (the royal gardeners) trimmed the holly hedges Dutch fashion, and the walks and grass, under the direction of these two men described in the *Spectator* as heroic poets, became very fine. Gentle Queen Mary, who in the absences of the king conducted the affairs of the nation with discretion, gathered round her men we still remember, such as the Earl of Dorset, Prior's friend; Prior himself; Burnet, the gossiping historian who afterwards became a bishop; Lord Monmouth, later Earl of Peterborough, the friend of Swift and Pope; and, of course, the playwright Congreve whose conversation she pleasured in.

William had the misfortune not to appreciate her love for him, her honesty, intelligence, and piety until he was on the point of losing her, and then his sudden grief is pitiful. Macaulay has described how she was seized with an illness which proved to be smallpox; how she locked herself into her closet, where she set her papers in order; and how William, his affection declaring itself at last, remained night and day at her bedside; and how, having received the sacrament from Archbishop Tenison, she sank rapidly. Many great and touching things have taken place in this palace, but this one is perhaps the most charged with the human element which suddenly endears the little Dutchman to our hearts, for while the Privy Council was gathered in a neighbouring room, the Duke of Leeds tiptoed into the queen's chamber to remove William, almost insensible, a few moments before the death of his devoted partner.

Scenes such as this seem to leave an imprint on their surroundings. That closet where the king's tears fell upon Mary's listless hand as he knelt beside her is still there, and from the window you may look upon the western

gateway with the tower and the clock therein, which Wren
was called upon by William to repair because it had become
old and decayed.   The panelling which saw William's grief
was ravaged by fire when incendiaries fell through the roof
during the Battle of London, and the chamber appears
ridiculously small and smells of damp and charred wood,
but somehow one begins to look amongst the wreckage
for the spot where the queen lay a-dying, and though the
walls are cold and reveal the naked brick, and though the
boards creak underfoot and in places appear hardly strong
enough to bear one's weight, the picture continues to haunt
the imagination and it is all so easy to reconstruct—the
tiny closet which opens out on a diminutive dressing-room,
which in turn is connected by a rather larger closet, now
without a roof, wherein the Privy Council paced up and
down, urging the Duke of Leeds to rescue the incoherent
Dutchman from his misery.   How all the rooms in this
suite must have crackled and burned on this terrifying
night when the almost deserted palace was nearly lost for
ever!   Twice historical are these three little chambers,
bathed in the soft glow of a wintry sun.   How often must
William, left a widower, have come back to look piteously
at the spot where his queen died, turning over in his mind
all the things he might have done to make himself more
agreeable to her!   Over the cobbles in that courtyard,
under the tower, they brought him back one evening laid
out in a coach, his horse Sorrel having stumbled on a mole-
hill at Hampton Court, causing him to fall.   His broken
collar-bone was reset twice during the journey, owing to
the jolting of the roads.   The taciturn little Dutchman who
was not made to be a king, knowing that the end was near,
sent for his friends Albemarle, Portland, and Auverquerque,
while Bishops Burnet and Tillotson read prayers by his
bedside.   After his death they found bracelets, made of the
queen's hair, upon his arm.

Anne built the orangery where the brocaded robe, the
hoop, and the fan made the music-room gay.   She drove

her open carriage through the park and drank chocolate in the evening. In the narrow, prim dining-room, with its draughty corners, Sarah Jennings, Duchess of Marlborough, fought vainly to recapture the ascendancy she once wielded over the queen. Whilst the queen lay dying, John, Duke of Argyll, and the Duke of Somerset presented themselves unexpectedly at the council and overthrew the design of Viscount Bolingbroke to recall the exiled royal Stuarts.

When George the First, Elector of Hanover, took up alternate residence at St. James's and Kensington, unable to speak our language and not very interested in our habits, St. James's Street and the Mall continued the places of wit and fashion, but during his reign it would appear that Kensington Gardens began its glittering promenades which were to last for over a century. Caroline of Anspach, the Princess of Wales, undoubtedly inspired them when she came to Kensington Palace with her lovely companions made famous by Pope and Gay—Miss Hobart, who was to become successively Mrs. Howard and Lady Suffolk, the sweet-tempered, patient mistress of George the Second; the ravishing Mary Bellenden who became Duchess of Argyle; the lovely Mary Lepell who married Lord Hervey; and the incomparable letter-writer Lady Mary Wortley Montagu who sometimes outwitted Pope. Persons of fashion, privileged to enter the gardens, would throng to see these youthful graces, and in due course the public was admitted.

In some ways it is easier for us to imagine the women in their hooped petticoats and the wits in their gay jackets with laced sleeves sauntering under the trees of the Broad Walk than along the Mall, whose modern counterpart has been, as long as most of us have known it, a swift motor way. In Kensington Gardens, even the youngest of us have recollections of more leisurely days, when children bowled their hoops along the gravel, and mammas and smart nurses took turns to push the perambulator with its cream coverlet and armorial bearings. Few of us cannot

remember the old women who sold the coloured balloons
at the entrance to the gardens where, in the days of Caroline
of Anspach, other old women, equally wrinkled, sat behind
their stalls gay with cheesecakes, marchpane, and China
oranges.   The fairies in the garden played their games by
moonlight as far back as in the early years of the solid
Hanoverian, George the First.   You may remember that
when Pope brought out the first volume of his translation
of Homer, he was extremely angry to discover that the
poet Tickell had also made a version published at the same
time, and, what was even more galling, Addison declared
that Tickell's was the better.   Tickell was a man of gay
conversation, whose whimsical turn of mind produced a
poem on Kensington Gardens.   He peopled the dell with
fairies who stole a baby boy of royal descent, whom they
fed on daisy roots and dwarf elderberries.   On the shelves
of the London Library you will find a first edition of
Kensington Gardens, published in 1722 by J. Tonson in the
Strand.   Tickell begins by giving a pretty picture of the
promenade when Caroline's beauties walked there:

> Where Kensington high o'er the neighb'ring lands
> 'Midst greens and sweets, a Regal fabrick, stands,
> And sees each spring, luxuriant in her bowers,
> A snow of blossoms, and a wilde of flowers,
> The Dames of Britain oft in crowds repair
> To gravel walks, and unpolluted air.
> Here, while the Town in damps and darkness lies,
> They breathe in sun-shine, and see azure skies;
> Each walk, with robes of various dyes bespread,
> Seems from afar a moving Tulip-bed,
> Where rich brocades and glossy Damasks glow,
> And Chints, the rival of the show'ry Bow.

His next stanza sings the glory of Caroline and her
virgin band:

> Here England's daughter, Darling of the land,
> Sometimes, surrounded with her virgin band,

Gleams through the shades. She, tow'ring o'er the rest,
Stands fairest of the fairer kind confest,
Form'd to gain hearts, that Brunswick's cause deny'd,
And charm a people to her father's side.

In some way or other the human baby was stolen from this gay and fashionable walk by the fairies. He grows up, and at dead of day, under the shade of a tulip, falls in love with a beautiful fairy princess called Kenna. The story becomes a trifle involved, but the Baby Walk may be said to trace its origin to his pen. Already he makes Kensington Gardens the English kingdom of the fairies, and the tale ends with the death of the little prince, who is changed by the weeping Kenna into a snowdrop.

George the First, 'not tall, of an aspect rather good than august, with a dark tie wig, a plum coat, waistcoat, and breeches of snuff-coloured cloth, with stockings the same colour and a blue ribband over all,' disappears from the Broad Walk, and the second George with his Queen Caroline, Sir Robert Walpole, and their picturesque chronicler Lord Hervey, people Kensington Palace where they scheme, gossip, and play quadrille by the flickering light of candles. George the Second continued to use Kensington Palace until his death in 1760, and all this time, in the Broad Walk, feminine fashions changed, head-dresses rose and fell, the fan remained a useful and picturesque adjunct, and muffs increased in size. No reigning sovereign has lived at Kensington since George the Second, but the weekly promenades continued until the Regency, and famous women of succeeding generations trod the gravel paths: Fanny Burney, the authoress of *Evelina*; Mrs. Trimmer of Brentford and Kew; Madame Récamier who appeared in the gardens *à l'antique* with a muslin gown clinging to her languid form, of whom Chateaubriand wrote that the trees had never seen so pretty a sight; and the beautiful and gifted Madame Du Barry, mistress of Louis the Fifteenth, who came to put her jewels in a safe place, not guessing that on her return to Paris she would be guillotined.

This statue reminds us that Queen Victoria was born at Kensington Palace and spent much of her childhood there. She would ride in a goat or donkey carriage, attended by her nurses. At 5 a.m. on 20th June 1837, the Archbishop of Canterbury and the Lord Chamberlain arrived here to announce to the young princess that she had become queen. They knocked . . . they rang . . . they thumped. At last they woke her up and she came into the room in a loose white nightgown and shawl, her nightcap thrown off, and her hair falling on her shoulders.

Kensington Palace became a royal palace when Dutch William of Orange went there in preference to Whitehall Palace, which was later burnt down. Queen Anne used it and so did George the Second.

The Duke of Windsor, when Prince of Wales, is said to have called it 'The Aunt Hill.' Princess Beatrice and Princess Marie Louise had apartments there. It is one of the loveliest of royal palaces which has temporarily ceased to make history. This painting was done from the Round Pond.

Now, a little girl, playing in these gardens, was to become the most important person of the century. The future Queen Victoria, living with her mother, the Duchess of Kent, in Kensington Palace, could be seen at the age of three, seated on a donkey caparisoned with blue ribbons, and accompanied by several ladies and two men-servants. The donkey had been given her by the Duke of York, whose statue tops the high column where once stood Carlton House. Princess Victoria came into the world when Nash was building Regent Street. London was changing rapidly, but it is not without interest that in her childhood there still existed, on the west side of Palace Green, a bath which Henry the Eighth had built for his daughter Elizabeth when she was three or four. The childish amusements of future great queens are more interesting in retrospect than to their contemporaries, but in the case of Victoria we are told that her eyes sparkled with fun, that she was not shy, and that when many well-dressed ladies, gentlemen, and children collected round the railings, she would walk towards them, curtsy and kiss her hands to the people, speaking to all who addressed her; and when her nurse led her away she would again and again slip from her hand and return to renew the mutual greetings between herself and her future subjects.

Thus the Princess Victoria grew up at Kensington under her mother's care. Her uncle Leopold, who became King of the Belgians in 1830, awakened her interest in foreign affairs, and she occasionally went to a ball, the play, or the opera. At five in the morning on 20th June 1837, the Archbishop of Canterbury, and Lord Conyngham, the Lord Chamberlain, arrived at Kensington Palace to announce the death of William the Fourth to their young sovereign. They knocked, they rang, they thumped for a considerable time before they could rouse the porter at the gate; they were again kept waiting in the courtyard, then were turned into one of the lower rooms, where they seemed forgotten by everybody. They rang the bell and desired that the attendant of the Princess Victoria might be sent to inform Her Royal Highness that they requested an audience on business of importance. After another delay, and again ringing to inquire the cause, the attendant was summoned, who stated that the Princess was in such a sweet sleep she could not venture to disturb her. Then they said:

'We are come to the Queen on business of state, and even her sleep must give way to that.' It did; and, to prove that *she* did not keep them waiting, in a few minutes she came into the room in a loose white night-gown and shawl, her night-cap thrown off, and her hair falling upon her shoulders, her feet in slippers, tears in her eyes, but perfectly collected and dignified.

The Diary of a Lady of Quality.

PRINCESS ELIZABETH—A COMPARISON

It is sad to record that after this pretty scene Kensington Palace was to fall into a long sleep. But roughly a hundred years later, at the other end of Hyde Park, our present Princess Elizabeth was playing with her sister in much the same surroundings as Victoria had enjoyed. One is tempted to make the comparison.

In 1935, when George the Fifth was celebrating his jubilee, and the Prince of Wales and the Duke of Kent were lending glamour to night life in the West End, the Duke and Duchess of York with their two young princesses lived at 145 Piccadilly. From the windows of his mansion the Duke of York looked across Piccadilly and the Green Park towards Buckingham Palace, where his august father resided. He had as neighbours Viscount Allendale, Lord Rothschild, and the fifth Duke of Wellington. The gardens of these mansions communicated by private gates with a strip of Hyde Park.

In this piece of woodland, with one or two very old plane-trees, a good deal of holly, some red and white lilac, and pretty lawns, to which all the surrounding residents had access by keys, played Princess Elizabeth, who nobody yet guessed would so quickly be heiress to the throne.

Nevertheless many Londoners did stop to gaze through the high railings at little Princess Elizabeth and her sister playing hide and seek under the shadow of Byron's statue or drawing a toy cart by turns along the gravel paths, as Londoners little more than a century earlier had congregated to look at Princess Victoria riding on her caparisoned donkey at the other end of Hyde Park, in the gardens of Kensington Palace. If one cares to look back three centuries before that, one may suppose that the villagers of Kensington were no less interested in Henry the Eighth's daughter Elizabeth when she was taken to bathe in that conduit he built for her, and who, then, would have believed that she was destined to become one of the greatest monarchs in the history of our nation?

The abdication of Edward the Eighth will doubtless inspire volumes in years to come, but from 145 Piccadilly, the Duke and Duchess of York and their two princesses moved to the great palace upon which they had looked on summer evenings across the leafy trees of the Green Park, and the royal standard floated above their heads, while the Duke and Duchess of Windsor moved from the south of France to the sultry climate of the Bahama Islands.

The lone German airman who tried to bomb Buckingham Palace by daylight during the Battle of London did nothing more than shake the windows, but during the dark winter months a direct hit demolished the mansion in Piccadilly the king and queen had lived in as Duke and Duchess of York, and cut off a slice of No. 144, used as the headquarters of a war relief fund. A year later, when the snow lay on the ground, men with acetylene lamps removed the high railings enclosing the strip of the park in which the princesses had played, and henceforth Londoners used these lawns as a short cut from Park Lane to Hyde Park Corner, and during ensuing Christmases, when holly was in short supply in the shops, they cut down the berried branches to carry them home or to decorate the posts of fire-watchers or wardens in Shepherd Market. The windows of Apsley House, blasted by. so many near explosions, were covered by temporary boards and looked as grim as when the Iron Duke had put up those shutters after the populace had thrown stones at him during the tumults of the Reform Bill.

In January 1946 a squad of men arrived in front of 145 Piccadilly to remove what was left of the historic house. The great stone boulders blasted by the bomb were raised and laid out in neat rows in the courtyard, and soon there was nothing left but the front door and the two pillars, each with its broken bell. On the door somebody had chalked the words: 'Gone to Lunch.' Brussels sprouts grew in the entangled garden, but there was a rustic seat on which the present king and emperor may well have sat while his children played on what was then a well-mown lawn. The great mansions which only a decade earlier looked so impervious to the mighty roar of London were in a sorry state. In one of the gardens the housekeeper kept chickens, whose cackle filled passers-by with envious thoughts about the eggs which might be obtainable by squeezing through the may bushes. A whole age had passed away. The years between wars appeared absurdly remote. The Prince of Wales's West End—the West End of the twenties and thirties—was reviving in a form he would not have recognized, and Princess Elizabeth, the future queen, who, when the Prince of Wales and the Duke of Kent had danced at the Embassy and Quaglino's, was a little girl tucked in bed after playing with her toy cart in the gardens of Hamilton Place, was now going to Wyndham's Theatre with a party of eight to see *The Years Between*, after which, according to the papers, the party returned to Buckingham Palace before going on to dine at Quaglino's. The princess was wearing a plain evening dress.

Thus a new generation was rising out of the ruins. This restaurant of Quaglino's will perhaps find a place in history

books because it was the scene in the 1930s of a great
royal romance which led to the abdication, and then in
the 1940s gave a glimpse of the future Queen Elizabeth
at play.

The houses adjoining the shell of 145 Piccadilly reflected
the shattering blows which a second gigantic war within a
lifetime had inflicted on the London private mansion. At
No. 143 the Radio Board, which for long had jealously
guarded the secrets of radar, had its quarters. No. 144,
belonging to Lord Allendale, had a notice on the front,
saying: 'KEEP OUT.' Soon, together with the shell of the
former royal mansion and No. 146, belonging to Anna Lady
Newman, it was to form the glittering Piccadilly 'empire' of
the film magnate, Sir Alexander Korda. Great films were
to be planned where a future queen had played. Soon I
was going to be invited to take my little boy (the hero of
so many of my books on London) there to have a film test
on the cool, pretty lawn, from which all trace of the Battle
of London had disappeared. We had flown, authoress and
child, from Normandy in the morning, and after lunch with
the director flew straight back to my farm.

No. 148, formerly the home of Lord Rothschild, was
occupied at the top by the Society of Motor Manufacturers
and Traders, and at the bottom by the Allies Club. Then
we come to the historic mansion known as No. 1, London,
our old friend Apsley House, which had changed but little
since the days of the Iron Duke. Given back to the nation
by the present duke, it was waiting to be turned partly
into a museum, partly into a residence for the Dukes of
Wellington. The gloomy, yellowish exterior, the most
characteristic landmark of Hyde Park Corner, sat squatly
in front of its garden with the circular lawn decorated with
a statue of a slain dragon the colour of verdigris, a holly-
tree begrimed by fog, and the wintry entanglements of a
climbing rose bush. When, one hot July evening of 1947,
Londoners were waiting for the official announcement of
Princess Elizabeth's engagement, Apsley House knew fame

again. To this house, wearing a green taffeta dress with a cape of royal ermine, the princess went to attend a coming-out dance for the daughters of the Hon. Robert and Lady Serena James. She did not wear her ring, and nobody dared mention the burning subject until it came out in the *Gazette*. The Duke of Wellington was present.

Kensington Gardens had suffered hardly at all from the six turbulent years, and amongst its aged trees softened by the January mist one fell insensibly into the realm of Peter Pan, who rules over greens and gravel walks where once the fairy princess Kenna fell in love with the human boy prince. In the distance, beyond the Broad Walk, still encumbered with army lorries, slept the royal fabric of which Mrs. K., a widow of the war of 1914–18, was the only remaining inhabitant, by virtue of her office of lady housekeeper, which post was once held by Horace Walpole's sister. I call her Mrs. K. because she said to me: 'I have lived such a secluded life during the past thirty-two years that publicity of any sort is distasteful to me.'

There was something wondrous strange on this cold misty morning, in pausing in front of the clock-tower entrance to this ghost-ridden palace. On the green some little boys were playing football in the mud. No chariots any longer drove over the gravel towards the delicately fashioned lamps with their golden crowns. No hooped maiden, fan in hand, leaned over the stucco balcony to steal a glance at a periwigged dandy passing underneath. One walked unchallenged under the clock-tower and into the courtyard, at the far end of which the lady housekeeper's friends knock at the modest door through which Congreve passed and William the Dutchman came back to die. Here Queen Anne's *chaise à porteur* must have stood, which for more than two centuries has been carefully preserved; here Lord Hervey rung to be ushered into the presence of his Queen Caroline.

The housekeeper's private apartments were a sweet reminder of what gay chintzes, a bowl of roses, and a bright coal fire can do to add the human, lived-in touch to red brick and oak panelling. Her drawing-room faces, across the lawns, the distant Round Pond upon which, by moon-light, Rackham has shown us Peter Pan, through those winter trees which take such strange human shapes. One supposed that in spite of the inability to get a servant, the harassing hours of shopping, and the increasing household burdens that we all know, there could be nothing more romantic than living in the heart of this deserted palace in which, by candle-light, up the king's staircase, along the king's corridor, across the cupola room, and into Queen Anne's dining-room one's heels must tap delightfully, and one's heart beat with pleasurable fear.

The grand staircase is Wren's, altered by Kent, and you can almost hear the guttural accents of George the First strike these walls, darkly painted with peering faces—the bewigged gentlemen holding ivory-topped canes, and the women, plump and homely, smiling from behind their fans. The housekeeper, to whom these figures are old friends (they have watched her coming and going in the years between the wars, and while the night sky, during the Battle of London, was painted crimson with fires), smiles back at them affectionately with the air of a person who knows their foibles. There we have Ulric, a German page of the stodgy Hanoverian king, two of his Turkish servants, and Peter the Wild Boy, a defective creature discovered in the woods of Hanover. The misty light from Kensington Gardens filters through the windows, and one could easily believe that a magic carpet had transported one to the hunting-seat of a German princeling. My hostess said: 'I am sorry you did not choose a better day. A little sunshine would have made all the difference.'

She stood with a hand poised on the slim, green banisters, and then, as if able to turn the pages of history backwards or forwards according to her caprice, led the way into that small panelled room where Dutch William's queen, Mary, was keeping the tea warm while her royal master was in

his closet at the opposite end of the gallery. Along the
polished floor little Lord Buckhurst drew his toy cart, and
there above the fire-place was the map of north-western
Europe, with its pointer communicating with a vane on
the roof. One studied this curious map with the same
childish interest as we are told did the semi-savage,
cruel, impish Peter the Great, crouching over the burning
logs with his glass of pepper and brandy. Listen to the
names of these foreign ports illuminated on the map:
Bordeaux, Rochelle, Rochefort, Ushant, Brest, Dieppe,
Dunkirk (which proved the ruin of the unfortunate Chancellor Clarendon), Rotterdam, Amsterdam, Emden, Ham-
burg! Each port heavy with history, but sounding now
like the repetition of Bomber Command's raids on the nine
o'clock news bulletin of those last anxious war years. One
supposed the czar of all the Russias must have been a little
vexed to find his snowy realms out of the map. One
reflected that not two hundred yards to the west of this
royal fabric stood the Victorian Gothic mansion in Kensington Palace Gardens, where lived Marshal Stalin's representative at the court of St. James's. Above its turrets
flew the red flag!

And what has happened to Dutch William's closet, where
he was working so hard when my Lord Buckhurst knocked
at the door? New scenes have been superimposed upon it.
The wallpaper is of pretty moss roses. Feminine hands
have lightened its heaviness, and a girl, using it as her
nursery a little more than a century ago, sewed the most
adorable bonnets for her doll with stitches so small and
exquisite that they look like Alençon lace. What pretty
hems! What cunning fingers! Casting her mind back to
this room, when she had become the great queen, living
at Buckingham Palace, Victoria wrote: 'I can remember
crawling on a yellow carpet spread out for that purpose.'
As she became a little older, was it by the window overlooking the Round Pond, that she sewed those bonnets?
Another closet, and then the bedroom, with singing birds

on the wall, where she was sleeping so soundly that morning when the most important people in the land came to tell her she was Queen of England.

Now through Caroline's drawing-room, where Lord Hervey kept up his tittle-tattle, to those three rooms which witnessed the death scene of Dutch William's queen, Mary. Yes, they smelt of charred beams and decay, but the Ministry of Works had built a temporary roof to keep the rain out. The thing happened at 7.30 on the evening of 14th October 1940. The fire-watchers came to the lady housekeeper with the news that incendiaries had fallen on the apartments of Lady Bertha Dawkins, and because of a high wind the whole palace might soon be ablaze. Lady Bertha was not in residence at the time. Indeed Mrs. K. was the only inhabitant of the palace. The fire-fighting people were summoned, but the fire was not brought under control until the clock in the tower had struck three. The palace was saved by bringing water from Peter Pan's Round Pond.

The lady housekeeper went to the window, by the powdering closet, and pointed to the prettiest of courtyards paved with flagstones, with here and there small squares, in which in summer the may-tree and the lilac wafted their heavy perfume over the old Dutch brick façades. Two lamp-posts with gilt crowns gave this garden the most curious effect. One imagined that in times past they offered flickering light to the chairmen who brought their sedans to the door. Fire had gutted the apartments occupied by Lady Bertha Dawkins, who in turn had passed away, after a long and kindly life as lady-in-waiting to our present Queen Mary, who as a child was brought up in the nursery where Queen Victoria dressed her dolls, and who, since the fire, had come to inspect the damage to the palace.

Almost forgotten royal fabric, when will the whim of some future sovereign bring you back to life? Successor to Whitehall, whose Tudor brick, tilt-yard, green lawns, and cool fountains are now only sport for the antiquarian, it is rather sad to see you sleeping, deserted, amongst the fairies of the Broad Walk whose glades are filled with petrol fumes of army lorries. Gone are the children, the nurses, and the coloured balloons. Dark is the king's grand staircase, at the bottom of which that January morning in 1946 the unframed portrait by Callet of Louis the Sixteenth, in coronation robes, stood upside down; the royal head which came to such a cruel end, powdered with the dust of the floor-boards!

LEICESTER SQUARE

THERE IS A FAMOUS and picturesque plan of London by Ralph Aggas, during the reign of Queen Elizabeth, which shows all the land now occupied by Leicester Square and Soho entirely devoted to country life and uses. We see the women milking the cows in the fields and bleaching their linen by spreading it over the grass; and there is a milkmaid walking along a footpath from the direction of Covent Garden with a pail on her head, a little boy behind her, and a dog with its tail up scampering by the hedge.

By the time Faithorne published his map in 1658 (the one showing Piccadilly Hall, the Gaming House, and the Windmill) two large houses with splendid gardens had been built south of the Military Yard where, it will be remembered, Prince Henry, Charles the First's elder brother, who died at the age of nineteen, used to do his exercises. The larger of the two houses belonged to Robert Sidney, Earl of Leicester, who in his youth had been a playmate of Prince Henry, sharing with him the pleasures of the Military Yard. The second house was built at about the same time by Sir William Howard, but took its name of Newport House from Mountjoy Blount, created Earl of Newport, who bought it in 1642. A close friend of the Leicesters, he had held his young neighbour, Robert Sidney, at the font.

Leicester House occupied the north-east side of what in due course was to become Leicester Square, whilst the Military Yard occupied what we now know as Gerard Street; the gardens of Newport House ran northwards, along the east wall of the Military Yard as far as our modern Newport Dwellings of which two blocks were demolished by that land mine which at the same time destroyed the Shaftesbury Theatre.

Leicester House was far bigger than either the Gaming House or Piccadilly Hall, and was more like one of those palaces which stood between the Strand and the Thames. It was built round a courtyard and its gardens were immense, effectually cutting short the future Coventry Street which here met Hedge Lane, our modern Wardour Street.

The Earl of Leicester was a descendant of Queen Elizabeth's favourite. In 1632, appointed ambassador to Denmark, he had set sail from Margate with his two eldest boys, Philip and Algernon, lads of thirteen and ten, to train them early to the knowledge of men, of business, and of foreign languages and countries. On his return to London, and before starting off on a more important embassy to France, he built Leicester House (between 1632 and 1636), and while it was building the family passed its time between their home at Penshurst, Kent, and Baynard's Castle, an old Thames-side palace facing the Globe Theatre and the Bear Garden.

While workmen were still in the upper rooms the earl went to Paris, where his allowances (paid with the greatest difficulty by Charles the First) were £400 a month. This was the most glorious moment of his career. The execution of his monarch, whom he supported but half-heartedly, the difficult years of Cromwell, the death of his wife, his eldest son estranged from him, and Algernon in exile— these things turned Leicester House at the Restoration into a sad place. Feeling himself too old for the gallantries of a new court, the earl went to the king and asked leave to retire into the country. The king, with a favourable and smiling countenance, said: 'With all my heart; but how long will you stay?' 'Sir,' said I (wrote the earl), 'to myself I have prepared to stay a good while, unless your Majesty command the contrary.' 'Whither do you go?' said the king, still with a smiling countenance. 'Sir,' said I, 'to my house in Kent.' 'Well,' said the king, 'and when will you come again?' 'Sir,' said I, 'it is for my health that I go; for if your Majesty's service require it, I shall not consider either my health or life itself, but will be where it pleases Your Majesty to command me.' 'I thank you,' said the king; 'but for the present I have no occasion to stay you; I wish you a good journey.'

On 28th January 1662, Charles the Second sent to Penshurst to ask a courtesy of the earl on behalf of his aunt, the Queen of Bohemia, that he would let her Leicester House, and immediately the earl answered the king, putting his poor house, himself, and all that he called his at His Majesty's service. This was the first time that this beautiful and tragic daughter of James the First had returned to London since her marriage at Whitehall, on St. Valentine's Day, 1613, amidst such pageantry as had never before attended the bestowal in marriage of an English princess. On his return from his embassy in Denmark, the Earl of Leicester had doubtless seen the princess in the first grief of her widowhood, and during his second mission to France, the restitution of the queen's eldest son to the throne of the Palatinate was the main object of his negotiations. Like most gallant men of the period, he had fallen under her charm, and now in her tragic years he wrote to her physician, Dr. Fraser:

I had no desire nor intention to let my house, for, as old as I am, I do a little consider my innocent pleasure, and I think that a pretty pleasant place. I consider my health and the air of the house. I consider my little private business, and the convenient situation of the house for it. I consider the honour of waiting on the King sometimes, when his Majesty will give me leave, and the nearness of the house to the King's Palace. But above all I consider my duty and obedience to the King's commandment; and next to that I consider the opportunity of contributing somewhat to the service of the Queen of Bohemia, whose humble servant I am and have been these many years. And I shall think it a great happiness to me if the air of my house may contribute to the recovery of her health or that I myself may be in any way serviceable to her Majesty.

Almost at once the unfortunate princess fell ill. Charles the Second, ashamed that this venerable aunt who had been so kind to him in exile should die in a hired house, proposed her removal to Whitehall, but it was too late. She, summoning the king and the Duke of York to her side, with the Lord Chancellor Hyde (Earl of Clarendon), made her dying prayer, and on the eve of St. Valentine's, her wedding day, expired while calmly seated on her chair.

Two years after the Fire of London, Leicester House lodged Charles Colbert, the French ambassador, brother of the great minister of Louis the Fourteenth. During a deputation to his excellency we find Samuel Pepys arriving rather late, whereupon he hurries away to show his wife the coach he has chosen for her at the coachmaker's in Cow Lane—that same coach in which he was soon to make such a sensation in the Ring.

Nine years later the Earl of Leicester died, but the house, thereafter much altered, continued to make history. Leicester House is all the early story of Leicester Square. Royally and politically it was now to enter its most important phase.

Since 1664 the planning of the West End had destroyed the countrified scene. You will recall that when Colonel Panton, having purchased Shaver's Hall, referred his building proposals to Christopher Wren, the great architect commended them on the ground that they would open up a new street from the Haymarket to Leicester Fields. Soon afterwards Henry Coventry took up residence in the Gaming House, and his tenancy gave the adjoining street its name. Leicester Square was now laid out, the buildings on the south side being finished in 1671, six years before the death of the aged earl. By 1672 Newport House had passed out of the possession of the Blount family, and a few years later it was pulled down. Newport Market, busiest on Wednesdays and Saturdays, sprang up on part of its grounds, and to meet the demands of those who had come to live in the neighbourhood, its butchers slaughtered up to four hundred bullocks and seven hundred sheep every week. Meanwhile, Charles the Second had granted to Lord Gerard a reversion for about thirty-six years of the land on

This lovely study of Leicester Square caught all the colour and movement on a January afternoon in 1948. Hogarth, whose statue was the only one of the four corner ones in the garden not to be destroyed in the nocturnal raids, was apprenticed to Gamble the goldsmith, in Cranbourn Street opposite. In Georgian days there was a palace in the square, the palace of Frederick, Prince of Wales. The cooks and émigrés founded foreign Soho.

Fanny Burney walked here when she was writing Evelina. Her father, Dr. Burney, lived in what is now the magnificent public library just out of this picture, to the right. It is good to think that the house where Fanny lived is so well employed.

For a century and a half Leicester Square has been London's chief amusement centre. The Feathers Public-house, John Hunter's anatomical exhibition, concerts at the Sablonnière, Wyld's Great Globe. . . . Oh, and how many others! The Empire Music-hall was built on the site of Frederick's palace, but in turn has been replaced by the cinema on your left. The minarets of the Alhambra (replacing Hunter's anatomical exhibition) have made way for the giant ebony cinema whose curious-shaped tower dominates this picture. Leicester Square is Cinema Square now . . . with a few milk bars, shoe shops, foreign newspaper stalls, and restaurants.

All over the world, millions of people still remember the words that sent the allied armies into the blood-bath of the First World War:

'Good-bye, Piccadilly, Farewell, Leicester Square.'

which the Military Yard stood; a licence to build being
attached to the grant. In 1681 Gerrard Street was formed
on part of the ground, and to this street came members of
the gentry and certain noblemen. Towards the end of the
century the ground in the centre of Leicester Square was
railed round, and, like other open spaces in those days,
served for duels.

Leicester House remained, of course, the most important
house on the north side. The house stood well back,
having a spacious courtyard in front, as well as its garden
in the rear. Immediately to the west of it was a house
belonging to the Earl of Ailesbury, but which in 1698
was occupied by the Marquess of Carmarthen, an eccentric
amateur sailor and shipbuilder, who with his son Peregrine
owned the fastest yacht afloat. When at the beginning of
1698 Peter the Great came to England, Dutch William, a
good judge of character, chose (in the words of Tom
Taylor, historian of Leicester Square) 'the very best man
in court for his cicerone, guide, and master of the ceremonies, the Marquess of Carmarthen, as keen a sailor,
as enthusiastic a shipbuilder, almost as hard a drinker, and
as bluff, blunt, and impatient of ceremony, as Peter himself.' The czar was then a magnificent young despot of
six-and-twenty, untamed, untaught, a unique combination
of practical sagacity, profound purpose and comprehensive
intelligence, with the habits of a sot, and the manners of a
savage. No man until Stalin was, like Peter, so anxious
to compress the work of years into days, determined that
his country should accomplish in years the progress of
centuries. Here it was that the czar, before going to the
theatre, besides a pint of brandy and a bottle of sherry,
floored eight bottles of sack after dinner. His real pleasure
was to sail all day with Carmarthen in his yacht, and to
drink with him all night at Leicester Fields.

The house passed into the Savile family through marriage,
and became known as Savile House.

In 1714, George the First succeeded to the English crown

through the Electress Sophia, daughter of the Queen of
Bohemia, who had died so tragically in Leicester House.
Prince George Augustus, Prince of Wales, and his wife
Caroline of Anspach, accompanied George the First to
St. James's Palace, having left their eldest son Frederick,
aged seven, behind them in Hanover.   Three years later
another son was born to the Princess of Wales at St.
James's, and it was at the christening that the quarrel
between father and son became so acute that the Prince
and Princess of Wales were ordered to quit the palace.
They sought a temporary shelter at Lord Grantham's in
Albemarle Street, but in January 1718 the prince rented
Savile House, where Carmarthen had entertained the
Czar of Russia.   At this time Leicester House was occupied
by Lord Gower, and as the Prince of Wales was anxious to
combine the two houses, Lord Gower consented to leave
at Lady Day, whereafter a communication was established
between Savile House and Leicester House.

Leicester House, the larger of the two, remained the town
house of the Prince of Wales until his succession to the
throne in 1727, and Savile House was used as a nursery.
Leicester House had been considerably altered, and the
front, towards the square, removed.   There were three
storeys of ten windows, each overlooking the courtyard,
into which the royal coach is pictured in prints of the
period.

The new court was graced by men of wit and by many
of the 'virgin band' sung by Tickell in his poem on
Kensington Gardens—Miss Lepell, afterwards Lady Hervey,
whose husband's memoirs show us Caroline in all her
moods; the beautiful Miss Bellenden; and Mrs. Howard,
who was to become the mistress of the future king and
end her days at Twickenham.

When in 1727 the Prince of Wales ascended the throne
as George the Second, Leicester Square was filled with
people and resounded with huzzas and acclamations; whilst
every room in the house was crowded with courtiers,

anxious to kiss hands, and to make the earliest and warmest professions of zeal for the new king's service. George the Second remained four days in town, during which Leicester House was thronged from morning to night. Then for a time the bright lights were no more, until in 1743 it became the residence of Frederick, the new Prince of Wales, who was to live on the same ill terms with his father as had produced the burlesque drama of the previous generation, re-enacted in the same setting.

Frederick Louis had been left in Hanover at the age of seven. He did not arrive in this country until a year after the accession of his father—impulsive, frivolous, twenty-one years old, and by no means welcomed by his parents.

In 1732 Frederick, now Prince of Wales, had purchased Carlton House from the Earl of Burlington and the necessay alterations were immediately made, the house being fronted with stone. Kent designed a cascade for the garden. Four years later the prince's marriage took place with Princess Augusta of Saxe-Gotha, a girl of seventeen, and immediately quarrels took place with George the Second and Queen Caroline on the question of allowance. Matters reached a public scandal when on 31st July 1737 Frederick carried off his princess, at the point of her first lying-in, from Hampton Court, at ten at night to St. James's, so that the child should not be born in the presence of the king and queen. Frederick was ordered to remove, with all his family, from St. James's as soon as the safety of the princess who was born there would permit, and they subsequently went to the White House at Kew.

From there they removed to Carlton House, and later, whilst certain repairs were being carried out at Carlton House, took the Duke of Norfolk's mansion in St. James's Square, where, on the 4th June 1738, just after the death of Queen Caroline, was born the prince who was to reign as George the Third.

The Prince of Wales's party was now in full opposition,

and a year after the downfall of Sir Robert Walpole, the prince, though still keeping Carlton House, took Leicester House for an alternative town residence.

The following year George the Second showed his personal courage at the Battle of Dettingen, where fought the little soldier whom he afterwards recognized selling apples in Hyde Park Corner; and we then obtain a glimpse of Leicester House in a letter which, because it is written by a woman, tells us just those trivialities which, after a long lapse of time, we most want to know. Mrs. Delany, who was later to be so much admired by Fanny Burney, the authoress of *Evelina*, had come to town from Ireland and lodged in Pall Mall. She wrote to her sister on 15th January 1746:

My lodging consists of one parlour (staircase is light and easy) and a drawing room, a size larger than what I had in Clarges Street: tapesty hangings, crimson stuff damask curtains and chairs, and tolerable glasses between the windows. The bed-chamber backwards, new and clean; crimson and yellow flaring hangings of paper, and a bed of the same materials as the curtains in the dining room; but it looks into a pretty garden, and over the Prince of Wales's into the park, which is cheerful and pleasant. The two pair of stair rooms and the garrets all very tolerable. The rent four guineas a week; the situation is next door to the Cocoa Tree. . . . On Sunday I go to Carlton House to pay my salutations to Their Royal Highnesses, and in the afternoon to Mrs. Montagu. I go to-morrow in my Irish green damask and my worked head; on the Birthday, which is on Tuesday next, in a flowered silk I have bought since I came to town, on a pale deer coloured figured ground; the flowers mostly purple, are mixed with white feathers.

In the next letter, dated 21st January 1746, also from Pall Mall:

Monday I spent the day at Whitehall settling *our Queen's* jewels, and yesterday we made our appearance at Leicester House. The Duchess of Portland was in white satin, the petticoat ruffled, and robings and facings. She had *all* her fine jewels on, and looked handsomer than ever I saw her look in my life, and in my eyes outshone in every respect all the blazing stars of the Court. There was not much new finery, new clothes not being required

on this Birthday. They curl and wear a great many tawdry
things, but there is such a variety in the manner of dress that
I don't know what to tell you is the fashion; the only thing that
seems general are hoops of an enormous size, and most people
wear vast winkers to their heads. They are now come to such
an extravagance in those two particulars, that I expect soon to
see the other extremes of thread-paper heads and no hoops, and
from appearing like so many blown bladders, we shall look like
so many bodkins stalking about. I never saw a greater crowd
than at Leicester House.

On 20th March 1751 Frederick, Prince of Wales, after a
few days' illness died in the arms of Desnoyers, who was
playing the violin at his bedside. The king was at cards
at St. James's when the news was brought to him by Lord
North. He turned pale and muttered: 'Fritz ist todt.'

The Dowager Princess of Wales continued for some time
to reside at Leicester House, though she spent much of her
time at the White House at Kew. It was in front of Savile
House, however, that her eldest son was proclaimed king
on the 26th October 1760, and a few days later the most
important people in the land thronged to Leicester House
to kiss the hand of the new sovereign, George the Third.

Not long afterwards the dowager princess deserted
Leicester Square, probably because her youngest son died
there in 1765 at the age of sixteen. After this she made
Carlton House her town residence, the palace which was
to play such a spectacular role in the not so distant future.

No London square has passed through such strange
vicissitudes as Leicester Square. Almost as soon as Newport Market was made on the gardens of Newport House,
the revocation by Louis the Fourteenth of the Edict of
Nantes brought to London a great number of French Pro-
testants who settled in this neighbourhood. Many were
silversmiths, and set up shops in front of houses inhabited
by the gentry. Newport Alley was predominantly French,
and thus behind the palace of the 'pouting princes' there
grew up a continental atmosphere which gradually colonized

Soho. Philip Audinet, the engraver, educated by an uncle, sometime minister of the French Protestant Church, was of Huguenot descent, and so was Matthew Liart, another engraver of merit, whose grandfather carried on a business of periwig-maker in Hog Lane. The forbears of many of our present Soho shopkeepers were doubtless traders in Newport Market supplying the kitchens of Leicester House.

This colourful fringe to the palace of princes was in itself sufficient to give the square a character of its own— less stolid and foggy than many another—but from the very beginning of the eighteenth century we find gracing it the first of those scientists, engravers, painters, and surgeons, who by an almost unbelievable turn of events were to transform it by degrees (when the glory of royalty had departed) into the centre of London's popular entertainment, which was to be sung nostalgically by millions of men going out to battle during the First World War.

It was to Ellis Gamble, one of the many silversmiths in tiny Cranbourn Alley, north-east of the square, that Hogarth served his apprenticeship between 1712 and 1719 when this footway for passers-by, not yet cut into a street, was a place where, in front of low shops whose windows displayed dish-covers, cutlery, and centre-pieces, street songs and broadsides, many of a scurrilous nature, were hawked and cried. There was nothing strange in an engraver of promise being apprenticed to a silversmith, for in those days family plate, watches, and shop plates were all elaborately ornamented with arms and devices which gave opportunities to the designer, just as shop signs did to the painter. Hither would come from nearby St. Martin's Street where he lodged, Sir Isaac Newton, Master of the Mint and President of the Royal Society. He could have seen the young Hogarth through the windows of Ellis Gamble, but that is not very likely, because, like many philosophers, he was always deep in his own thoughts. The wits of the day flocked to his house, attracted partly by his conversation,

but even more by his charming niece Catherine Barton
who kept house for him from 1710 to 1727. One day, it
is told, the antiquary Dr. Stukeley called by appointment.
He was told that Sir Isaac was in his study, having given
the strictest orders not to be disturbed; but, as it was near
dinner-time, the visitor sat down to wait. In a short time
a boiled chicken was placed on the table. When an hour
passed and Sir Isaac did not appear, the doctor ate the
fowl, and, covering up the empty dish, desired the servant
to have another dressed for his master. Before it was
ready the philosopher opened the door, apologized for his
delay, and added: 'Give me but leave to take my short
dinner, and I shall be at your service. I am fatigued and
faint.' Saying this, he lifted up the cover, and without
emotion, turned to Stukeley with a smile. 'See,' he said,
'what we studious people are! I forgot that I had
dined.'

On 23rd March 1729 Hogarth carried off Jane Thornhill
from the paternal mansion, and four years later set up for
himself in Leicester Square under the sign of the Golden
Head, made out of pieces of cork glued together to represent a bust of Vandyck, which he gilded and placed over his
door. He built a painting room behind the house and here
he wrought unweariedly, employing in time a large staff
of engravers, most of them French—Ravenet, Scotin, Baron,
Grignion, Aveline, Le Cave—but with them also clever
Englishmen like Luke Sullivan. 'Southwark Fair' was
executed the same year that Hogarth set up for himself in
Leicester Square; 'Rake's Progress' came in 1735, and
'Marriage à la Mode' in 1745. In the taverns, such as
'The Feathers' in the east corner, were held jovial clubs
of artists, actors, and tradesmen of which he was a leading
member. The central enclosure of the square then had
a handsome basin surrounded by a dwarf wall, but in
1748, on the birthday of Frederick, Prince of Wales—such
an occasion as Mrs. Delany has described for us—an
equestrian statue of George the First was uncovered on

the site of the basin.   We may imagine Hogarth stepping
out in his sky-blue coat to examine it.   'The Golden Horse
and Man' (for the statue was gilt) was a great sight for
country people up in town, giving the more simple amongst
them the impression that the streets of London were paved
with gold.

Between March 1760 and October of the same year when
George the Third was proclaimed king before Savile House,
Joshua Reynolds, in the full tide of his popularity, removed
from Newport Street to 47 Leicester Square.   Four years
later, on 25th October, Hogarth, ailing in health, left his
house in Chiswick to drive in his coach to town.   He was
welcomed by his housekeeper Mary Lewis, the daughter of
George the Second's harper, who looked after the sale of his
prints.   The journey had tired Hogarth, but he was cheerful
and went into his study to answer a letter, but this exhausted
him and he retired to bed.   Soon after, Mary Lewis heard
a violent ringing of the bell, and running into the bedroom
found her master suffering from a heart attack.   She
supported him in her arms until he died.

Now the dowager princess left the square for good, and
Dr. Burney, Fanny's father, went to live in that house in
St. Martin's Street where Sir Isaac Newton had dwelt half
a century earlier.   While Fanny Burney was writing *Evelina*
which, later championed by Samuel Johnson, was so justly
to make her famous, Sir Joshua Reynolds was receiving
sitter after sitter, usually for an hour at a time, in his
painting room, and in the evening gave those convivial
dinners at which every one called for what he wanted,
whilst the great artist was attentive to all that went on
within range of his ear-trumpet.

Meanwhile Savile House, deserted by royalty, was now
occupied by Sir George Savile, an intimate friend of Sir
Joshua, who, after introducing into Parliament the Roman
Catholic Relief Bill to repeal the odious laws against that
religion, found his house the goal of the desperate mob
incensed by Lord George Gordon and the fanatical

Protestant associations. It was a Monday, and from the windows of his house Sir Joshua, who had cancelled all his sittings, saw the howling crowd break into Savile House, smashing the windows with the railings they had torn from round the Golden Horse and Rider in the centre of the square. All the furniture was thrown into the street and set fire to, and soon the flames spread to the house and gutted it.

Three years later a new arrival came to Leicester Square who was to change its entire aspect. John Hunter was then fifty-five years old, the most famous surgeon of his time, who was earning what was then the stupendous sum of £6,000 a year. He bought No. 28 on the east side, and at the back, on ground leading to Castle Street, started to build premises for his Museum of Comparative and Pathological Anatomy which had previously been housed in Jermyn Street. In 1785 the museum was placed in its new home. The newest and most sensational exhibit was the skeleton, eight feet tall, of O'Brien the Irish giant which Hunter had acquired by an extraordinary ruse while the corpse was being taken for burial at sea. Already the famous surgeon was suffering from repeated heart attacks, which used to make him say that his life was at the mercy of any rascal who liked to irritate him. He sat, rather grudgingly, to Sir Joshua, who found him a bad sitter, till Hunter, lost in a reverie, assumed so powerful an expression that the painter turned the canvas on which the head was already painted and started again. It was one of his last great paintings, for in 1789, the year Dr. Burney removed to Chelsea, he lost the sight of his left eye, and within four years both the painter and the surgeon were dead. Hunter was seized with a fatal attack, just as he had foretold, during an altercation in the board room of St. George's Hospital.

Now the glory was to fade from Leicester Square—or rather, it was to begin a period of transformation before becoming the playground of the town. Unwittingly, John

H

Hunter had laid the foundations for a place of entertainment which, after passing through many phases, still bears
a magical name, but the Leicester Square of royalty, of
engraver, painter, musician, authoress, and surgeon, had
to be shaken, pounded, and mixed like a plum pudding
before emerging into its new character.

The change began towards the end of the century.
Hunter's Museum had lost its appeal—nobody wanted it—
but on the site of the 'Feathers' public-house, Hogarth's
favourite place of call, Charles Dibdin, a sixty-three-year-
old actor, dramatist, and song writer, opened a one-man
cabaret called the Sans Souci, on the lines of the Paris
chansonniers, and he became famous for his sea songs.
Next to the theatre was a music shop where he sold his
songs. His success ended in 1805, but just as he closed his
doors, Savile House, the nursery of princes, having been
rebuilt, a Leicestershire woman of good family opened a
show of pictures in needlework there which pleased the
aristocracy and the gentry. While the first carriages rolled
up at this exhibition Leicester House was being pulled
down and, the lease of Hunter's house having expired,
the contents of the museum were being taken away. Miss
Linwood was a gifted show-woman, and her tapestries
were designed to conjure up the same emotions in her
public as Madame Tussaud was evoking at the Lyceum
Theatre with the waxworks she had brought over from
France in 1802. Tom Taylor remembered having being
taken there as a child, through the long gallery hung with
scarlet and approached by an imposing flight of steps.
There was 'King Lear' after Sir Joshua Reynolds, and
the 'Shepherd in a Storm' after Gainsborough. A mysterious passage had entrances to prison cells into one of
which one peeped at Lady Jane Grey. Next yawned a
gloomy cavern with a tigress, a lion, and a lioness, all in
needlework.

Miss Linwood's exhibition lasted till her death at the
age of ninety, after which the tapestries were put up for

auction and Savile House became the home of a multitude of curious shows, panoramas, and cabarets. Meanwhile the central enclosure of Leicester Square was becoming as dingy and as unkept as most of the once famous houses that over-looked it. Cranbourn Alley was made into a street connecting Coventry Street with St. Martin's Lane, and the last of the silversmiths' was pulled down. In 1851 the Golden Horse and Rider disappeared under an immense globe which covered the once trim lawns, and our Victorian ancestors could inspect the world at leisure by following an attendant, staff in hand, who pointed out the features of the snow-covered Rockies or the tropical banks of the Amazon. Wyld's Great Globe touched off that travel fever which was soon to send our grandfathers shooting lions in Africa and building an empire which was to have its centre in the Piccadilly Circus of the nineties, and while this was going on, a feverish interest in the wonders of modern science inspired a Moorish palace on the site of Hunter's deserted pathological museum, which opened with a great flourish under the name of the Royal Panopticon of Science and Art.

One senses through all these varying phases the heart-beats of a nation on the eve of great discoveries and fresh conquests. Soon great fortunes were to be built up and squandered by a younger generation in amusement and champagne with little less restraint than in the days of the great Prince Regent.

The Panopticon, incorporated by royal charter and opened with prayer, was turned within six years into the Royal Alhambra Palace Theatre where incipient interest in the wild west, inspired Howe's and Cushing's American Circus season, a pointer to the time, not so far distant, when Augustine Daly would run up the Stars and Stripes over his theatre on the north side of the square.

Music-hall was only elbowing its way into popularity, and for a time the Alhambra swayed uncertainly between circus and ballet. The Victorian song and supper room had not yet emerged from its chrysalis stage when, in return for a trifling payment at the door, a voucher entitled each guest to drink or tobacco at the usual rates, which he could consume at scattered tables in front of the chairman's platform. Soon the immense profits earned by the London Pavilion would appeal to the imagination of the most conservative investors.

Wyld's Great Globe was soon removed, leaving the ground in the centre of the square exposed in all its hideous nakedness, overgrown with fetid vegetation, and covered with the debris of tin pots, kettles, cast-off shoes, old clothes, and dead cats. The Golden Horse and Rider, chipped and weather-beaten, became the subject of every kind of practical joke, and His Majesty, having lost all his limbs, was finally beheaded. The horse was spotted like the leopard, and the royal trunk collapsed under its belly, where it was propped up with a broomstick.

While the statue was passing through this long process of humiliation the second Savile House was destroyed by fire. The Prince of Wales, the future Edward the Seventh, arrived on the scene and, borrowing a fireman's helmet, viewed the final destruction of this house where his ancestors had held their princely courts. The thing had started at six o'clock on the evening of 28th February 1865, when the cellar-man of a house called the Wine Shades went to inspect a leakage of gas with a lighted candle! Savile House, like the Golden Horse and Rider, had suffered fearful degradation, having been the home of the ill-famed El Dorado Music-hall and Café Chantant. So powerful was the explosion that a furniture shop next to the house was blown into the middle of the square, and the flames spread towards Stagg & Mantle's, the drapers.

Nobody has left us a very faithful account of the El Dorado Music-hall and Café Chantant, which by then was closed, but with the help of a very curious book called *London in the Sixties*, written before the war of 1914 by an anonymous gentleman reviewing the nights of his youth, one obtains a glimpse of the Wine Shades and haunts of a similar nature, frequented by the bucks of the time who never opened their mouths without swearing, and who indulged, between bouts of champagne, in practical jokes that leave one quite aghast at their manners.

Leicester Square [he writes] was then a barren waste of ground surrounded by rusty railings, trodden down in all directions; refuse of every description was shot into it; whilst in the centre stood the dilapidated statue which assumed various adornments as the freaks of drunken roysterers suggested. The Shades was a low-class eating house in the basement, approached by steps, where every knife, fork and spoon was indelibly stamped 'Stolen from the Shades' as a delicate hint to its patrons. On the opposite side stood a huge wooden pump. . . . At the adjoining eastern corner were the *tableaux vivants* presided over by a judge in wig and gown, where more blasphemy and filth was to be heard for a shilling than would appear possible, all within one hundred yards of such harmless, if disreputable, haunts as Kate Hamilton's, which was overhauled nightly. . . . Panton Street was a sink of iniquity. Night houses abounded, and Rose Burton's and Jack Percival's were sandwiched between hot baths of questionable respectability and abominations of every kind. Stone's Coffee House was the only redeeming feature, and as it existed in those days, was a spring of water in a dry land.

On the site of Hogarth's house had risen the Sablonière Hotel, kept by an Italian called Pagliano and frequented by foreigners. It was pulled down during the Franco-Prussian War, by which time the Alhambra was besieged every night by dense crowds, some of whom sang the *Marseillaise* and others the *Wacht am Rhein*. These partisan fights drew the town as well as all the bullies and sharpers of the West End, most famous of whom was a gigantic negro known as the Kangaroo. If a party of people were seated at the Alhambra watching the performance, a black arm would suddenly appear, and glass by glass was lifted and coolly drained. Occasionally the Kangaroo met somebody stronger than himself, whereupon he was thrashed and thrown into the square to begin his tactics again in an adjoining night-house.

By 1873 nothing had been done to resuscitate Savile House. The blackened hole left by the fire was partly hidden by a bill board on which it was announced that an elegant theatre, to be called the Denmark, would there be erected, larger than Drury Lane, and to provide the grandest musical and spectacular effects yet seen, but, alas, nobody came forward to take up the shares. Meanwhile £50,000 was offered by an aquarium company for the ground in the middle of the square. What remained of the Golden Horse and Rider had been sold by auction for £16. After an immense amount of litigation, the Master of the Rolls announced that the vacant space in Leicester Square 'is not to be built over, but will be retained as open ground, for the purposes of ornament and recreation.' A defence committee was established, and 'Baron' Albert Grant, the most spectacular financier of the period, was led to make an offer to purchase the ground.

This Baron Grant, one of these meteors of the City such as we have seen so many since, determined to present it, as a people's garden, to the citizens of London. The principal ornament was to be a statue of Shakespeare, an exact reproduction in marble, by Signor Fontana, of that designed by Kent. Water was to spout from jets round the pedestal and from the beaks of dolphins, at each of its corners, into a marble basin, and at each corner of the garden was designed a bust on a granite pedestal. To the south-east, Hogarth, by Durham; to the south-west, Newton, by Weekes; to the north-east, John Hunter, by Woolner; and the north-west, Reynolds, by Marshall.

This gift cost Baron Grant £30,000. 'One can see him now,' wrote the author of *London in the Sixties*, 'arrayed in white waistcoat and huge button-hole, accompanied by an unpretentious bevy of councillors and Board of Works men, over whom a few bits of bunting fluttered, presenting his gift in a speech that was quite inaudible. When asked whether he gave or retained the underground rights in addition to the recreation ground, the great man, in the zenith of his success, replied: "Yes, yes; I give it all."

He was just then building a mansion for himself in Kensington at a cost of a quarter of a million pounds, the largest private residence in London, containing a hundred rooms, some of them of the most magnificent proportions and exquisitely decorated. Along the garden front ran a marble terrace 220 feet long, with three flights of steps. The grounds of this house, probably the most splendid edifice built since the Earl of Clarendon put up his great palace in the days of Charles the Second, contained an Italian garden, an orangery, an aviary, a skating rink, a bowling alley, and an ornamental lake with two miniature islands. The whole was screened off from Kensington High Street by chocolate-and-gold iron railings. Like Clarendon House, Kensington House was demolished almost as soon as it was built.

Baron Grant lost all his money, and years after, when poor and friendless, hearing that the underground works had made the subsoil in the centre of Leicester Square more valuable than the surface, he inquired whether some remnant could not be claimed by him, but met with a curt denial. He died in penury with no friends round him.

The plan to build a Drury Lane on the site of Savile House came to nothing, and those who remembered the panoramas for which it had been famous after the death of Miss Linwood, put up a building in which they planned to recapture an atmosphere which, in truth, was no longer in keeping with the times. Alexander Henderson then founded his playhouse known as the Alcazar, but when in turn this failed, Daniel Nicolas Thévenon of the Café Royal in Regent Street, now at the height of his success, became its owner, and the former French peasant appointed as his nominee and manager Mr. H. J. Hitchins, who was inspired to call it the Empire.

But neither Nicols nor Hitchins had yet discovered what Londoners wanted.

Making the same mistakes as their predecessors, they opened the Empire on 17th April 1884 with the opera *Chilperic*, in which Hayden Coffin joined the company as a chorister. They then tried a season of Gaiety burlesque, and, searching this way and that, even tried a military pantomime. One can picture the rotund Nicols sitting grimly in his box, wondering whether he had made a bad investment after all.

One supposes that Nicols, driving from his restaurant to his theatre of a night, watched with considerable interest the making of Shaftesbury Avenue, which was to change so radically the appearance of Piccadilly Circus. The little buildings and alleys disappeared under the pick, and the Pavilion Music-hall, which had emerged in the sixties as a dingy hall where once there had been a swimming pool and an undertaker's shed, was now pulled down and rebuilt on its present site, its façade glittering with light.

A year later, during Christmas week of 1887, the Empire was reopened as a music-hall. The theatre became world-famous. Ballet and music-hall turns produced profits at the rate of sixty per cent. Nicols turned his genius to making that entertainment which the Sassoons gave to the Shah of Persia a thing to be talked about. Famous actresses of the regular theatre appeared in music-hall for the first time, and its promenade was made a matter of country-wide discussion by the Nonconformist party.

The Alhambra and the Empire had stolen from the palace of the princes and the homes of Reynolds and John Hunter the glory of Leicester Square. The cycle from one century to the other was complete. Flowers blossomed round the marble dolphins in the central enclosure where the plane-trees gave shade to the statues of the great. But even while music-hall was capturing the imagination of the whole country with apparently limitless possibilities, a

finger was pointing to the day when all these pleasures
would be considered out of date.

The thing happened even before the London Hippodrome
was built.

Robert W. Paul, a London craftsman of delicate and
ingenious scientific instruments, working at his Hatton
Garden workshop in the small hours of a winter night in
1895, suddenly endowed his experimental pictures with life.
His men uttered a great shout of victory and a passing
policeman broke in, whereupon he was given an impromptu
exhibition of the cinematograph.   Meanwhile the brothers
Lumière, Parisian photographers, had arrived at similar
results.   On 9th March 1896, Lumière's cinematograph was
introduced into the programme at the Empire, and a
few days later Paul's animatograph was shown at the
Alhambra.

Now Daly's and the Hippodrome added to the lights of
Leicester Square.   Archbishop Tenison's Grammar School,
having moved from Castle Street, replaced the Sablonière
Hotel on the site of Hogarth's house, and Puttick &
Simpson the auctioneers occupied the former residence of
Sir Joshua Reynolds.   The new century brought shining
new buildings—the dental hospital at the corner of St.
Martin's Street; and Thurston's, the billiard-table makers,
who opened up on the west side of the square after being
rendered homeless by the construction of Kingsway.   The
Edwardian era brought fresh success to the Empire and the
Alhambra, and the Leicester Lounge began its hectic life.

Soon the B.E.F. was marching across the plains of
eastern France to the tune of *Tipperary*:

> Good-bye, Piccadilly, Farewell, Leicester Square.

The Alhambra, after searching for a revue to meet the
thirst for enjoyment by men back from the blood bath of
the trenches, announced in April 1916 the first night of
The Bing Boys, for which the house will be for ever
remembered. *The Times* dramatic critic wrote on this

* H

occasion: 'Mr. Oswald Stoll, in his efforts to revivify the
Leicester Square house, has called in three genuine experts
in humour: Mr. George Robey, Mr. Alfred Lester, and
Miss Violet Loraine. Mr. Robey is immense. It is, we
believe, his first appearance in revue.' At the Empire,
Ethel Levey and Joseph Coyne were playing in *Follow the
Crowd*. The Hippodrome produced *Joy Land*, with Shirley
Kellog and Harry Tate, and the London Pavilion, still with
its flower-girls and boot-blacks, embarked on its successful
run of *Pick-a-dilly*.

This was the year of *A Little Bit of Fluff*, but *Chu Chin
Chow* had not yet begun. In Orange Street, between
Leicester Square and the National Gallery, an Italian of
the name of Luigi had turned Ciro's into the smartest night-
club in town. The Café de Paris was a place for teas and
cheap dancing dinners. In Panton Street the sinks of
iniquity had long since disappeared.

As we look back on the Leicester Square our generation
has known, we see it, between wars, loosening the shackles
that bound it to music-hall and revue, just as music-hall,
ballets, and circuses drove away the panoramas, the needlework exhibitions, and the scientific and anatomical toys
which in their days had jostled out the painters and the
princes. The lords of the cinema, at the peak of the great
boom of the twenties, pulled down the Alhambra and
dropped the curtain on the last performance of *Lady be
Good* at the Empire. Daly's crumbled to give place to
Warner's. Puttick & Simpson's, with Sir Joshua's staircase, bowed its head before the shining new premises of
the Automobile Association. The house in which Sir Isaac
Newton's boiled chicken was eaten by his guest, and in
which Fanny Burney wrote *Evelina*, became by a pretty turn
of events the splendid public library of the Westminster City
Council. A new Regent Street, a new Café Royal, and a
new Leicester Square shone in the brief sunlight of easy
money. The Café de Paris, under Poulsen's direction,
became as exclusive as once Ciro's had been, and Luigi had

formed in Bond Street his Embassy Club, the like of which may never again be known. A new Prince of Wales dined at the Café Anglais and patronized the '400'—between the former homes of John Hunter and Hogarth—a bottle party newly invented to permit the drinking of liquor after midnight without contravening the law.

Then came the abdication, the coronation, and the great black-out.

Four months before the war began a famous *restaurateur* called Bellometti had removed from premises at the south-west corner of Leicester Square to a new site on the south side, between the Royal Dental Hospital and the Leicester Galleries which are actually in Irving Street. The premises he vacated were quite famous between wars, having been originally occupied by M. Boulestin, a noted French gourmet and writer who had moved to Covent Garden; after which, and before Bellometti took over the lease, there had been another restaurant of the same kind called the Maison Doré.

M. Boulestin's tenure during the early twenties had brought back to Leicester Square something of the literary, scientific, and artistic atmosphere which, in another age and in very different manner, had made justly famous the Feathers Tavern, where Hogarth and his friends spent so many joyous evenings. In Boulestin's days also, a little beyond the Leicester Galleries in what was then Green Street but is now Irving Street, there was a long narrow shop devoted to the sale of French tobacco, books, magazines, and newspapers, aptly named the Coin de France. Every French statesman of importance who came to London—men like Tardieu, Briand, Herriot, and Blum—were to be seen there, and the atmosphere was rather of a club than a shop, the most picturesque figure being a certain Mme Colette who was the double, both in name and features, of the great French woman writer.

Panton Street to the south-west of the square, and Green Street to the south-east, were both streets of enormous personal character whose individualism gave warmth to the square itself, which might otherwise have been simply a collection of monster modern cinemas. Green Street, in addition to the Coin de France and the Leicester Galleries, had a famous theatrical costumier's where you may still be fitted out as Marie Antoinette or Napoleon; the Garrick public-house; a stamp dealer's, and a store devoted to the sale of American newspapers. Panton Street had the Comedy Theatre; Stone's chop-house, of historic memory; and one of the most famous print-shops in London, owned by John McMaster, whose family has been associated with Leicester Square for well over a century. The McMasters started as shoemakers in Castle Street before the Alhambra was a theatre and when the Golden Horse and Rider had not been mutilated. The McMasters, each in turn, went on making shoes until the end of the last war (they removed from Castle Street to Panton Street in the eighties, when Charing Cross Road was built), but gradually the multiple shops came in and the individual craftsmen, as always happens, were squeezed out. The John McMaster of that period was, in addition, a man of letters who collected old prints and wrote a history of St. Martin's-in-the-Fields which remains to this day a valuable text-book. He therefore switched from boot selling to print selling. The son, who now owns the business, was at Archbishop Tenison's Grammar School before the last war. As a youngster he used to watch the cabbies drive up their growlers, hansom cabs, and early motor cabs outside a fried-fish shop in St. Martin's Lane. Two old cronies filled their lamps with oil (and sometimes with oil and water) at a penny a time while the drivers ate their meals; as a scholar at the grammar school he and his fellow pupils listened to the involuntary laughter of the patients at the dental establishment opposite when gas was administered.

Now the taximen go for their meals to a small café in Panton Street, next to McMaster's print-shop, and sometimes pause to look at the old prints in the window showing

Leicester Square as it was when the Golden Horse and Rider was still there. The house of McMaster is merely an example of how deep are the roots of those who set up their signs in our ancient streets and squares.

At three in the morning on the night of the 17th–18th October 1940 a land-mine dropped on the entrance of Bellometti's former restaurant and utterly destroyed the south-west corner of Leicester Square, reducing to rubble the empty restaurant, the flats above, and the offices of the Swedish Airway Company; blasting beyond repair the Studio, the Green Room Club, and Thurston's billiard rooms. Five months later, before midnight on 16th April 1941, Stone's chop-house in Panton Street, a landmark for over a century, was blown up, and a few seconds later the north-east corner of Leicester Square collapsed under the weight of high explosives which destroyed the Café Anglais, Jones's cake and bun shop, a public-house, and other less famous property. This was the night when two wings of Newport Dwellings and the Shaftesbury Theatre were laid low by a land-mine which fell between them in the narrow street. The north-east corner of the square caught fire, and in the dull light of morning this immense conflagration surpassed all the lurid scenes which Leicester Fields had known during its two and a half centuries of existence.

As the flames leapt skywards and the beams crackled, one thought instinctively of Reynolds, peeping from behind plush curtains at the mob burning the furniture thrown out from Sir George Savile's house; at Edward Prince of Wales, borrowing a fireman's helmet to watch the flames which destroyed the Wine Shades, whose stores of liquor doubtless burned with the same violet tinge as the whisky in the cellars of the 'King's Head'; but now the disaster was not confined to one spot, for half London was writhing from the magnitude of the night's raid, and through the April sky there floated clouds of mist and smoke.

Shakespeare's right hand had been cut off, fragments of
taxicabs hung from the trees whose branches were not yet
breaking into leaf, and the marble busts of Newton and
Reynolds and Hunter had been hurled from their pedestals
and now lay disfigured or beheaded in the dust.

During this terrific scene, Bellometti was clearing the
debris in his restaurant on the south side of the square.
He had jumped behind a partition as the bombs dropped
the previous night and had just escaped the settees, tables,
and chairs projected against the opposite wall. He had
been busy that evening, and his last guests had only just
gone when the aeroplane circled overhead. Now he determined to open as best he could for lunch. One of his
waitresses, by name Tina, had been buried for seven hours
under the debris of her flat in Newport Dwellings and was
in hospital with forty stitches in her back.   John McMaster,
over against Panton Street, was knee-deep in prints of Old
London, many of which were in shreds—for his shop was
exactly opposite Stone's chop-house. In Newport Street
distracted folk were waiting for news of their dear ones
buried beneath a mountain of bricks, who, less fortunate
than Tina, were yet undiscovered. The Odeon and the
Empire were strewn with broken glass; the Leicester Square
Theatre, which between wars had risen on the site of the
National Society for the Prevention of Cruelty to Children,
was deeply pockmarked from the explosion of the land-mine
which in October had destroyed the south-west corner.

As London became a city of streaming khaki; as soldier
and airman, sailor and commando, not only of our own
immense empire, but of a dozen countries whose languages
we did not even understand, flocked to the capital on short
leave; as the Americans came over in waves, outnumbering
by three or four to one, in our streets, the fighting people
of both sexes belonging to the old world, one became
conscious that London was not designed to offer the gay
street scene which would have allowed these men and

women, strangers in our city, to enjoy the spectacle of
booth and café.   In truth, we would have needed a modern
Bartholomew Fair to enliven these spells of precious leave.
Piccadilly was wide and steeped in history.   It glittered at
lunch-time and even surpassed all it had seen during two
and a half centuries, but in the evening it was dark and
morose.   The parks, mysterious in the moonlight, offered
the attractions of Rosamond's Pool, but when the wooing
was finished, human nature called for noisy laughter and
the fun of the fair.   The café and the restaurant, even more
than the ale-house, was what our visitors felt an urge to
seek.   One street alone offered this tinsel forgetfulness of
camp and battle school, and of an evening it seemed that
a hundred thousand feet tramped in the direction of Piccadilly Circus, whence Coventry Street led to Leicester Square.

This short half-mile became the beaten track, during
the long months of the war, for millions and millions of
people from all over the globe, who will remember for ever
its rather childish attractions—the fun fairs and the milk
bars, the ice-cream shops and the music vendors, Lyons'
Corner House and the Prince of Wales's Theatre (well and
truly named), the Rialto and the dingy door which once
led to the Café de Paris's glittering night cavern, the noisy,
lovable Wardour Street with its parakeets and print-shops
pointing towards Soho, the barrows, with all the fruit the
housewife could not find to relieve the monotony of her
daily menu, the street hawkers and the map vendors—and
then the giant cinemas of Leicester Square!

Strange shadows haunted the central enclosure, where
Shakespeare, gazing morosely at the terrific success of *Gone
with the Wind*, was beginning to know the disintegration,
if not the profanation, of his predecessor (the chronology
is a trifle confusing), George the First.   United States
marines sat on the battered head of Reynolds chewing
American gum, or stumbled in the semi-darkness over the
shattered bust of John Hunter.   Bellometti's Roman sheep-
dog, an immense white fluffy thing, took his nocturnal

airing whilst his master attended to the needs of his wealthy customers in the restaurant whence all the window-panes had been blown out. The sheep-dog was a character of the square. His whiteness was almost phosphorescent, wherefore he was named Lumaio, which means a lamp-lighter. The Café Anglais had painted what was left of it in bright blue, and the management placed evergreens in pots outside. Archbishop Tenison's Grammar School, where McMaster had strained at his desk to listen to the unfortunate patients under laughing-gas, was boarded up. The site of the Maison Dorée, at the south-west corner where the land-mine dropped, was a gaping hole; that of Jones's bun shop, and the 'King's Head' at the north-east corner, had been turned into an immense deep-water sump in which you could have sailed a boat.

When the lights went up the Americans departed, and suddenly made us sorry to lose them. The gardens in the central enclosure were tidied up, and Shakespeare, his wounds dressed, was given a bath. Now, again, traffic sped round the square, and there came an evening in the autumn of 1948 when I was to see the name of my nine-year-old son Bobby who had achieved fame suddenly for his part in Carol Reed's *The Fallen Idol*, blazing across the façade of the Empire cinema. It seemed a long time since I had wheeled him in his pram past smoking wreckage or since authoress and child had hidden in the grass of the Green Park sheltering from flying bombs.

BOND STREET

BOND STREET is the only fashionable promenade left in town.

Though severely gashed by the bombs of the battle of London, which destroyed many of its quaint Georgian houses and shops facing each other across the narrow carriage-way, it still attracts a great number of those who hurry along Piccadilly from St. James's Street to the Prince's Arcade, looking in at Fortnum & Mason, whose hampers of edibles delighted Charles Dickens, or turning over the latest books at Hatchard's which has been a feature of Piccadilly since the eighteenth century.

Bond Street, though congested and shabby, provides the only picture at all comparable to what St. James's Street must have looked like when the wits and the beaux sauntered along it in the shadow of the palace clock-tower. It contains a large share of all that is elegant in the capital—an elegance much attenuated by two world wars and against which it has become the rule to scoff; but the roots of Bond Street lie two and a half centuries deep, and as long as there are women with a mind to dress, and men not too old to look at a pretty face or a spring hat, Bond Street may hope to shimmer in the sun.

You will recall that Bond Street, Stafford Street, Albemarle Street, and Dover Street were built on the site of the Earl of Clarendon's magnificent mansion from which the Chancellor was obliged to flee almost as soon as he had taken up residence.

Before it was pulled down, Clarendon House had for a short time belonged to the second and last Duke of Albemarle who, to pay his debts, sold it to the highest bidder. The house and grounds fetched £35,000, and the purchasers

formed a syndicate, headed by Sir Thomas Bond, a devoted
follower of Charles the Second, to whom when the king
was in exile he had advanced large sums of money. Henry
Jermyn, Earl of Dover, nephew and heir of Henry Jermyn,
Earl of St. Albans, to whom Charles the Second had previously given all the land south of Piccadilly, was a member
of Sir Thomas Bond's syndicate, and his name is perpetuated
in Dover Street.

When the first houses were going up in Bond Street,
St. James's Church, Piccadilly, had just been consecrated,
its porch facing Jermyn Street, a stone's throw from the
picturesque St. James's Market. At the western end of
Piccadilly (still called Portugal Street) the turnpike faced
Berkeley House with its superb gardens, on either side of
which Lord Berkeley's widow, on the advice of her friend
John Evelyn, was building Stratton Street and Berkeley
Street. The diarist deplored that the sweet place and noble
gardens should be so much straitened by these two streets,
but the mansion of the late Lord Chancellor Clarendon,
being all demolished, there was some excuse for my Lady
Berkeley letting out part of her ground for the excessive
price offered.

At first Bond Street did not go beyond Burlington
Gardens, which then really were gardens behind Burlington
House, extending to the end of what is now Cork Street.
Beyond this was an open field known as the Conduit Mead,
and a thief who stole a silver mug from Dr. Sydenham's
house in Pall Mall, being chased across Piccadilly, was able
to lose himself in the bushes. Soon after 1700 Bond Street
was extended as far as Clifford Street, and that part of it
was named New Bond Street. The old and the new street
were now more or less the same length as Dover Street
and Albemarle Street, which remain as they were to this
day, forming a picturesque old-fashioned maze between
Berkeley Square and Bond Street.

While peaches ripened in the gardens of Burlington
House, and the nobility and gentry were taking up houses

in Bond Street, St. James's Street and the Mall were the high spots of the town. St. James's Coffee House was the fountain-head of information, and the outward room buzzed with politics. The wits and theorists argued amid the steams of the coffee-pot, and outside the door there was a globular oil lamp, newly invented. Brooks's Club was well established, and the Cocoa Tree Tavern, already fashionable, was the lounging place of the wits, the dandies, and the adventurers.

Soon Dr. Swift would be writing to Stella (20th December 1711): 'I dined, you know, with our society; and that odious secretary (Lord Bolingbroke) would make me president next week, so I must entertain them this day se'night at the Thatched House Tavern, where we dined to-day. It will cost me five or six pounds, yet the secretary says he will give me wine.' These were the days of the *Tatler* and the *Spectator*, of Lady Mary Wortley Montagu, of John Gay and Alexander Pope.

The third Earl of Burlington, having transformed his Piccadilly mansion, curtailed his garden and started to build some small houses, scattered irregularly up and down what is now Burlington Gardens. Cork Street was built in time for two of the most famous figures of the reign of Queen Anne to live there—the kindly Lady Masham, who supplanted, in the favour of the queen, her cousin, the Duchess of Marlborough; and Dr. Arbuthnot, the physician, wit, and man of letters. It was the building of Burlington and Cork Streets which led to a new extension of Bond Street —across the fields towards Oxford Street.

While the poets of the Augustan age sang the glories of the town, St. James's Street, Bond Street, Albemarle Street, and Dover Street remained purely residential. John Macky, in his *Journey through England* (1714), states that Earl Paulet, late Lord Steward of the Household, 'hath a magnificent palace at the end of Bond Street, with a fine prospect to the adjacent country, and indeed all Bond Street are palaces; the Earls of Orkney, Portmore, and many others of the nobility have sumptuous lodgings round that quarter.'

Between them grew up the smaller houses on the lines of those built by the Earl of Burlington on the site of his orchards. Nevertheless, in Burlington Gardens there was also a mansion known as Queensberry House where the poet Gay enjoyed the hospitality of the Duke and Duchess of Queensberry, who quarrelled with the king when a licence was refused in 1729 for the production of *Polly*, the sequel to *The Beggar's Opera*. Thackeray has accused the duke and duchess of over-feeding the poet, who 'was lapped in cotton, and had his plate of chicken, and his saucer of cream, and frisked, and barked, and wheezed, and grew fat, and so ended.'

Quite obviously Bond Street was not yet in any position to compete with the attractions of St. James's Street, but what did happen was that, unlike its neighbours, it gradually introduced gay shops of feminine apparel, the first of which, early in the century, was that of a mercer who hung up the sign of the Coventry Cross on account of the silk ribbons manufactured in that town.

Lodging-houses also sprang up in the street, which explains why so many of the most distinguished residents were merely birds of passage. And so, very quickly, indeed as early as in 1717, we hear in the *Weekly Journal* of a special class of fashionable persons known as Bond Street loungers.

Great figures come and go in those early days of Bond Street. One August evening in 1727 you might have seen Dr. Swift, freshly arrived from Pope's villa at Twickenham, driving up to his cousin Lancelot's house over against the 'Crown and Cushion' in New Bond Street. He had long given up his lodgings in Bury Street, St. James's.

Mrs. Delany, whose memoirs and letters you may read to quieten the tempo of your busy life, came to live here for a short time in 1731 when she was still married to her first husband, the aged and impotent Pendarves, who

wasted so many years of her youth. Then there was the
pieman Austin (he seems to call up a memory of our
nursery-rhyme days!) who took up his abode here—those
succulent pastries wafting their odour across the narrow
street. He was a disciple of Braund, the cook, who hung
up a painting of his own head for a sign, to show that in
the art of cookery there were men as great as your Eugenes
and Marlboroughs had proved themselves in the art of war.

Surely Bond Street is already a-moulding a character of
its own?

Do you suppose that the saunterers did not stop to
admire Lavinia Fenton, the original Polly in Gay's *Beggar's
Opera*, getting into her carriage; or look up at the window
where the charming poet Thomson, author of *The Seasons*,
lodged above a milliner's, a fact even more interesting
than that he seldom rose early enough to see the sun do
more than glisten on the opposite windows. A milliner
and a poet! A charming bonnet and a lovely summer
morning! Are these not a pretty combination to attract
the saunterer? There at least we have something to tempt
the crowds away from the smoky taverns of St. James's
Street, and those club windows behind which the men sat
all by themselves.

And now if you read Fielding you can dip again into
Tom Jones, and notice that Bond Street was a very good
part of the town where our hero was led by circumstances
to take up his residence in a house where he found a very
good friend in the landlady. From here we pass on to the
1760's, by which time George the Third had mounted the
throne and was deserting St. James's for what we call
Buckingham Palace. Literary figures were creeping into
Bond Street, like Gibbon who, young and fresh from
Lausanne, studied in the midst of the fashionable world.
'While coaches were rattling through Bond Street, I have
passed many solitary evenings in my lodgings with my books.'

There are few more touching scenes than the last hours
of Lawrence Sterne, the author of *Tristram Shandy*, who lay

miserably on a shabby couch on the first floor of No. 48 Old Bond Street, while pretty faces peered at the silk bags displayed in the window of the shop above which he lodged. We owe the death scene to a footman, whose curious book was discovered by Isaac D'Israeli:

'John,' said my master, 'go and enquire how Mr. Sterne is to-day.' I went, returned, and said: 'I went to Mr. Sterne's lodging—the mistress opened the door—I enquired how he did. She told me to go up to the nurse. I went into the room, and he was just a-dying. I waited ten minutes; but in five, he said: "Now it has come!" He put up his hand, as if to stop a blow, and died in a minute.'

While this scene was being enacted we may imagine Johnson's friend, Bennet Langton, tall, thin, and long-faced, standing as was his custom on one leg like a stork, on the pavement in front of Rothwell's, the perfumer, above which he lodged.

Now Boswell came to Bond Street where, besides the inevitable Dr. Johnson, he entertained at dinner Sir Joshua Reynolds (come over from Leicester Square), Garrick, and Goldsmith. Here are the giants we find so vividly brought to life in the memoirs of Fanny Burney—Dr. Johnson, who treated her with paternal affection, doing all to launch her novel *Evelina* towards its lively success; Sir Joshua Reynolds, whose amiable character she draws so vividly for us. Here, too, came to live in due course Sir Thomas Lawrence, whom she first saw as a youth in his parents' inn. We shall keep on meeting in her memoirs the gentle Mrs. Delany, who by then was grown old and of whose health Queen Charlotte always inquired when Fanny became lady-in-waiting.

To Bond Street went our authoress to see, from time to time, an exhibition of pictures. The place was crowded and fashionable in the extreme—fashionable in the double sense that its shopkeepers proved people of superior taste, and that the narrowness of the street allowed the loungers to obtain a nearer glimpse of the beautifully dressed 'and generally titled ladies that pass and repass from two to five o'clock.' The Prince of Wales, the future Regent, himself liked to saunter along Bond Street, sometimes with Charles James Fox, the Whig politician, who in 1783, when Foreign Secretary, lodged in Grafton Street, this, five years after Fanny Burney had published *Evelina*; and there is a pretty story of how Fox laid the Prince of Wales a wager that he would see more cats than he did in their saunter. Fox, knowing that cats like sunshine, took the sunny side of Bond Street and counted thirteen, while the prince, on the shady side, saw none.

The Princess of Wales Tavern had become the resort of literary men, while the Clifford Street Coffee House gathered round its fireside such men as Lord Charles Townshend and the youthful George Canning, who here first practised his oratory on such subjects as the French revolution.

Now a succession of colourful scenes help us to imagine the Bond Street of these last years of the eighteenth century. We can picture, for instance, Mrs. Fitzherbert, for whom the Prince of Wales declared himself ready to renounce his rights to the throne, leaning out of her window in the year 1796 surveying the curious crowd jostling on the pavement. The scene has been handed down to us in detail in a print you may still obtain for a few shillings—the curious little men with their white trousers, ill-fitting jackets with velveteen collars, high neckerchiefs, and beaver hats; the women, with dresses floating behind them like sacks inflated with air, their hair in ringlets, and feathers standing up to a height of two feet or more. 'High 'Change in Bond Street; or, la Politesse du Grand Monde,' it is called, and one may add that the men are pushing the women into the gutter. In the background is the Three Pigeons Inn.

Almost at the same time—within a matter of months— Admiral Nelson came to lodge at No. 141 after the expedition against Teneriffe, where he lost his arm. Southey tells us that he had scarcely any intermission of pain, day or night, and that Lady Nelson attended the dressing of his arm herself. One night he returned early to bed with a

dose of laudanum, but soon the family was disturbed by
a mob knocking loudly at the door.   The news of Duncan's
victory had become public and the house was not illuminated, but when the mob was told that Nelson lay there in
bed, they cried: 'You shall hear no more of us to-night.'

The Bond Street beau was now a character depicted in
poems and plays like the wits of St. James's Street and the
lounger of the Mall a century earlier.   A Cambridge don,
facetious as a judge, bequeathed his jackdaws to the Bond
Street beaux, his rooks to the club at Brooks's, and his
geese to the heads of his university.

The bookshop, the music shop, the picture gallery, and
the silversmith flourished in Bond Street.   So did a certain
Mr. Savory, apothecary, who early in the 1800s was presented with a handsome silver cup in return for his services
to Lady Hamilton, who had once begged for bread in the
streets of Soho.

Burlington House was now sold by the Duke of Devonshire to his uncle, Lord George Cavendish, who greatly
altered the interior and built the Burlington Arcade, which
was then divided from Bond Street by fine trees and a
low wall.

Meanwhile the hub of the street was increased by the
appearance of three hotels which figure prominently in the
history of the town during the nineteenth century.

There was Long's, at the corner of Clifford Street, which
if you are old enough you may still remember in its
declining years.   Lord Byron haunted it as he haunted
Stevens's Hotel on the opposite corner, but it was at Long's
that Sir Walter Scott saw Byron for the last time—the date
was 1815—'never so full of gaiety and good humour, to
which the presence of Mr. Mathews, the comedian, added
not a little.'   On the site of Long's smoking room and
billiard room now stands Truslove & Hanson's, the
book shop.

Later, with a frontage also on Albemarle Street (already
famous for Grillion's, where Louis XVIII lodged in exile),

there came the Clarendon, considered the only public place
where a genuine French dinner could be obtained.

We find these hotels constantly bobbing up in the books
and memoirs of our grandparents. Long's and Stevens's
were certainly rowdy places from the days of the Regency
(when it was no uncommon thing to see thirty or forty
saddle horses or tilburies waiting outside) to the ill-
mannered sixties when the young bloods drank brandy and
played cards till the morning sun streamed in.

Long's Hotel forms the background of a jolly print showing the brilliant company sauntering in front of its elegant
exterior in 1820. Gentlemen greeted one from horseback;
no traffic but an occasional cabriolet prevented one from
crossing slowly from pavement to pavement in gay attire.

While Bond Street was tidying itself up after the Battle
of London, the director of one of its famous art galleries,
talking to a client, told her that he was in the habit of
lunching at Long's until the war of 1914. Its glory, of
course, had somewhat diminished because, from the eighties
onwards, these family hotels could no longer compete with
such places as the Berkeley, the Savoy, Claridge's, and the
Ritz. But the fact that there are still Bond Street people
who talk to one quite easily of Long's show how deep in
the past are the roots of the street. One finds these everywhere—even when booking a couple of stalls for a theatre
at Ashton & Mitchell's in Old Bond Street. The original
John Mitchell, in his early days, was employed by William
Sams who started the system of selling tickets for fashionable
entertainments which, often connected with a circulating
library, has been a feature of Bond Street for over a century
and a half. Mitchell opened a library at the corner of
Stafford Street in 1834, and while carrying on the business
took over the Lyceum Theatre, newly rebuilt after the fire
of 1830, but his season of Italian comic opera not proving
a success, he introduced French plays and players to the
St. James's Theatre.

The drugs we buy at Savory & Moore's remind us of
that Mr. Savory who was apothecary to Lady Hamilton.

Almost everybody in the street will tell those of us who
are too young to remember such things, that until 1914
hardly any man walked down Bond Street unless in a
top-hat, frock-coat, and gloves. Our mothers dressed
differently to go down Bond Street than for any other
street. They left their carriages in Piccadilly with orders
to pick them up in Oxford Street, thus allowing their
pretty feet to saunter the whole way down, and later, if
it was a sunny morning, they would drive to the Achilles
statue in Hyde Park to sit for a while.

It is quite true that our modern fashions are necessarily
attenuated. The motor-car and the week-end habit deeply
affected Bond Street between the wars. The bombing
wrecked many of its trim little shops, smashed a hundred
windows, and everywhere left hideous scars. The immense
hole between Keith Prowse (another theatre agency!) and
Bruton Street with its chickweed, begins to look like a
meadow of the Conduit. The only building left standing amidst this desolation is the distant 'Coach and
Horses!'

But Bond Street is different, all the same, to any other
street in town—different in spite of the double-decked red
omnibuses and the commercial trucks which encumber the
narrow roadway, filling the pavements with their exhaust,
and using the street merely as a short cut between Piccadilly
and Oxford Street.

Before lunch-time, and even during it, Bond Street
mirrors everything that is elegant and fine. Consider now
its rivals and see how they have come and gone: the Mall,
where Lady Castlemaine showed her yellow feathers; Kensington Garden, sung by the poet Tickell; the Queen's
Walk in the Green Park where Lady Mary Coke walked
under the lilac-trees, admiring the deer and the cows; the
Achilles statue, and those paths alongside Rotten Row,
fashionable until the outbreak of war in 1914. What was

more splendid than those Sunday morning church parades of Edwardian, even early George the Fifth, days? What is left of the glory of the Mall, the Broad Walk, the Queen's Walk, or Hyde Park? Nothing at all. People of fashion do not even remain in town on Sunday. They have gone off in their pagan motor-cars. Dukes and generals no longer ride in Rotten Row. None of us would dream, even on a sunny week-day, of hurrying to any of the royal parks in our new Paris hat to see what is being worn.

Is there something in an alley of trees, green lawns, a bed of tulips, or a border of rhododendrons to make it more liable to fluctuation than a street? But the streets, all but this one, have been obliged to drop their sceptre, each in turn —the Piazza of Covent Garden, the Strand, St. James's Street, yes, most famous of all, and the spoilt infant, Regent Street, now shorn of its colonnades as well as of its loungers.

Where then must we turn to search for the secret of Bond Street which attracted the notice of the *Weekly Journal* in 1717? Two hundred and thirty years is a long slice, even in the history of London, when one considers the shifting sands of popularity, the continual heaving of fashion this way and that—a process of fermentation if you will, that turned Park Lane from a path to the gibbet into an avenue of millionaires, and then felled its mansions to replace them with hotels, flats, and business premises!

One suspects that even in this utilitarian age there remains in many of us a need, from time to time, to gaze upon what is pleasing to the senses—the portrait which Reynolds painted, the book which Samuel Johnson may have handled, the piece of china we can almost see through, and at Sotheby's saleroom every fascinating treasure from a lace parasol to a Louis the Fifteenth tapestry.

Such are doubtless the real attractions of Bond Street. Even though the lover of pictures can spend his or her lunch hour at the National Gallery which, since the war, has provided both the sandwich and the Rubens, the hot coffee and the Goya, the appetite may still demand other

courses—the satisfying glimpse of a piece of Chippendale
in the hall of Frank Partridge, the shepherdess in Dresden
at The Antique Porcelain Co., or a pair of Queen Anne
silver candlesticks in the window of century-old Tessier's.

Perhaps the fashionable parade is the result of the
accumulation, along one narrow street, of the treasures
of the past, the craftsmanship of three centuries, all there
for the seeking.

The people of Bond Street are aware of the precarious-
ness of their good fortune.　Before 1914 three-quarters of
the firms were old-established.　If new-comers, unmindful
of the street's traditions, do not give the saunterer his
aesthetic pleasure, if the little Georgian houses and shops
are everywhere replaced with steel and cement, the upper
storeys filled with offices, the ghosts of Swift and Gay,
Fielding and Sterne, Boswell and Reynolds, Byron and
Scott, Nelson and Lady Hamilton will be driven away.

Bond Street is an aristocrat.　Not quite of royal blood,
like St. James's, it ranks high in the peerage and wears its
scarlet and ermine with ease.　Even at its most dowdy
moments one is never surprised or shocked to see diamonds
and rubies glittering in its shop windows.　A royal car
threading its way through the traffic appears quite a normal
happening.　One expects to be greeted by a succession of
Gainsboroughs and Van Dycks, which are just as much at
home here as in the picture gallery or the ball-room of any
ancestral country house.　When one visits the Fine Art
Society one takes for granted the Turkey carpet, the splendid pieces of furniture, the log fire crackling in the old
fire-place, the faint smell of oriental tobacco, and the
pleasing sight of William Fullarton with his red coat and
tight trousers painted by Sir Henry Raeburn.　The gilt
French clock, the pretty staircase leading to the first floor full
of the etchings and engravings of Dürer and Rembrandt are
all in tone with the atmosphere.　Thus the hatter delivers his
goods, as he did throughout the bombing, in a box carriage
with a prancing horse; and one is treated with the sight

of a Louis the Fifteenth hand-painted fan which nobody would dream of taking any longer to the non-existent ball!

But Bond Street does more than present tastefully so many of the glories of the past. We find here the best of what is modern. More than any other street, it champions the individualistic craftsman. Almost on the site of the gay milliner's above which lodged the poet Thomson, Italian straws and velvet ribbons delight the eye. The diamond bracelet which tempts us at Boucheron's, the clip or the vanity case, are representative of a craft in which modern taste is remarkable, and far more advanced than in the days of Benvenuto Cellini. Nobody can say that Europe is not making masterpieces for the museums of to-morrow. In Bond Street the shoemaker like Delman makes one's bag in the leather with which one is shod. Elizabeth Arden has not merely studied all the secrets of feminine beauty since the days of Nefertiti and her sisters of the burning Egyptian desert, she has invoked science to her aid and hers is another art which shows amazing progress. The nightgown and the blouse at the White House, at Lydia Moss's, or in other shops of the kind, is made with ethereal silks and satins of a beauty undreamt of not long ago, and is often garnished with hand-made lace so fine that, as the French say, one should kneel in front of it. In Bond Street also you will find the craft most typical of the present. Watch the girls seated behind bow windows who mend the ladders that so easily happen to our silk or nylon stockings. How quick and nimble are their fingers! How gay they are! One is glad to be a woman in the paradise that is Bond Street!

Bond Street nestles up against its powerful relation. On the most intimate terms with Piccadilly whose ancestry, after all, is lost in its ruts and highwaymen, its coaches lumbering past green fields and orchards, through the turnpike, to the west country, Bond Street clings to the immutable strength of our most famous thoroughfare. One is almost inclined to say that it feeds at its table, for the people who come to it come from Piccadilly. There is no dividing the one from the other. If Piccadilly is the head, Bond Street is the right arm.

The days when Dover Street and Albemarle Street and Grafton Street were entirely filled with fine private houses are no longer. The finance corporations of the City, the art dealers, an airway company, and a few hairdressers and beauty parlours have adapted to their different uses those Georgian houses which still exist.

In Grafton Street there is, however, a house that is so much more beautiful than any other that you can quickly imagine the coach at the door and the servants in livery bowing and scraping. The double doors have heavy knockers fashioned like lions. Every morning at half-past ten the parlourmaid steps out of the front doors to polish the two brass bells, each with a lion to match the knockers. Then the butler, holding his head very erect, comes out to sniff the air and to glance at the freshly polished brass.

Are we describing ghosts of the past who have come back, in spite of the petrol fumes, to haunt the house where, according to Wheatley, Benjamin Franklin used to come of an evening to play chess with Admiral Earl Howe and his sister, which innocent games cloaked important conferences of American affairs? Nay, within this house lives Mrs. Arthur James, godmother of the present Queen of England! A cousin of the late Countess of Strathmore, the queen's mother, Mrs. James was so devoted to this backwater of Bond Street that she never left it during the entire war, going down with her servants to the shelter during the noisier nights of the Battle of London. Is there not something fine in this last distinguished resident of Grafton Street—clinging through fire and high explosive to her house? The voice of the perfect butler echoes softly through the great hall. He can remember Bond

Street when the omnibuses were drawn by horses. The bell which the parlourmaid polishes so ardently every morning is seldom rung to admit visitors to the vista of Italian marble, which stretches, as if to the infinite, up the staircase bathed in the red glow of its warm texture. 'We have a country estate,' says the butler, 'but we prefer London.'

How soft is his voice! What splendid sentiments!

A little while after these lines were written, during the summer of 1948, I was passing this house when, on the steps, I met a niece of its gracious owner. She told me that Mrs. Arthur James had just died, and that the house was being sold. It would probably be turned into offices. Thus does London change before one's eyes!

The encroachment of business premises into this back-water of Bond Street often reflects, in particular cases, the shifting tide of fashion. One sees these old firms jumping forward, reign by reign, like the men on a draught-board until one almost hears them crying out: 'King!' and adding a new storey to their height. One likes, for instance, to think of the print-shop, Parker's, starting the game at Cornhill in the year 1750 and then leaping over its adversaries in easy stages—in 1790, to Wardour Street in the wake of the westward migration of London's wealthy citizens; in 1843, to Panton Street, then the centre of collectors from all over the world; in 1905, a sort of side move to Whitcombe Street; and so on, until finally it settled in Albemarle Street, overlooking St. James's and the red-brick palace so often featured in prints behind its plate-glass window. What a mellow satisfaction to reflect that your game has gone on from great-great-grandfather to yourself, during nine reigns! Can you wonder, after all this, that there is something particular in the atmosphere which makes one tread these pavements with respect? There is a bookshop, also, in Grafton Street, which began

playing its game of draughts a century ago in Castle Street
which one thinks of in terms of Leicester Square, and then
careering across the board to Piccadilly, before settling at
the turn of this century where it is now, its sombre front
redolent of all that is splendid in the book trade.

Occasionally there are fresher memories. Charred ruins
of the Battle of London are apt to be monotonous, but the
Grafton Galleries provided a panorama that made the flesh
creep in much the same way as a visit to the Chamber of
Horrors at Mme Tussaud's. There should have been somebody to collect a shilling entrance fee at the Grafton
Galleries which, if you had a mind to, you could enter across
the most picturesque mass of broken stained glass that any
Wren church in the City could put down. There was a
horrible smell of burned timber, and a curious echo that
was for ever holding back one's timorous footsteps, making
one wonder if the floor would not give way and hurl one
into the unknown. Obviously one had no business to be
trespassing in this forgotten land. One felt extremely
brave and quite definitely in the wrong. A wide staircase
twisted and turned. The sunshine, through the open roof,
cast eerie shadows, but suddenly one was rewarded by the
sight of a temple with a domed roof much damaged by
fire, and beyond, double doors opened on a view of the
seemingly infinite, but in reality, on the great hole between
Bond Street and Bruton Street, where tables and chairs still
clung to buildings cut in half, and swaying over the new
Conduit Mead with its grass and chickweed growing on the
crazy pavement of erstwhile cellars. What were these
Grafton Galleries? Who remembers that during the
war of 1914–18, little boys from Eton and young girls with
fresh complexions danced here to the tune of *Beautiful
Katie* and the song hits of *The Bing Boys* from that
Alhambra which now, alas, exists no longer?

One recalls curiously that aroma of Turkish tobacco
which our Guards officers smoked, for is it not strange
to reflect that those gentlemen had not yet accustomed

themselves to the vulgar weed from Virginia to which they
only gave way towards the end of that far-off conflict?

We came to Grafton Street to examine the environment
of Bond Street. We should study with equal diligence
that other backwater—from Burlington Gardens to Clifford
Street, through which Cork Street and Savile Row run
with historic ease. What strange layers of interest coat
this little world where the elderly courtiers of Queen
Anne came to spend their declining years. Our good
friend Dr. Johnson was always running round to Cork
Street to visit Mr. Diamond, the apothecary. Even to the
time when Napoleon was first consul, George the Third's
dentist lived in Bond Street, and there was a surgeon
residing there of the name of P. Elizee, so you see that
there was nothing strange in Lady Hamilton's Mr. Savory
practising amongst the bonnets and the beaux! But one
suspects that the tailors had already planned to oust the
doctors from Clifford Street, for by 1814, when the Prince
of Orange came to pay his addresses to Princess Charlotte,
the Regent's daughter (you will recall that she jilted the
Dutchman in favour of Prince Leopold who was so much
better-looking. Alas, poor child, she died in childbirth),
the Prince of Orange, then, while he believed he could win
her hand, lodged above his tailor's in Clifford Street where
was Mr. Stultz, the fashionable cutter, who had half the
members of the clubs of St. James's on his books.

And now what has happened to Clifford Street, and
Cork Street, and those other streets once merry with my
lord's apple blossom?

When the temple of the Grafton Galleries echoed to the
tune of *Beautiful Katie*, there were chambers in Cork Street
where the wealthy and fashionable resided, because as yet
there were none of those gigantic structures of steel and
cement which, between the wars, rose upon the mansions
of the mighty. The flats of those days already appear very
antiquated to us but, in truth, they had a comfort all of
their own—a comfort based on the Edwardian conception

I

of lofty rooms designed for large, decorative furniture and thick Turkey carpets; and, in their proper place, big square baths in which the most corpulent lord could float with ease. Experienced housekeepers looked after these buildings, and there was generally a fine, roomy kitchen on the top floor with skylights to let in the fresh air from heaven. People gave dinner parties of a leisurely character, and gathered their friends round them. Some still hunted the fox in the shires, and many had not quite rid themselves of the habit of going to church on Sundays and parading the park. The kitchenette and the tin of sardines had not entered into their lives, in spite of the mud that was oozing on the Somme.

It is a strange business to trace the twilight of such Edwardian flats until their final curtain when, during the Second World War, many became dormitories for American troops. To-morrow most of them will put up the commercial plate. The typewriter will play its symphony where the leisurely splashed in their baths. The Edwardian flat mansions were already squeezing out the last of the private houses, but the tailors of Regency days, or their successors, clung to this part of the town and, according to tradition, seldom sent in their bills.

There are still tailors hereabouts, and Savile Row has become synonymous with their trade, as Harley Street is now famed for the consulting rooms of the medical profession who, in Victorian days, removed thither from the purlieus of Bond Street. The tailor's shop is probably still something of a club. His premises are dimly lit, and weekly magazines can be seen scattered on faded leather couches. One imagines that somewhere in a back room must be hidden those morning coats and velvet smoking-jackets which will soon, together with the gold-knobbed cane and the shining silk hat, be relegated to the theatrical costumiers in Wardour Street.

While the fox was being shot by the wartime farmer, or even by the land girl, the aged cutters of the last war put

the hunting pink on dusty shelves, and bent over the
dismal lengths of uninspiring khaki. Tailors who were
bombed out sought the hospitality of their neighbours.
The ladies' habit makers in Cork Street who have made
riding habits for women in the shires for so long took in
the partners of a men's tailors who were bombed out.
They have since become such good friends that when I go
there to order a skirt I pass through what has become quite
a meeting place for officers and diplomats. A fashionable
dressmaker, back from the wars, began to set up business
in the very heart of Savile Row—even in the house where
Sheridan had lived—breaking into this male sanctuary much
as if Clarissa or Doris had walked straight into Brooks's
Club or the Cocoa Tree Tavern with a band-box of gay
bonnets under her arm. It seems strange and charming to
order a dress in Savile Row.

In spite of these events the little streets retain, like
Grafton Street, something that does not yet allow one quite
to forget the past. There are small houses a century or
more old—quaint little houses, with creaking staircases.
Often the craftsman plies his trade in basement and on street
level. Then when he has put up his shutters for the night,
when Bond Street has become suddenly quiet, as if stilled
by a breath of hot wind, when the diamonds and the rubies
are sleeping in strong rooms, when the Gainsboroughs are
covered up with dust-sheets, when the grandfather's clock
is ticking the seconds in the deserted sale room and the
street lamps twinkle mysteriously, when the lounger of
the daylight hours is nodding behind his evening paper
and his glass of whisky in clubland, then the courtesan
treads the ground where Clarendon's palace rose and
where Burlington's apple-trees displayed their delicate
blooms.

Whence has she come?

Why, a century ago you would have found her in the
Strand. Did not Lady Louisa Stuart write in the year
1827 about some person of her acquaintance that she was

of a class of women apparently desirous 'to proclaim that it is not the principle, but want of sufficient temptation alone, that hinders their walking the Strand'?

Yes, and before that it would have been in the vicinity of the Piazza in Covent Garden.

Thus the painted cheek and the winning smile have, in tune with the lithograph and the vellum binding, been hopping from square to square on the London draught-board in the great game in which the men move farther west through each century.

Did we not say that Bond Street has different characters, like a sort of Dr. Jekyll and Mr. Hyde? By day it is like this; by night it is thus; and on Sunday mornings it is so deserted that you may look down it from Piccadilly to Oxford Street, and even beyond, without so much as seeing one of those cats for which Charles James Fox and the Prince of Wales searched so diligently.

We who trip down Bond Street on high heels, showing off a gay hat, when the sun glistens on the windows of the street, would not dare to tarry when the moon bathes the shutters with its milky glow, and, as for the week-end, the place is quite beneath our notice!

BERKELEY SQUARE

BECAUSE OF THE nightingales that are supposed to sing in the shrubs in the garden, and the picturesque link extinguishers in front of the few private houses which have not yet been pulled down, there is a lingering romance in Berkeley Square which makes it of world renown.

In truth, we see here a fading picture of the London of other days, when rich people built their town house in the leafy quietness behind the noble mansions of Piccadilly.

You will recall that just about the time when Lord Chancellor Hyde, who made such a lot of money in the days of Charles the Second, was building his sumptuous palace facing the top of St. James's Street, another rich man, Lord Berkeley, of Stratton, an able officer who had served in the royal army under Charles the First, built a fine mansion where Devonshire House now stands.

Berkeley Square did not begin to take shape till the last years of William the Dutchman. By this time there was nothing left of Clarendon House. Lord Chancellor Hyde's palace had come and gone like a meteor.

During the reigns of Queen Anne and George the First, Berkeley Square grew up lazily against the gardens of Berkeley House. Berkeley House was bought by the first Duke of Devonshire, burnt down, and rebuilt for the third duke in 1735 from designs by Kent. Henceforth it was to be known as Devonshire House.

The accession of George the Third (1760) saw the next important change. The Earl of Bute, the new king's favourite, required a big town house to mark his appointment as Prime Minister and he built himself a house on the south side of Berkeley Square. Whereas Devonshire House faced Piccadilly, Lord Bute's house, of course, faced Berkeley Square, but their gardens merged.

But the Earl of Bute became as maligned as the unfortunate Lord Chancellor Hyde a hundred years earlier, and the house in Berkeley Square was sold in an unfinished state in 1768 to the Earl of Shelburne who became Marquess of Lansdowne in 1784. Then it became known as Lansdowne House.

A narrow passage, sunk below the level of the ground, was now built to divide Lord Lansdowne's garden from the Duke of Devonshire's garden. A flight of steps led down to it at one end. It was called Lansdowne Passage, and it still exists. The iron bar which you will see by the steps was put there because a highwayman, having done a deed of violence in Shepherd Market, rode through.

Devonshire House was pulled down in 1925 and the iron gates erected in the Green Park. The great steel building of modern flats perpetuates the name.

Lansdowne House was demolished half way between the wars, and modern flats were built there also. The sunken passage dividing the gardens fell into disuse, and alongside it, but on higher level, was built a new Lansdowne Passage flanked on one side with shops, amongst which the pekinese kennels are perhaps the best known. Looking down Lansdowne Passage you may see the big building in Curzon Street which had been arranged during the Battle of London as an alternative home for the king and queen if anything had happened to Buckingham Palace. Those of us who remember Lansdowne House with its beautiful lawns and tall trees can doubtless form a tolerable picture of what Berkeley Square used to look like in the eighteenth century with its linkmen, its sedan chairs, and cumbrous family coaches. Footmen ran by the side of their masters' carriages. There were flowers and more trees in the middle of the square, and here Princess Amelia, of Gunnersbury Park, put up an equestrian statue of George the Third. The rich and titled lived all round in compact houses with nice iron-work and clean white steps in front.

This is Berkeley Square. These words bring to one's mind thoughts of a more leisurely age, more picturesque, perhaps, with its linkmen, its sedan chairs, its chariots, its gay window-boxes, and large houses well staffed with powdered footmen and lace-aproned maids.

In the house opposite lived, when this picture was painted, a very gracious old lady who had been given it as a present when she was young and very pretty and newly married. She drove a four-in-hand, and her hats were so becoming that they were copied all over the world. But now that her husband was dead and her lease was nearly finished, she wanted to die with her house. Of late years her only amusement was looking out of the window at the traffic in Berkeley Square. There was little left in her house but an iron bed on which she slept. She had given all the rest away to her relations.

After this book was first published her lease fell in and she went to live with friends in a mews near Park Lane. She died almost immediately but the house in Berkeley Square was still there in 1950 —grim and neglected.

In Victorian days, fine ladies drove on summer afternoons to eat ices at Gunter's against Hay Hill. There was pretty colouring from their bustles, their parasols, and from the green leaves rustling in the warm air. Lady Lindsay of Balcarres, whose portrait by G. F. Watts is the painter's masterpiece, would drive there with the poet Browning.

While the people who lived in the square visited one another, their servants and coachmen drank beer at the 'Running Footman' in Hay Mews, whose signboard still represents a tall man in gay dress running with long easy steps. In his hand is a long light stick with a metal top. Underneath are the words: 'I am the only Running Footman.'

The new Lansdowne House was the first giant to implant itself in the square, but almost immediately afterwards all the small houses between Bruton Street and the south corner were pulled down for an even larger building, which was scarcely finished when the war of 1939 broke out. The Government commandeered it for various ministries, and that part of the street level which should have been shops was bricked up. Meanwhile the railings were taken from the garden in the middle of the square and trenches were dug across the gardens. Later a steel water tank was erected at the south-east corner.

Lord Rosebery's house, on the south of the square, collapsed after being damaged in a raid. The house on the north-west corner was blown up by a time-bomb at six on a Wednesday morning. One of the turrets of the new Lansdowne House was hit by a flying bomb on a Sunday morning in August 1944.

Because people walked all over the flower-beds and the lawns in the gardens in the middle of the square, the ground became hard like clay baked in an oven, but in spite of this a number of crocuses and daffodils pushed up their heads each spring and actually flowered.

During the winter of 1946 the square was fenced round and landscape gardeners set about restoring its beauty.

In a way the war had done less to alter the looks of the square than the years between wars, which had brought along those giants of steel and cement.

But every year some private family left some private house and it would become flats, or a shop or a bank.

Unconsciously there seemed to be a race between the shops and high commerce to wrest the remaining houses from the nobility, but the tendency was for the square to commercialize itself—not to become a shopping centre. However, Maggs the fine booksellers settled on the west side during the war, after being bombed out and were here bombed again, but not too seriously. On the north side a coat of arms designated a dressmaker and a *modiste*, who both on occasion supplied the queen.

Yet the ancient spirit of Berkeley Square still persisted, pushing up its head like the spring flowers had pushed up theirs through the hard-baked mud round the air-raid shelters.

Throughout the war, for the benefit of my child, I bought a chicken every week from a poulterer in Mount Street whose façade testifies his long association with the residents of Berkeley Square. Because the shop closed at one o'clock on Saturday, and because it was generally difficult for me to call before early evening, the bird would be left for me with an old employee, Mr. Trigg, who lived over the stables at the back. This arrangement went on during the difficult years which followed.

Now it happened that on one Saturday evening during the summer of 1947, though I rang loudly on Mr. Trigg's bell against the wooden gate there was no answer. Disappointed, I decided to return home through the gardens surrounding the Catholic church in Farm Street where the last king of Spain worshipped during his visits to London, and, making my way towards Charles Street, by the mews past Lachasse the dressmaker, I suddenly, from the other side, saw a little man emerge from the public bar of the 'Running Footman,' crying out:

*1

'Are you looking for me, madam?'

Of course it was Mr. Trigg.

He said, to excuse his presence so far from home: 'They told me you were coming at four o'clock.'

'I know, Mr. Trigg. I'm sorry. I had so much to do.'

'It doesn't matter. I'll be with you in a moment.'

He rushed back into the public bar, and in a few moments caught up with me, having quickly emptied his tankard and paid for it with the florin I had pressed into his hand. He appeared very happy and talkative.

'How is the little boy, madam?'

'He's in the country, thank you, Mr. Trigg.'

He began to be very eloquent about the various great families—his customers mostly—who for a multitude of reasons had been obliged to leave the square.

Then as he took out his key to open the big wooden doors of the stables over which he lived, he said:

'The link extinguishers, the grand folk, and the nightingales will soon be no more. They will pass away with the once lovely Mrs. Cloete who sits every day waiting for death as she looks through the curtainless windows of her empty dining-room—dreaming of the past, waiting to rejoin her husband in heaven. What? You don't know Mrs. Cloete—Mrs. Montrose Cloete—Mrs. Cloete of the corner house against Charles Street—the loveliest, oldest house in the square, where all the royalties since Queen Victoria have dropped in for tea or dinner? She's not proud. You should go to see her. Often as I hurried past her window, she would tap against the pane, and invite me in for a sherry. She has lived in the house since she was a bride, and now she's eighty-six. But lately, madam, I don't know why, I haven't been to see her. But you should go. She'll receive you very kindly.'

He hurried across the courtyard into the shop by the back entrance, and opening the enormous refrigerator brought out the chicken already tied up in a parcel. He saw me back into the mews, and repeated:

'Do as I say.   Call on Mrs. Cloete, and another time,
if I'm not here, remember to look for me at the "Running
Footman."'

Really, I never intended to call on her.

But when I reached the corner house and saw the wrought-
iron torch-snuffer and lantern on the railings by the squat
heavy door, and realized that externally, at any rate, it
retained all the picturesqueness of a disappearing age, I
longed to go inside, and reflecting that this of all hours
was the least impolite for a visit, I bravely mounted the
white steps, and rang the bell which echoed against the
still dark walls of the servants' area.

There were steps, and after some clanking of chains, a
comfortable middle-aged woman appeared, framed in the
coolness of the hall.

'Is Mrs. Cloete in?' I asked.

'What name shall I say, madam?'

'It wouldn't be any use.   Mrs. Cloete doesn't know me.
I'm simply interested in Berkeley Square, and I thought
—well, I thought Mrs. Cloete might be so very kind as
to tell me something about her house.'

She hesitated, obviously wondering what to do with me,
when suddenly from the depths of the narrow hall, a
frail but imperious voice began to ask what the visitor
wanted.

'You had better go through,' said the woman.   'She
won't like me talking to you behind her back.'

So I hurried in the direction of the voice.

She was a very old lady with white hair done in a bun
at the back, and she had raised herself slightly on her bed,
twisting round her neck to inspect me critically as I came
along.   As soon as I arrived into what for the moment I
shall call her room, though in reality it was merely a corner
with a dark window behind the stairs where, when the
house was properly kept, the guests might have washed
their hands and left their coats and umbrellas, she said:

'Sit down, my dear, and make yourself as comfortable as you can.'

I was so surprised by this mixture of ease and penury that I sat down obediently on the kitchen chair, the one, the only chair in the tiny space between the foot of the bed, the window, and the marble wash-stand. Then she recited what seemed to be a set piece, running (as far as I can remember), thus:

'Yes, my dear, I am eighty-six, and I have lived in this house for fifty-five years. The lease has only another eighteen months to run, but though I've asked the landlord to renew it, he's going to pull it down and build a big block of modern flats on the site. No, it's not his fault. Besides, presumably by Christmas 1948 I shall be dead. The house and I have another eighteen months to live, and then we shall disappear together. What is there left for me to do? All my nearest and dearest have gone. I have no regrets. I have not left undone many of the things I ought to have done, and I haven't really done many of the things that I shouldn't have done. I have had a long and splendid life, and now that I'm the last survivor of a Berkeley Square that is disintegrating, I'm ready to go when God calls me.'

She had been fingering the stained coverlet with hands blue and black with veins, but she exclaimed with sudden eagerness:

'I will show you my photographs.'

To my amazement, she jumped lithely out of bed and I saw that she wore a black woollen dress and stockings. She explained:

'I'm getting up or lying down, so I remain in my clothes. My dear, pour yourself out some beer. The doctor advises it. I used to have eight servants. Now, I'm alone except for the woman who let you in, and she only comes from time to time.'

'Do you sleep alone in the house? Aren't you terrified?'

'Oh, my dear, why should I be frightened? There's

nothing left in the house. It's empty, empty from top to bottom. I've given everything away before dying, not to have anybody squabbling over my last possessions.'

'But who cooks?'

'The woman makes me an egg for lunch. I have to force myself to eat it. But what was I saying? Oh, yes, the photographs. There are not many. The family are always tearing leaves out of the album, but you shall see what I have. First of all, open the window behind your back. You will see where I built my stables. They cost me £2,800, and I kept eight horses.'

I put my handbag, and the parcel with the chicken in it, at the foot of the bed, and struggled with the recalcitrant window. She went on:

'My husband was a great sportsman. He kept his golf clubs and his guns in a closet behind the wash-basin, but I've turned it into a lavatory. There, now you can see where I had my stables, up against the back of the "Running Footman." Yes, leave the window open a moment. I like to have a little air. In summer, on hot days like this, Montrose, my husband, used to play cricket at Lords, and after lunch I would drive there in my tandem. The men would throw the gates open for me. I was the beautiful Mrs. Cloete!'

She laughed without affectation.

Her wealth, her importance, her situation, and her past happiness were things nobody could take away from her.

Turning to a rusty iron door in the wall she pushed it open and said:

'This was the strong room for the silver and plate. Come and give me your arm, my dear.'

We switched on the light and penetrated this recess. It appeared empty except for a bundle of papers and some beer bottles.

'There!' she exclaimed, clutching a faded album. 'Come and sit on the bed and tell me what is written on each page.'

On the fly-leaf, scribbled in pencil, were some names and dates.   They appeared to make no sense, but because she was bending over me and kept on asking: 'Well?   Well?' with a touch of impatience, I began:

'Philip van der Byl—the Eerste River——'

She arrested me with a bony hand:

'Philip van der Byl, my father, left South Africa when he was a young man to take his doctor's degree at Edinburgh. They gave him a gold medal, but one of my cousins or nephews sold it for a fiver.   His mother offered to buy it back from the dealer, but I answered: "What's the good? As soon as I'm gone, somebody else will sell it!"   Are you sure you won't have a beer?'

She was beginning to deviate from the straight path of the story, so I said firmly:

'I see two names written here—Simpson and Gladstone.'

'My father travelled on the Continent with Simpson, but later he gave up medicine and sat in the House of Commons under Gladstone.   When I wanted to marry Montrose Cloete—he was seventeen, and I was sixteen—my father wouldn't have it because we were cousins, and poor Montrose was banished to his brother's ranch in Mexico.'

'So what did you do?' I queried, encouraged by the beginning of a love story.

'I waited for him,' she snapped.   'I waited for him for ten years.   During that time I was asked in marriage thirty-two times.'

'Thirty-two times!' I exclaimed.   It needs some imagination to think of being asked in marriage by thirty-two different men.   There must have been a look of admiration about me, for she made this answer rather offhandedly:

'Oh, it wasn't altogether for me, I expect.   They probably thought I was rich.'

I began to wonder who these thirty-two suitors were. Some had presumably been famous, or at least, had become so.   It was indiscreet, but I asked her to tell me something about them.

'Let them alone,' she answered. 'Those are questions one doesn't ask. Anyway, one day papa said to me: "Do you still want to marry Montrose?" "Yes, papa, I 'll never marry anybody else." "Then," proclaimed my father, "you 'd better write and tell him to come back." "No, papa," I answered. "You must do that."'

One sensed she had always been a woman of character, but what I liked best was the way she pronounced the word 'papa'—the tone of respect and affection was very pleasant to the ear.

'Turn the page,' she ordered.

I announced (after reading a little):

'You were married in a village near Winchester on 9th February 1888. This is an account of the wedding cabled back to a newspaper in South Africa. ' "The villagers lined the streets, and the bride and bridegroom saw on every side evidence of the pleasure their union occasioned——"'

'Read on. Read on.'

' "After the ceremony, bells rang out in a merry peal, and there was a *feu de joie* in a meadow, a friend lending the cannon. As the bridal party reached the porch, Mr. and Mrs. Cloete halted and were successfully photographed by a local photographer. I cannot imagine [it was a woman reporter writing] a more embarrassing situation than being photographed in one's bridal array before the gaze of a throng of spectators. The idea is certainly novel. I am glad to hear the proofs were successful."'

We both remained quiet for a few moments while the sun streamed through the dirty window-pane, shedding a rainbow of dust on the cracked wall. She explained:

'Four years after my marriage my mother gave me this house as a present. I used to say to myself in those days: "Is it possible that I really live in Berkeley Square?" It was so quiet, so leafy, so full of friends. Tradesmen were not allowed in the square. They used to pull up in Charles Street. The Prince of Wales—the future King Edward the

Seventh, you know, would drop in for lunch with the
Princess of Wales. Often sixty uninvited guests would
arrive. That was the fun of it. There was always plenty
to eat and to drink. Why, even in the servants' quarters
I would put a baron of beef and a barrel of beer on a table
for any tradesmen who liked to help themselves when they
came to deliver anything. Yes, and the nightingales really
sang. I heard them a hundred times. I heard one the
other day, but now the traffic drowns their singing.'

I asked meekly:

'Were you very pretty?'

'They said so. I was referred to as Mrs. Cloete, "whose
personal attraction is so well known in Berkeley Square."
It sounds old-fashioned, doesn't it?'

I turned the pages of the scrap-book and found a reproduction of her portrait hung in the Royal Academy in 1892.

'Oh!' I exclaimed, 'it's amazing. I see the resemblance.'

It really was extraordinary how the main characteristics
remained—the angular features, mysterious but noble like
a quarter-moon—the imperious blue eyes and the fine
deportment.

I asked:

'Did you have any children?'

'I had one when I was newly married, but it died the
same year.'

She threw up her head proudly, but a tear rolled down
her wrinkled brown cheek, and I could feel that under
the wizened exterior her thoughts had become tender
and young.

'Some months later,' she continued, 'I went to see my
mother, and while we were talking with friends in the
drawing-room, a young woman arrived with a baby. "Oh,
mama! Mama!" I cried, covering my face with my
hands. "I can't bear to see it." But my mother said:
"Mary, don't be absurd."'

She repressed her tears. Her mother's reproof must still
have echoed in her memory. She was hard, or, more

exactly, she knew how to curb her feelings, like the
aristocrat she was. Suddenly she said:

'Come back, my dear, whenever you feel like it. Make
the house your own. Even when I'm in bed, you may
go into the empty dining-room and look out on Berkeley
Square.'

To look out on Berkeley Square! She was offering me
the only possession left to her and I would have been unkind
not to make use of it.

The next day which was Sunday I lunched out of town,
but as soon as I was back I went up the steps of Curzon
Street into Berkeley Square.

As soon as I had crossed Charles Street I saw her frail
figure at the dining-room window. Her eyes met mine,
but for a moment she appeared not to recognize me. Then
suddenly they lit up and she rose quite excitedly, making
signs that she was going to open the door.

I next saw her through one of the narrow panes of glass
at the side of the massive nail-studded front door whose
paint was wrinkled and cracked. She probably wanted to
make sure that I hadn't made off during her journey from
the dining-room window to the hall. Her features were
quite radiant. Obviously she thought of me as a slight
diversion during the long lonely hours.

There was some play with bolts and chains, and then
when she had opened the door she took my arm and helped
herself back into the dining-room.

She had begun her recitation, saying: 'Yes, my dear,
I am eighty-six, and I have lived in this house for fifty-
five years . . .' but as I knew that part of it by heart,
I centred all my attention on the room.

To a height of about four feet from the floor it was
magnificently panelled in dark oak. The fire-place was of
the same carved wood, and so was a heavy sideboard next
to the window where she liked to sit. The only other
piece of furniture was a fine Persian rug. The walls above
the panelling were quite bare.

I exclaimed: 'What lovely panelling! I suppose your mother had it put in when she gave you the house?'

'Oh, no,' she answered. 'This is what happened. William the Conqueror gave an oak beam to Winchester Cathedral to repair something or other, but the beam was never used. Just after our marriage, the dean gave it to a carpenter called Thomas in lieu of money the cathedral owed him, and Thomas offered it to my husband. Montrose made the design and Thomas carved it. He came to stay for a fortnight in the house. I put him up with the coachman in the stables and I sent him to a different theatre every night. Yes, indeed, it's very pretty, but, my dear, there were such lovely things in the house. I had sixty pictures on the staircase alone.'

'It's very kind of you to invite me,' I said. 'I would have brought some flowers, but it's Sunday and all the shops are closed. I will bring some to-morrow.'

'Oh, no, don't do that!' she cried. 'I wouldn't know what to put them in. There isn't a bowl or a vase in the house. There's nothing, nothing.'

Well, I thought, I would bring her a growing plant.

She now insisted that I should begin to enjoy the view from the window as if it was time to keep still and watch the curtain go up for the play. Because I had spoken of flowers, the subject must have stirred memories. She said:

'When I was a young married woman each house had window-boxes full of flowers, and then there was the gardener who tended the beds under the plane-trees and cut the grass. It smelt so good you would have thought yourself in the country. Every year I gave him a Christmas box until one year he disappeared, and now I think he's just died off, and I really don't know who looks after the garden. Think of it, I've seen nine different families occupy the house next door. How long did I say I'd been here? Why yes, fifty-five years.'

All this was very well, but I really cared only moderately about the gardener and the families next door. I wanted to know what she had looked like when she was a young married woman, and I asked her what sort of hats she wore. She answered without any hesitation:

'Oh, my dear, there was even a Cloete hat which was copied all over the world. It had a crown of velvet and Tuscan lace, and it was trimmed with plumes and bows of ribbon.'

'Did you go walking in Bond Street in the morning?'

'No woman ever walked alone, just as no man would be seen carrying a parcel. I have a brother who even now wouldn't be seen carrying anything. He hails a cab immediately to hide his guilt. But only the other day, looking out from this window, I saw one of the duchesses walking along with a cabbage in her hand!'

'Where did you buy your dresses?' I was really most tenacious in sticking to the point.

'Oh,' she answered, 'at Jay's, and of course there were so many places. Do you know, that one afternoon Mr. William Whiteley came to see my aunt, Mrs. Alexander, at her house in Porchester Terrace, and told her that he was thinking of opening a little shop of his own. And do you know what my aunt did? She took him into her drawing-room and made him kneel on the carpet to ask God to prosper his enterprise.'

She began to look out into the square again.

I tried to make her reconstruct the room in which we were.

'The cold buffet was up against the far wall. People liked to serve themselves.' She rose and explained where each piece of furniture had stood. Then she looked down at the carpet and said stoically:

'I'm giving it away to a young niece who has just got married. It will be my wedding present.'

'Then your floor will be bare.'

'Yes,' she answered. 'There will be just the planks.'

The next day I bought a blue hydrangea in Shepherd Market and took it round to her. Later, passing that way, I saw that she had put it on the sideboard by the window, and it seemed to fill all the house with colour.

THE HAYMARKET

CONSIDERING THAT the Haymarket is as old as the 'way to Readinge,' one is a little aggrieved to find that after a long, and often naughty, existence, it has become such a colourless artery. Perhaps it is too wide. Possibly it has reverted merely to its original function of a link between the cross-roads and Charing Cross. Nobody saunters along the Haymarket. The red omnibuses and the traffic spin along it in two waves, both going the same way—towards Trafalgar Square.

When it was bordered by green fields, Suckling the poet, Clarendon the future Chancellor, and Panton, dreaming perhaps of what he would do when he made a lot of money at cards, walked or drove past the courting couples holding hands by the hedgerows to the Gaming House by the cross-roads. Robert Baker's widow would be picking herbs in her garden hard against the windmill, and the coaches would be lumbering down the muddy road to Brentford and the west country.

On the site of the Gaming House there is to-day one of the prettiest little shops in London, whose two bow windows date from the reign of the first George. The wits and the beaux bought their snuff here in 1720, when the rough pavements of the Haymarket were protected by chains suspended from stone pillars; at night the swinging oil lamps were supplemented near the Opera House by the torches of the masqueraders arriving in their coaches and sedans. Hanging signs creaked over the doors of all the houses. Over the bookseller's shop, on the Broad Stones, near the little gate of the Opera House, those who had not yet obtained their masquerade habits could buy them at reasonable prices until the very moment the ball began. Across the way from the Opera, the King's Head Inn, where carters and hay dealers had refreshed themselves for many years, had just been pulled down to make way for the Little Theatre, so called to distinguish it from the Opera House. The Haymarket must have been a fine sight on such evenings. Is it not miraculous that a piece of it, in the shape of the two bow windows of this snuff shop, should remain absolutely unchanged? Let us therefore feast our eyes upon them, and allow our imagination to fill in the picture with the sedan chairs, the hoop dresses, the powdered hair, the fans, and the bewitching smiles.

The foundation stone of the Opera House had been laid during the reign of Queen Anne, only a few weeks after Marlborough won his victory of Blenheim. In a garret, up two shabby pairs of stairs, in the Haymarket, Joseph Addison, the poet, had been living, when suddenly an emissary from the Government came to ask him to write a poem about the duke's victory. He wrote:

> But, O my muse! what numbers wilt thou find
> To sing the furious troops in battle join'd?
> Methinks I hear the drum's tumultuous sound
> The victor's shouts and dying groans confound.

The poem landed him in the sinecure of Commissioner of Appeals. Within two years he was made Under-secretary of State.

'O angel-visits!' wrote Thackeray, 'you come "few and far between" to literary gentlemen's lodgings!'

Meanwhile the Opera House had been going up, a pretty building of the Doric order, under the eyes of John Vanburgh or Vanbrugh, author of some of the most witty and sparkling comedies of his generation, who was just beginning to turn architect.

A man of many parts was Vanbrugh, a 'sweet-mannered gentleman and pleasant,' whose late father, of Flemish descent, had been a sugar baker at Chester.

Recently he had designed, between versification, Whitton Hall, near Twickenham, for Sir Godfrey Kneller who, like himself, was a member of the Kit-Cat Club, and it was while so doing that he had written to his friend Jacob Tonson, the Strand bookseller and publisher, who was the club's secretary, that he had negotiated for the purchase of land in the Haymarket upon which he would put up the Opera House in honour of Queen Anne.

So Vanbrugh and Congreve, the queen's favourite playwright, with the help of the Whig party represented by this famous club, became very busy, and on Easter Monday 1705 opened the new Opera House with *The Triumph of Love*.

The same year Vanbrugh was chosen to draw up the plans of Blenheim for the Marlboroughs. Wren was getting old and Vanbrugh was thought to be his logical successor. Work started at Blenheim while *The Loves of Ergasto* was playing at the Opera House, but three years later neither Congreve nor Vanbrugh was able to make the new theatre pay. On 27th July 1708 Vanbrugh wrote to the Earl of Manchester:

'I lost so much money by the opera this last winter that I was glad to get quit of it, and yet I do not doubt that operas will thrive and settle in London.'

Now Queen Anne died at Kensington Palace, the first George came to St. James's Palace, and while Vanbrugh, during the new reign, was running into all sorts of trouble in the building of Blenheim, the gay world flocked to the Opera House—which was no longer his—to attend those masquerades which had caught the fancy of the town.

Sir John must have looked rather bitterly at the chairs carrying these unmusical revellers to their evening's frolic, but already he was planning to build a little house of his own amongst the ruins of Whitehall, a house so small that Swift called it rudely a 'goose-pye.'

The 'goose-pye' was finished just about the time that our snuff vendors set up their business at the top of the

Haymarket.   A few months later a certain George Wickes, a goldsmith, opened a shop at the corner of Panton Street and the Haymarket, displaying in his windows all sorts of jewels and curious works in gold and silver.

The goldsmiths had been migrating westwards from the City for some time, and young Hogarth had just finished his apprenticeship with Elias Gamble in Cranbourn Alley, at the north-east corner of Leicester Fields, and had a modest place of his own in the same narrow passage.

Hogarth was now tramping the streets of the town, taking in all those sights which he was later to portray, and in the evenings he would have passed Mr. Wickes's new shop on his way to the Haymarket, where the Little Theatre, opposite the Opera House, was newly opened and leased to a company of French actors who were drawing not only the noble families but also the French émigrés who lived and worked in the vicinity of Leicester House. Colonel Panton's widow was still alive, though very old, and lodged in the street which bore her husband's name.

During the next ten years while Hogarth was developing his talent, passing from the stage of the accomplished apprentice who had chased salvers and tankards for his master, to that of the penetrating genius who produced the 'Harlot's Progress,' wooing the pretty daughter of Sir James Thornhill in whose house he lodged before the elopement and the setting up of his own married establishment in Leicester Square, George the Second had mounted the throne, and Frederick Prince of Wales had come to England from Hanover.   Mr. Wickes's shop had by now become as important as that of Elias Gamble, whose sign of the angel flourishing a palm branch had been engraved by Hogarth during his apprenticeship.   Frederick Prince of Wales, a year before his marriage at St. James's Palace, appointed Wickes to be his goldsmith, jeweller, and silversmith, and his Royal Highness purchased there a fine cup, and a bread basket weighing eighty-seven ounces.   Now

Wickes also produced a series of artistic trade cards on which was mentioned the fact that his establishment was 'à deux portes du Marché au Foin.'

The Haymarket and Panton Street were crowded and picturesque at the time of the marriage of Frederick Prince of Wales to Augusta, the daughter of the Duke of Saxe-Gotha. Handel was directing operas and oratorios at the Opera House, the Little Theatre was doing good business, the beaux gossiped at the sign of the Rasp and Crown where they bought their snuff; and the Norfolks, the Gordons, and the Carmarthens, following the lead of the heir apparent, ordered their silver from Mr. Wickes, who had just put up his sign of the King's Arms and Feathers. These signs must, by their picturesqueness, have made up for the evil smells of the gutter. Three chemists, two of them under royal patronage, sought to cure all the ills of the system by their strange elixirs—Thomas Townshend, Chymist-in-ordinary to George the Second; a certain John Oldham (what would the great poet have said?), Chymist to the Duke of York, who, at the sign of Boerhaave's Golden Head sold King's Honey Water and a famous tincture for the gout and the rheumatism; and Richard Siddell whose lavender water and Galenical medicines were of great avail. In Panton Street John Doig made perukes at the sign of the Rising Sun and Lock of Hair, and over against him, Mr. Richard Lee carried on business at the Golden Tobacco Roll whose trade card had been designed by Hogarth himself.

The young women who danced at the Opera House bought their shoes at the Hand and the Slipper as to-day they buy them from Gambia's in Soho; a French confectioner made *massepains* and pralines at the Sign of the Royal Bisk-Cake; an Italian had set up a warehouse whose sign bore the pretty title of the Orange Tree and Two Jars.

Undoubtedly the Haymarket was colourful in the days when Hogarth was newly living in Leicester Fields. This

is the street one likes to picture when passing the two bow
windows of our friends Messrs. Fribourg & Treyer.

For some time after the marriage of Frederick Prince of
Wales, his purchases at the King's Arms and Feathers were
sent to Carlton House, newly purchased for him. In 1737
a service of plate costing £3,000 was delivered here, and
soon we hear of a Mr. William Garrard being employed
by the firm. By the time the Prince and Princess of Wales,
having been dismissed from St. James's Palace by George
the Second, moved to Leicester House, Mrs. Hogarth had
deserted the Golden Angel in Cranbourn Alley where her
husband had served his apprenticeship, and bought a buckle,
a girdle, and a pair of brilliant earrings from Mr. Garrard
at the King's Arms, at the corner of Panton Street and the
Haymarket.

After Frederick Prince of Wales had died so pathetically
at Leicester House a new warrant was granted to George
Wickes, making him goldsmith, jeweller, and silversmith
to their Royal Highnesses the Prince and Princess Dowager
of Wales, and when this prince became George the Third
in the year 1760, the royal arms were put up. The firm
which had appeared of so little importance when Hogarth
was making the house of Elias Gamble a name for ever to
be coupled with his own, was now on its way to becoming
the English crown jewellers. The ledgers of Wickes's, or
Garrard's as we know it to-day, unfold pretty scenes—the
coronets and swords that were conveyed by chairmen for
the marriage of George the Third to his queen Charlotte,
the setting and adorning of the sovereign's crown of state,
the queen's circlet, and three sceptres and the globe. The
yellowed parchments give bright glimpses of those people
whom we continually meet in the letters of Lady Mary
Coke, Horace Walpole, and Mrs. Delany, and tell us of
their foibles and their vanities. We even find Sir Joshua
Reynolds sending his teapot to be mended and his tea-chest

The Haymarket was once a country lane along which people from Charing Cross walked on summer evenings. At the top, at the right, was a gaming-house with a bowling green. A certain Colonel Panton made a lot of money here and invested it in land. Panton Street leads into Leicester Square.

In the eighteenth century the Haymarket was famous for its hay sales and for its foreign operas. The forerunner of His Majesty's was opened by John Vanbrugh and Congreve, in 1705 with The Triumph of Love. The chief singer sang in his native Italian while all the rest sang in English. Fifteen years later a carpenter built the forerunner of the Haymarket Theatre. The lovely building you see here was put up in 1820, not quite on the site of the old one. It was designed by Nash, who is associated with Regent Street. Since then nearly all our leading actresses and actors have played at this theatre. You can be sure of seeing the best plays at the Haymarket, just as originally people said it was the only theatre in town where they could be certain of seeing the standard English comedies such as The School for Scandal.

In the nineteenth century the Haymarket had the best eating-houses for after-theatre crowds. Now the street goes to bed early. Besides its two famous theatres, it has two monster cinemas, a very old tobacconist's shop, and lots of travel agencies.

to be fitted with a new lock. Then, in reverse, so to speak, we go back to the letters we love to read, and find Mrs. Delany hurrying down the Haymarket, past the king's jeweller, for a shopping expedition. 'I have not been able to get your silver scoop yet,' she writes to her brother from St. James's Palace just before Christmas in the year 1774, 'tho' I bespoke it immediately, for I could find none ready made. I would not wait for it, as I thought you might want the fruit; but I have tucked into Mrs. P.'s parcel an ivory one, *en attendant*. There goes also, tied on that box, a small one with superfine jarr raisins, as the confectioner, Koffin in the Haymarket, assures me; they have now made up in those little boxes; if they are not what you like let me know sincerely, that I may mend my hand. Smith grumbles extremely that the fruiterers will not now allow *more* than fifty to the half hundred! Apples in general this year are small. There are no good French plums to be yet had.'

While Mrs. Delany was shopping in the Haymarket during these last days before Christmas, Fanny Burney's thoughts were engrossed in her first novel *Evelina*, already in the making, the story of a young lady's entrance into the world with the vicissitudes that attended it. Born after Fielding and Richardson had finished their best work, Miss Burney, in the words of our brilliant contemporary writer, Elizabeth Bowen, comes in time to contribute the woman's view of the Age of Reason and its society. In view of the prejudice against women writers, Miss Burney wrote in secrecy and with some sense of guilt, and when the manuscript was finished, it was to the Orange Coffee House in the Haymarket that she requested Mr. Dodsley to address his reply to the proposal she made him anonymously for its publication, and here her brother Charles received the discouraging reply which caused them to negotiate with Mr. Lowndes of the City. The novel to which Dr. Johnson was later to give his approval was eventually published by the City firm in 1778.

The Little Theatre, the Haymarket Band-box, as some people called it, had become the Theatre Royal by virtue of a licence granted to Samuel Foote, the actor, who having soon after the accession of George the Third gone hunting with the high-spirited Duke of York, became a victim of one of His Royal Highness's practical jokes by which he was made to ride a too lively horse, was thrown and suffered the amputation of a leg. The Duke of York made amends to the actor by helping him to buy the theatre he had previously leased and procuring him the patent. By the time *Evelina* was published Foote was dead, and George Colman, the elder, had bought his interest, but the Little Theatre justified its new name by the frequent visits which George the Third and his family made to it.

In the year of the French Revolution the Opera House opposite was burned to the ground, the leader of the orchestra having set fire to it during rehearsals to spite the manager, for whose benefit the next evening's performance was to have taken place. It was rebuilt in 1790, but already the Haymarket was beginning to shake and turn, and take on a different aspect.

The periwigs have gone, the shining silk hat and the kid gloves are in fashion, and Dickens is describing the town which Richardson and Fielding wrote of and Hogarth portrayed a century earlier. The linen-drapers in Regent Street and Oxford Street close at nine, and the Theatre Royal, Haymarket, the old Little Theatre, has been rebuilt by John Nash, the maker of Regent Street and the two circuses, with the Corinthian portico of six columns which have been retained for our pleasure to this day. The two bow windows of Fribourg & Treyer, the snuff-men who now sell all sorts of other tobacco are, of course, unchanged, but at the corner of Panton Street, the business of George Wickes the jeweller has come into the possession of the Garrards. The Duke of Wellington had bought his coronet there and had trotted up the Haymarket on his old white charger to cut the first facet of the Koh-i-Noor, and the

Crown Jewellers, as they are officially named, had fashioned the jewelled pendant which Queen Victoria presented to Florence Nightingale. The Opera House, now called Her Majesty's Theatre, rebuilt after the fire, after the designs of Novosielski, together with the adjoining Opera Arcade, had been refronted with a colonnade by Nash to harmonize with his Theatre Royal opposite.

Midnight has just struck. The date is 1859, and George Augustus Sala gives us a splendid picture of the Haymarket.

The street was already wide—the Theatre Royal on its eastern side, and the colonnaded opera house opposite; a street with a fair number of shops of a general nature, but most of all crowds of hotels, restaurants, cigar divans, coffee-houses, and establishments for the sale of lobsters, oysters, and pickled salmon. But the Haymarket before midnight was not the Haymarket which suddenly came to life after the clock of St. Martin's Church struck twelve.

As though Harlequin had smitten the houses—and the people also—with his wand, the whole Haymarket wakes, lights, rises up with a roar, a rattle, and a shriek quite pantomimic, if not supernatural. Midnight; the play is over, and the audience pour from the Haymarket Theatre. The aristocratic opera season is concluded by this time of the year, and the lovers of the drama have it all their own way. Crowds of jovial young clerks and spruce law students cluster beneath the portico, yet convulsed by the humours of Mr. Buckstone. Happy families of rosy children, radiant in lay-down collars, white skirts and pink sashes, trot from the entrance to the dress-circle under the wing of benevolent papa and stout good-humoured mamma, with a white burnous, and a tremendous fan, expatiating on the glories of the concluding tableau, with its tinsel and gold leaf, its caryatides of ballet girls, and its red and blue fire.

Supper was now the great cry, for in those days there was no problem of transport, no lack of restaurants. For the wealthy, the Haymarket offered Dubourg's, the Hôtel de Paris, or the upstairs department of the Café de l'Europe where cunning cooks prepared pheasants and partridges, mushrooms and truffles; and where cellarers produced in an instant Roederer's champagne, the fragrant Clos Vougeot, the refreshing Laffitte, or the enlivening Chambertin.

Above everything else, the Haymarket was famous for its oyster bars—rude, simple, and primitive, with hustling, joking customers standing at the counters, plying the pepper castor and the vinegar cruet, calling for crusty bread and pats of butter, and tossing off foaming pints of the brownest ale, after which they contentedly wiped their hands on the jack towel on its roller.

But [says Augustus Sala] if you be yet lower in pocket, and your available wealth be limited to the possessions of the modest and retiring penny, you may, at the door of most of the taverns, meet with an ancient dame, of unpretending appearance, bearing a flat basket lined with a fair cloth. She for your penny will administer to you a brace of bones, covered with a soft white integument, which she will inform you are trotters. Eat them, and thank heaven, and go thy ways, and take a cooling drink at the nearest pump with an iron ladle chained to it, which is, if I am not mistaken, over against St. James's church in Piccadilly.

But supposing the Londoner of Sala's day had not even a penny to sup with, he might visit the Royal Albert Potato Can at the Coventry Street extremity of the Haymarket, where at that three-legged emporium of smoking vegetables, gleaming with brazen ornaments, he might for a halfpenny obtain a refreshment at once warm and nourishing, the potato in its jacket, taken from its hot blanket bed, and garnished with salt and pepper, and even with Irish salt grease that went by the name of butter.

What is left of the picturesque, rather naughty Haymarket?

The two bow windows of the snuff house have not changed. The Theatre Royal, though rebuilt internally, displays the Corinthian portico of six columns designed by Nash. His Majesty's Theatre opposite, recalls, though only by name, the Opera House of Vanbrugh and Congreve, of Handel, of the boy Mozart, of Frederick Prince of Wales and of his son good George the Third, of Samuel Johnson, Mrs. Delany, and Fanny Burney. Erected afresh by Novosielski after the fire of 1789 to echo to the voice of Mrs. Billington, who had delighted Napoleon by the time she appeared there; then beautified by Nash, it was burned for the second time in 1867; rebuilt after the Franco-Prussian War, and finally pulled down in 1892. On the ground it occupied now stands the Carlton Hotel. The theatre which we call His Majesty's was put up next door to its predecessors for Sir H. Beerbohm Tree in 1896, but if you have a mind to stray into Charles the Second Street, you will come upon M. Novosielski's Opera House arcade.

At the turn of the century and for eleven years afterwards, the King's Arms and Feathers, founded by Mr. Wickes but now bearing the name of Garrard, Crown Jewellers, remained like the bow windows of the nearby snuff-men, an eighteenth-century period piece. Their business was becoming more romantic. For the coronation of King Edward the Seventh and Queen Alexandra the whole of the regalia and plate was checked in their workrooms, and both the crown known as St. Edward's and the imperial state crown were altered to the requirements of the new sovereign, but this task was small compared with that carried out for the coronation of George the Fifth, when Londoners gathered in the panelled rooms to see the royal crowns and the sceptre of the empire into which the jewellers had introduced portions of the Cullinan diamond, henceforth to be known as the Stars of Africa. No monarch had ever worn two such valuable gems as those which then lay in the little shop where Mr. Wickes had sold a girdle and a buckle to Mrs. Hogarth, and mended Sir Joshua Reynolds's teapot, but at the very moment when the King's Arms had risen to heights that not even Elias Gamble could have dreamed of, the pickaxe was waiting to turn the corner house in Panton Street to rubble and ashes, scattering its pretty façade to winds as cruel as those which carried off the low house in Cranbourn Alley where Hogarth had bent, as an apprentice, over his first trade card.

There is no more Mr. Wickes, no more King's Arms and Feathers at the corner of Panton Street and the Haymarket. Tempted westward to the purlieus of Bond Street, the house of Garrard rose in that year newly built on ground in Albemarle Street and Grafton Street where once flowered the roses in the great Earl of Clarendon's garden. They carried with them all sorts of jewels, and some of the panelling of their old home. To-day royal limousines drive to their elegant doors, just as Frederick Prince of Wales's chariot stopped nearly two centuries ago in Haymarket there to call on the periwigged Mr. Wickes.

The Carlton was one of those hotels which, though continually modernized, clung in its great public rooms to the gentle palm-court atmosphere of the Edwardian epoch. It was younger than the Savoy, a little older than the Ritz, but between the wars it neither adapted itself to the gay supper life of the Savoy, with its rising floor and shafts of coloured light, it clowns and dancers, shimmering against a background of upturned faces, nor to the lunch-time fashion parade of the Ritz. The marble and brass of the Carlton foyer, the inner windows with their beflowered balconies, the smooth carpets and the traditions of Escoffier, the cunning cook, brought to this hotel the Briands and the Tardieus, and before them, the great Foch, who during a succession of victory, peace, and disarmament conferences, discussed the future of Europe over the pheasants and the partridges, the truffles and the fragrant Clos Vougeot which, in an earlier age, had diverted the patrons of the Haymarket's Dubourg or Hôtel de Paris.

During those gloomy, nervous days of the first winter of the next war, after all those peace-time conferences had failed, and when a blanket of rumour and darkness had descended on the streets, Neville Chamberlain and his military advisers, Daladier and General Gamelin, sought under the roof of this hotel to prepare for the great German offensive that would break without warning from the east. How pathetic now to look back on those secret meetings which no newspaper could divulge—our guests dropping in from the air with their black brief-cases, to exchange their hopes, to count their aeroplanes and plan their tanks, and finally to toast in fragrant wines their very meagre resources.

Then it was that *The Beggar's Opera* which had delighted our forefathers—yes, that same *Beggar's Opera* came back to the Theatre Royal, Haymarket, the date being 5th March 1940.

Eight months later, on 16th November, during the height of the Battle of London, a bomb whistled over the roof of Nash's theatre and crashed upon a great store at the north-west corner of Trafalgar Square which burst into flames, whereupon the enemy, using this mighty conflagration as a target, dropped a high explosive at twenty minutes past two in the morning through the roof of the Carlton Hotel, the bomb exploding with terrific force on the third floor. The stairs from the top of the building to the first floor disappeared altogether and the lights went out. One hundred and six people were sleeping there, but only two were killed—a Belgian diplomat and a cashier. M. Gelardi, the manager, standing in the hall, was buried under boulders of marble, and though when rescued he had multiple injuries of the arm, did not leave his post until daylight.

Consider now what had happened in these eight months! Neville Chamberlain, the Prime Minister of that dark, bleak period before the Germans struck, had been replaced and was dead only a week. Daladier was in a fortress, and Gamelin, his pretty uniform a mockery, was languishing, despised and forgotten—the fair country of these two once-mighty captains enchained by the enemy. This piece of

K

London clay bordering the Haymarket was lit by torches more magnificently bright than ever attended the most august patron of Queen Anne's Opera House. Two theatres had gone up in flames, another had been pulled down, and now the Edwardian palm court, where Foch had walked, where Briand had dreamed of a Europe at peace, and where the statesmen of a dozen nations had planned to whittle down their mighty fleets, was broken marble and swirling dust. The theatre we call His Majesty's remained intact, having had the good sense, half a century earlier, to side-step impending disaster, and when morning came on that 17th November, the pillared portico of the Theatre Royal, on the opposite side of the road, remained a stately and charming reminder of the builder Nash and the great Prince Regent.

Nocturne

On the evening of 9th March 1946 a quarter-moon, reddened by a raw, white mist, was shining over the London Pavilion whose façade, behind steel scaffolding, advertised a film called *The Diary of a Chambermaid*, with Paulette Goddard in the leading role. The great clock, high above the circus, between the Monico and Saqui & Lawrence's, showed that the time was eleven-twenty. The Saturday night crowds were still milling up and down Coventry Street, thickest near the Lyons Corner House whose exterior was quite dark, but gradually as one watched the moving mass of people in which khaki was no longer the predominant colour, one sensed that the flow was diminishing, being drained off by the cavernous depths of the underground tube station whose last train would soon be rumbling home.

Lights still burned in Scott's restaurant, which was founded long ago by a promoter of the London Pavilion in the days before it was rebuilt and when there was a chairman who tapped his hammer on the worn table, but in a few minutes the last of the supper crowd would have left this famous restaurant, and the grid would be padlocked.

The façade, whose wide glass had not yet been put back, was covered by paintings of the old windmill with some gallants dressed as in the days of Charles the First, a wartime reconstruction of what Windmill Street looked like when Piccadilly Hall was standing beside the cross-roads.

Two doors away tinned music and the click of the penny-in-the-slot came from the fun fair whose electric globes illuminated the pavement. The uniformed porter of the Criterion Restaurant was saying good night to a very important personage who was stepping into a shining police car whose driver sat upright at the wheel.

This was the hour which Augustus Sala chose to portray the sudden coming to life of the Haymarket, as though Harlequin had smitten the houses—and the people also—with his wand, 'when the whole Haymarket wakes, lights, and rises up with a roar.' As if conscious that something really was impending, the passing crowds in Coventry Street paused for a moment to look at three policemen placing squat lighthouses with black-and-white bases and red lamps, across the road to close it to traffic.

Fribourg & Treyer's slept behind its smooth, curved shutters, but a little farther down, the Chicken Inn was ablaze with light, and amongst the ferns and flowers in the window, a ginger cat was curled up next to the menu card which read: 'All day menu: Chicken Salad, Ice Cream or Waffle, 5s. Open till 11.30 p.m.'

Across the way the lights were going out at the Gaumont picture house, where the big film was *Spanish Main*. On this site, in the twenties, stood a dance club called the Kit-Cat, which had nothing to do with the Whig party!

The Haymarket was silent except for an occasional footstep, but down by the Theatre Royal, the one-time Little Theatre, arc-lamps lit the middle of the street. Here was the very spot where Sala opened his story. From the theatre with its six fluted columns put there by Nash, darting out amongst the excited crowd of theatre-goers, all thinking of oysters and merriment, would come Harlequin with his wand! As if to announce his arrival there was a sudden crash, and then, in truth, all the lower part of the street woke to life.

What great performance was being staged for the benefit of the three girls and the laughing sailor who had suddenly turned into the Haymarket from Charles the Second Street? Midnight was indeed the magic hour. The three twenty-eight-yard-long surface shelters which had stood in the centre of the street during all the war were to be spirited away before business resumed on Monday morning, and everything that was new in science had been brought on the scene to accomplish this miracle of speed.

Leading the assault were tall cranes from which dangled a steel ball weighing a ton or more which now started to pound the reinforced concrete until it shuddered and collapsed into the roadway. Then each crane crawled sideways like a prehistoric monster, gently pushing the rubble out of its way with the same steel ball which a moment earlier had crushed the fabric.

The pretty fluted columns of the Theatre Royal, ochre at their summit, bright red at the base, quivered to think that the slightest accident might send them falling down after nearly a century and a half of delicate existence. But the cranes, which, with their heavy weights, could shatter a modern shelter, at other times played with the debris like a kitten with a ball of wool, and though these bulky contrivances operated within a few inches of the pillars, they never grazed them.

What had happened to the playgoers of the Haymarket, where *Lady Windermere's Fan* filled the bill? They had gone home like good children three hours ago, for the evening performance had started at 6.45, and no theatre manager in town yet dared to revert to the pre-war custom of ringing up the curtain after eight o'clock.

Already the Chicken Inn had evicted its last customer, and the ginger cat had the place to itself. No wand could bring to life, after 11.30, a single eating-house in the Haymarket. Not an oyster or even a potato at this hour tempted those theatre-goers who, rightly, insisted that the show should be over in time to let them seek out something more substantial than the two fountains which, at the touch of a button, sent up meagre sprays of drinking water along the only part of the wall left standing in front of St. James's Church in Piccadilly. The halfpenny, which in Sala's time would have purchased a satisfying meal at the Potato Can, was useless to the new generation when the bells of St. Martin's struck twelve. Three halfpennies and a long wait might allow the weary traveller to jump on an omnibus speeding to its garage, but even the omnibus after midnight was rare. Nocturnal traffic had disappeared like the woodcock, which the old chroniclers claimed to have seen in this part of London during the reign of Queen Anne.

In these circumstances few were the people who watched the midnight performance outside the Theatre Royal whose curtain was down and whose pit was deserted, only the inevitable policeman and, for as long as it amused them, the three girls and the sailor who had fallen upon it by accident.

But the performance was worthy of a much larger audience, and at least a hundred men were taking part in it, re-enacting the siege of Troy with their stone-throwers and battering-rams, their flares, and eager upturned faces covered with particles of flying dust. Thirty lorries were waiting to run a shuttle service with the debris to a dump near the County Hall, and men with oily heads stood beside complicated mobile plants, brought there to deal with possible breakdowns.

The front of the Carlton Hotel, on the site of which had stood Sir John Vanbrugh's Opera House, was scarred by high explosive and the metal was singed of its paint, for little had been done to remove from its face the effects of the bomb which exploded on the third floor. The new His Majesty's adjoining it was bright with ferns and gay posters advertising *Follow the Girls*, the modern equivalent of those gay comedies of two and a half centuries ago. A little farther along the Carlton Cinema rivalled the Gaumont with a drama of the sea, and a murderous individual, twice human size, was climbing up a papier-mâché mast which stretched half across the façade.

Through the misty night, to the tune of the pounding of the steel ball and the whine of the caterpillar wheels, came memories of the bountiful twenties when Yankee trippers crowded the American Express, spending lavishly the money they had made during the last war; memories of the thirties when Air France collected its passengers over against St. James's Market to take them to Paris in an hour and a half; memories of 1940–1 when the tailor who, according to his blasted shop-front, was appointed to the King's African Rifles (shades of desert sand sung by Kipling!), was obliged to seek a new home in Suffolk Street because there was so little left of his old one.

Oh, battered Haymarket, curious is your illogical mixture of interests—a theatre, as old as any in London, an opera house which has side-stepped into new life and echoes to the tunes of *Follow the Girls*, two cinemas, a half-wrecked hotel, and all sorts of shipping companies from the Khedivial Mail Line (that goes well with the King's African Rifles, don't you think?) to the office which once housed polite little Nazis who sang to us the merits of the *Bremen* and the *Europa*, in which it was so terribly fashionable to sail when British companies were in the depths of despair.

The three girls and the sailor made off along Panton Street where, inside the Comedy Restaurant, a waiter or a night watchman (who knows?) in his shirt-sleeves and without collar or tie, was smoking a cigarette at a table on which stood a vase containing a tulip and a daffodil! In the Haymarket the steel ball continued to pound the reinforced concrete. A heavy van drove up with a jolt, opened its sides, and revealed a mobile canteen for the actors of this all-night show. Coffee and tea, sandwiches and hot potatoes in their jackets, and all free! Why, George Augustus Sala, what have you got to say about this?

A FAIRY-BOOK WEDDING

PRINCESS ELIZABETH, who played in the gardens behind Hamilton Place in the same way as the future Queen Victoria in a white dress and pink sash played behind Kensington Palace, who had appeared with her parents on the balcony of floodlit Buckingham Palace at the end of the second war against Germany, and who had gone to a party at Apsley House, Piccadilly, on the eve of her official betrothal, was in November 1947 at Westminster Abbey the fairy-book bride of the most romantic wedding of the century.

The white dress with the long train and the satin roses, the veil and the glass coach were all there, out of the pages of Grimm. The fairy prince was young, and his voice was golden, and the bridesmaids with garlands in their hair looked like delicate figures of Dresden china.

That so many could have believed that because of instability on the Continent and austerity at home, a love story like this could be minimized seems, in the light of what really happened, almost unbelievable. The enormous, spontaneous rejoicing of Londoners proved that the fairy-book lure still held sway, and that for the time being there was no doubt whatever about the affection of the people for their monarchy.

London had changed a great deal since the end of the war, but mostly unseen, like the rumbling of hot lava which, after bubbling and oozing, gradually alters the crust. We were not at all the same people as two years earlier. The men had lost their knights-in-armour spirit engendered by the bombs and nocturnal conflagrations. Also these heroes of the blitz had been outnumbered by younger men returning from abroad who were anxious as quickly as possible to readapt themselves to civilian life. Cat burglaries, lorry thefts, a black market run on continental lines, and the evil creakings of a class war were to be found in our magnificent London where during night raids, in the black-out, one could have walked anywhere without an escort, leaving the home doors open.

Concurrently with this, London had been preening herself more than some would have cared to admit. There was lots of new paint, thousands upon thousands of new windows, a tremendous carting away of wreckage, and, in the West End, a very lively business in works of art and all things beautiful which may not have been altogether unconnected with a fear of inflation.

In the City the great expanses of desolation had lost some of their romance because of the brick walls and corrugated-iron hoardings which hid many vistas. But the stone cutters worked between St. Paul's and the ruins of St.-Mary-le-Bow (Bow Bells), carrying on their craft as in the earliest days of our civilization. In the West End the great stores had put back enormous plate-glass windows behind which there took place the battle for the longer skirt, with the Government (for once interesting itself in a feminine topic by taking sides, for economy's sake, but quite uselessly) against it.

The wedding of the young woman whom one of the French newspapers described as La Princesse Elizabeth d'Angleterre came right on the heels of the ban on petrol and foreign travel. For a short time it was spoken of in such hushed terms that one might have thought it 'unpatriotic' to talk about it. From the stories about police searches and shorter routes for the royal procession, one might have supposed that half the country was waiting to murder the lovely bride. And then on the damp and sometimes cold night of 19th–20th November there arrived from nobody quite knew where great multitudes of people who were determined to squat all night in the Mall, in Trafalgar Square, in Whitehall (in whose gay gardens a

* K

former Elizabeth had so often strolled), and all round Westminster Abbey.

A breeze of excitement whistled round the historic corners of the town almost as soon as it was dark. Lights were put on in St. James's Palace, for instance, revealing to the passer-by through uncurtained windows strange pictures to quicken the pulse of those who love the story of the town. If you had wandered into Friary Court you would have noticed in a lighted gallery above you halberds, spears, and lances hanging from crimson walls, and in a lower room a gentleman in a gorgeous red uniform writing most solemnly in a book. On the other side of the carriage-way which leads from the junction of St. James's Street and Pall Mall into the park, lights also showed up the inside of the Queen's Chapel, designed by Inigo Jones and completed in the reign of Charles the First, in what was then the garden of St. James's Palace, as the private chapel of his French queen Henrietta Maria. On the marriage of Charles the Second to Catherine of Braganza in 1661, it was refurnished for the new queen. The iron gates by Pall Mall were still twisted by the famous bomb which dropped outside St. James's Palace on the night of 23rd February 1944. In front of the red-brick palace the sentinels wore plain khaki, but they hit the worn flagstones with their thick boots so loudly that they made the night air quiver. In Ambassadors' Court there were more lights revealing interiors many people had never thought about before— gilded ceilings, tapestried walls, and ambassadorial red carpets and chairs. On the opposite side of the yard a lamp threw a ribbon of yellow light against some foliage between the offices of the Duke of Gloucester and the yellow-plastered walls of the former home of our Prince of Wales, whose slim figure will always haunt this part of the town. There was no light here, only dark shadows whence emerged a policeman on duty. Here in our life-time had happened a great drama. A car slipped in and out of here bearing King Edward the Eighth, as we called him

St. James's Palace was built by Henry the Eighth, and on May mornings be rode out of it wearing a beautiful hat to gather blossoms in Hampstead.

St. James's Street arrived in the Augustan age. Poets and wits drank coffee and pretty women gathered for tea. Nearly three centuries of London court and fashion tread the street. There is a man's hatter on the left where Napoleonic headgears are displayed. There is a courtyard where Beau Brummell had a duel, and beyond it is a wine shop whose premises are nearly as old as the street.

The palace is a history book where kings and queens still play their parts. During the February–March raids of 1944 it was nearly demolished by bombs intended for General Eisenhower's headquarters in St. James's Square. Look at it with affection as well as pride. Sometimes one has the feeling of being in front of a mirage.

then, just before his abdication. These tense moments seemed to have left their mark upon the walls and in the shadows where the policeman had been hiding. There is no use in trying to forget so tremendous a happening on a night like this, when a young woman who perhaps will be our future queen is being married. The flagstones of Ambassadors' Court are heavy with history since that May morning when Henry the Eighth first rode out, all shining on horseback, to gather blossoms out Hampstead way. A black cat darted across the yard towards the kitchen of Sir Alan Lascelles's residence, whence came an appetizing smell of dinner.

Across the carriage-way Lancaster House was asleep, with more policemen in the shadows. Here would meet the Four-Power Conference described by Ernest Bevin as the most vital in world history, though, alas, each conference since Versailles had been graced with this compliment. Britain, the United States, the Soviet Union, and France were to make a desperate effort to restore the splendid wartime spirit which had quite disappeared. Round the green baize table moved the ghosts of former diplomats who, on a multitude of questions, had tried so hard to reach agreement, and failed. From the darkened room with its cream and gilt walls, they would look across to Buckingham Palace where the princess's bridal dress had just arrived. The fairy-tale across the way was for a few hours more important to at least half the world than the bickerings between Russia and the Western Powers. On the other side of the carriage-way stood Clarence House, with many lights on the first floor, suggesting that workmen or servants were making the place ready for the princess and the young man who was soon to be her husband. The contents of this residence had been put up for auction just after the battle for London. The Duke of Connaught had lived here, and before that it had been the home of his brother the Duke of Edinburgh. So two dukes will have lived there within a hundred years. Before

that it had been the home of a future king—yes, for it was
built for that Duke of Clarence who became William the
Fourth.

The Duke of Edinburgh (Queen Victoria's son) re-
modelled the building and made the portico overlooking
the garden. The new Duke of Edinburgh would doubtless
remodel it a second time, for the Duke of Connaught's iron
bed was in a room where the windows were so incom-
modious and high that he could not even look out at the
Mall, so pretty when they cut the grass in summer. There
was one prehistoric bathroom partitioned off at the back
with no access whatever to light and air. A few Londoners
attended the auction in 1942, on a sunny afternoon when
the green lawn that is common to the whole of St. James's
Palace was girdled with golden daffodils. But probably if
people had known who would soon come to live there, the
crowds would have been great. There were crimson carpets on the stairs and in the halls, but the pictures, or what
was left of them, were stacked on the floor. The reception-
rooms, where some of the windows had suffered from blast,
were filled with furniture of mid-Victorian period, though
on the first floor there were some lighter rooms in French
Empire style. One would have thought that the reception-
rooms would have overlooked the garden—a regal view for
a royal residence—but they all overlooked the street.

In the darkness of this pre-wedding night one passed
between Clarence House, symbol of past and future
royalty, and Lancaster House where Mr. Molotov's
henchmen would soon surround him (the Russian people
would be denied all news of the wedding in their papers).
The carriage-way was in itself picturesque, with the granite
kerbstones placed there in the days of coaches. The
narrow sentinel-box, looking so much like a toy, outside
Clarence House, the two lamps surmounted by gilt crowns
on the posterns, and this little brass tablet: 'Central
Chancery of the Orders of Knighthood,' made one dream.

In the Mall people were already making themselves

comfortable, or as comfortable as they could, to spend the
long hours of the night grouped against the gutter in which
flowed lazily the rain which had fallen early in the evening
but had not yet had time to fade from the hard surface of
the road. Most of the people had made encampments
round the lamp standards, for there were not so many that
they could not choose their ground. But even as one
watched, new-comers kept on arriving, with the result that
soon the space between the lamp standards began to be
filled in. From the direction of Trafalgar Square came a
long stream of costermongers. Some had barrows of
grapes and apples, others pushed braziers which filled the
night air with the odour of hot chestnuts, yet others had
streamers and programmes, and in the middle of the Mall
acrobats and singers who normally worked outside theatre
queues had come to amuse the crowds, who were curling
up on carpets of gaily coloured plastic materials which
they seemed to have chosen by common accord to keep
themselves dry and relatively warm.

The authorities had not thought it worth while to put up
a single decoration along the whole stretch of the Mall, and
in many places only one out of every two lamps was
burning, but soon after Big Ben struck midnight the place
began to look like a fair ground. Accordion players knelt
in front of improvised fires while the curled-up brown
leaves from St. James's Park danced round them. A family
of eight had come down from County Durham, a bus driver
with his leather coat arrived to find his wife already in her
chosen place, half a dozen French girls had come over from
Paris, where soon there would be no government and where
the Communists would call a general strike. A young
woman reporter from an American magazine jumped out
of her car and walked alongside the crowd with two
photographers at her beck.

At this early hour it was a crowd mostly composed of
women, women who would never have a say in the prob-
lems which Bevin and Molotov and Marshall would soon

be discussing round the green baize table in Lancaster House, women who were simply left to struggle with the housework and the shopping queues while the men planned strikes, filled in their football pools, and thought it stupid that any of us could be interested in a glass coach and a wedding gown.

The Admiralty Arch to Trafalgar Square had become the centre of the fair ground. All sorts of refreshment bars on wheels had arrived, and their owners were doing a fine business. There was the juke-box, there was one which specialized in hot dogs, and others which sold fish and chips, but most of them served hot tea and sandwiches. Youths on tricycles sold ice-cream, as if the night were not cold enough already. Charles the First was looking on from his commanding position on horseback, but because his statue is the finest, with Eros, in London, the authorities had wisely boxed up his legs with corrugated sheeting, against which peanut vendors and toffee apple sellers plied their business.

Little night winds, treacherous and cold, came sweeping in, blowing and eddying round one's legs. Back in the Mall men were selling rosettes, and women pushed prams full of food and blankets uncomfortably reminiscent of refugees in front of an invading army. Prams with blankets: France in 1940, the nocturnal raids of 1940 in London, and now for our joyful tribute to a young princess! Soon we shall queue up not out of necessity but for pleasure. In front of Buckingham Palace coloured streamers fluttered in the night, and a B.B.C. television van was being put into place. This was the only invention still in the stage of a toy, as wireless was after the war of 1914–18. The dark beauty of the Green Park was made more impressive, more mysterious by a magnificent Union Jack on a dazzling white flagpole bathed in light on the roof of the Ritz Hotel.

This was the Green Park of the Bombers' Moon, the balloon site, the National Fire Service lake, and of what

those of us who used to sit with our children in summer in
the shade of the five Cornish elms used to call the Drawing-
room.   On this side of the gravel path was the mound
where American soldiers played baseball.   Farther towards
the Ritz had stood the air-raid shelters with tall thistles
growing round them.   But except for a certain roughness
of terrain where the grass on the lawns was thin or partly
stifled by weeds, the bulldozers had done their work with
good effect, and these things were merely memories, gone
for ever like the Water Board's lake of 1820, of which a
splendid and most rare print had just been shown in a
Bond Street gallery.   The façade of noble houses along
Queen Caroline's Walk had not changed outwardly, but
Wimborne House had just given up the uneven struggle
to remain a private mansion.   Only a few hours earlier
the earl had sold the family place to the chairman of an
insurance company, who said: 'It can never be used as a
private house again.   Its upkeep would be too costly.'

Spencer House with its delicate lines and lovely statues
had, by courtesy of the present Earl Spencer, become the
new home of Christie, Manson & Woods, whose building
in King Street, St. James's, consumed by fire during the
nocturnal raids, had not yet been rebuilt.   But what a
splendid stroke of luck for Spencer House to be the setting
for the world's treasures, as week after week they were
displayed in the noble but tired rooms overlooking its
own garden of tangled weeds and the autumn-tinted Green
Park!   By rather a strange coincidence the original James
Christie held his first sale in Pall Mall about the same time
as the foundations of Spencer House were laid.   Nothing
was more enjoyable than to spend an hour on a sunny
autumn morning admiring the pictures hanging for sale on
the walls of this mansion, inspecting furniture or silver
brought there for our delight and education, and handling
jewellery and miniatures one momentarily coveted.

On the morning of the royal wedding a small crowd of
people stood against the railings of Apsley House watching

the guests drive through the park gates towards the abbey. The traffic was so thick in Hyde Park Corner that from time to time it came to a standstill. Waves of people poured across the Green Park towards the Mall hoping, though late, to see something of the procession.

Though no public holiday had been proclaimed, anybody walking along Piccadilly or in Regent Street or Bond Street at this hour had the impression of a most curious emptiness —a city where the shops were open but in which there were no shoppers. Girls were grouped together, listening to radios whose commentaries and music came through open doors into the street, repeated from building to building. Bond Street had reason to be proud of itself—roses, carnations, and arum lilies in every shop window amongst the jewels, the old masters, the Chippendale chairs, the silver candlesticks, the lingerie, the baby lace, and the calf-bound books. Then suddenly from everywhere at once came the first strains of the National Anthem.

AUTUMN 1947

As Christmas approached there were some days, fresh and cold, but so sunny that one might have believed they heralded a second summer, and in this invigorating atmosphere the heart of the town looked really lovely. Shaftesbury Avenue, the grimy but lovable Cinderella of the arteries, was changing quite a little. Rainbow Corner, the home of American soldiers during the end of the war where the G.I. found his cigarettes, his candy, his chewing gum, and his juke-box, Rainbow Corner, while waiting to be turned by its new owners into a magnificent milk bar, had been lent by them to the Canadian province of Ontario to further its drive for emigration. Right across the façade in immense letters were the words: 'Emigrate by air now to Ontario, Canada. Air passages for 7,000 young British workers—Agriculture, Forestry, Mining—£67 fare.' Who now could say that our youths could not pick up adventure,

like gold, on the pavements of the town? Between Rupert
Street and Wardour Street, *Tuppence Coloured* was playing
at the Globe, Jack Jacobus's, the shoe shop, was having its
front artistically redone, and the poor Queen's Theatre,
destroyed during the raids, was newly enclosed in
scaffolding.

In Coventry Street, foreign films had come back to the
Rialto where after the Roman resistance film, *The Open
City*, Londoners could now see Jean Cocteau's rendering
in French of *Beauty and the Beast*. The Automobile Association was inviting motorists to sign a petition, whilst across
the way, Stagg & Russell were showing us how to make
our lingerie by unpicking nylon parachutes.

In Leicester Square, Shakespeare, whose left hand was
amputated at the wrist, continued to look jealously at
Margaret Mitchell's tremendous success, *Gone with the Wind*,
still playing here as it had played at the very beginning of
the war, before Paris had fallen. Unless, of course, the
poet's gaze, which seems unlikely, was sometimes distracted
by the shoes at Dolcis. Hogarth, whose three distinguished
companions had been shattered during the bombing, having
himself suffered nothing more than a bad fall, was now
back on his perch at the south-east corner of the square,
his velvet cap pulled over his right eye. The shelters had
been removed. The lawns were trying to make themselves
pretty for the spring.

Panton Street was looking much its old self in spite of
the fact that Stone's chop-house was not yet rebuilt. The
Haymarket was doing rather well. The pillars of the
Theatre Royal were beautifully repainted in cream and red,
with gold lettering across the top, and the Carlton Cinema
was bedecked with flowers for Sir Alexander Korda's screen
version of Oscar Wilde's *Ideal Husband*. The shipping
offices had made themselves smart, and so had Air France
which, after beginning in this street as a tiny venture
called something else just after the 1914–18 war, now
advertised services to fifty-one countries all over the globe.

Though petrol had been reduced, the 'way to Readinge' was still immensely busy, and every day at lunch-time, Piccadilly was, as in the eighteenth and nineteenth centuries, the meeting-place for the most fashionable people in the town. Hatchard's, booksellers to the king, one of the oldest firms in the street, had just taken new premises next door. The West End offices of the *Sunday Times* portrayed the week's events in magnificent photographs. Swaine Adeney Brigg & Sons showed their hunting-crops, Roberts & Carroll, across the way in Cork Street, were immensely busy, not only making riding-habits but also lengthening skirts of their customers' tailor-mades. Fortnum & Mason, whose windows were a joy throughout the war, and remain so, showed us lace blouses and perfume from Paris. The charred roof of St. James's Church had not been mended. The garden built between Jermyn Street and Piccadilly by the generosity of Lord Southwood bore these lines by Dorothy Frances Gurney (1858-1932) on a plaque at the foot of a plane-tree:

> The kiss of the sun for pardon,
>   The song of the birds for mirth,
> One is nearer God's Heart in a garden,
>   Than anywhere else on earth.

OXFORD STREET

THE crowds in Oxford Street never seem quite the same crowds as those in other London streets. They roll and thunder like the waves on the seashore. The stores are the great attraction. People say they are not so smart as the stores in Regent Street. In a way, this is true, but the fact is that we all go to them in that moment of despair when a ribbon or a piece of material has to be matched. The Oxford Street stores gather all the riches of the world. They have become palaces in the sense that the Cumberland Hotel and the Odeon Cinema are palaces. They dazzle with light and magnificence.

Oxford Street is a sort of 42nd Street, built on a road which is dark with history. From Marble Arch to Tottenham Court Road tube station is a mile and a half. In the days of highwaymen and hangings we would have said that it was the Tyburn road from the turnpike to St. Giles's Pound that was one and a half miles in length. The names have changed.

The Tyburn gallows, or Tyburn Tree (or Deadly Nevergreen) was the public place of execution for criminals convicted in the county of Middlesex. It existed in 1196 in the reign of Richard the First, and moving from one site to another ended up in Connaught Place or Connaught Square.

The gallows gave the road a bad reputation, and no wonder, because people went there to make a day of it when some unfortunate man was to be hanged. The highway was developed rather later than Piccadilly and, of course, in a mean way. But in 1725 James Figg opened an academy of cudgelling and pugilism, and his pupils taking offence at appearing in the Tyburn road, changed the name to Oxford Street, though Wheatley points out that it may have received this appellation at a still earlier date, because a stone let into the wall at Rathbone Place bore the inscription: 'Rathbone Place in Oxford Street, 1718.'

In its youth Oxford Street was not a savoury place. Thomas Pennant, who was born just about the same time as the boxing academy, looking back on his early recollections of Oxford Street recalled it as a deep hollow road, full of sloughs, with here and there a ragged house, the lurking place of cut-throats, and added: 'I never was taken that way by night, in my hackney coach, to a worthy uncle's who gave me lodgings in his house in George Street, but I went in dread the whole way.'

In 1724 a magnificent double avenue of walnut-trees was planted between Cumberland Gate and Hyde Park Corner, along what was then Tyburn Lane and is now Park Lane. In Oxford Street the coaches for the west started from the 'Hog in the Pound,' which in 1726 gained notoriety by a murder committed by its landlady, who cut off her husband's head, put it in a bag, and threw it in the Thames. Mrs. Hayes was burnt alive at Tyburn.

Long before the great shops came to Oxford Street there arose a place of amusement between Argyll Street and Poland Street which prepared the way for the music-halls which were to make it famous.

The Pantheon, for so it was called, was opened in 1772 for concerts, balls, and promenades to compete with Mrs. Cornelys in Soho Square. It was a sort of winter Ranelagh and became extremely popular.

The Pantheon was really very smart. Horace Walpole says all sorts of nice things about it and, of course, the Prince Regent, when Prince of Wales, went there. He gave it the same cachet as our own Prince of Wales, before becoming Edward the Eighth and Duke of Windsor, gave to the Embassy and to Ciro's between the wars. Many things happened to the Pantheon after this, and by the time

Nash was building Regent Street it had just been turned from an opera house into a bazaar.

The building of Regent Street opened up a new way into Oxford Street. The new circus was specially admired. But round Cumberland Gate the land continued to have a bad name because the gallows were still in people's memory. Nobody wanted to live on the flat, marshy ground, and the only good thing about it was the tea gardens, where in summer people ate shrimps and bread and butter and home-made jam.

Almost as soon as Nash had made his Regent Street, George the Fourth, as you will remember, got it into his head to beautify Buckingham Palace. In front of it he wanted to have a monument to Nelson made in marble, with statues and bas-reliefs. But George the Fourth died, Nash was removed from office, and the young Queen Victoria had all the carvings destined for the marble arch sold. One of these carvings, which was going to be Britannia, was turned into Minerva by chipping Nelson's head off her shield, and it was set up over the eastern entrance to the Royal Academy, where you may look at it next time you pass.

Quite a long time after this—in 1847—when Queen Victoria was remaking the façade of Buckingham Palace, she decided to get rid of the marble arch. Sir Charles Barry wanted to put it in the Green Park opposite Bridgewater House, but happily it landed up beside the Cumberland Gate of Hyde Park, where it glitters on summer days. The Marble Arch has brought brightness and fortune to Oxford Street, where its presence is as welcome as the Arc de Triomphe in the beautiful Champs-Élysées of Paris.

THE BIG STORES—MARSHALL & SNELGROVE

A few of the big stores in Oxford Street began in a modest way even before music-hall came to the street. James Marshall, for instance, opened a shop in Vere Street in 1837. John Snelgrove, who was to become his partner, was a few years younger and started by working under him. The shop we know to-day, and over the entrance to which hangs the royal coat of arms, has grown little by little over and round the first tiny shop where young Marshall sold his bonnets. That is why, when we go there, we go up a few steps, down a few steps, from one delightful surprise to another. The vast building is a conglomeration of different houses welded lovingly together, and fragrant with more than a century of Oxford Street history. When one goes to see the manager one discovers that his office is the prettiest room in what must once have been a charming residence. On a wall facing his desk is a painting of the store when it was still a tiny place, with a fruiterer and a haberdasher forming the corner of Marylebone Lane. Ladies wearing crinolines are sauntering past.

JOHN LEWIS

John Lewis, born in 1836, was apprenticed to a draper in Wells, from where he moved first to Bridgwater and then to Liverpool. Upon a sudden impulse he borrowed a sovereign from a Frenchman and came to London, where, before he was twenty-five, he had become buyer of the silk department of Peter Robinson. This was a wonderful situation for so young a man, but John Lewis did not like working for others. He used to look at the costermongers in Oxford Street and envy them because they, at least, owned the fruit on their barrows. One day, just after his twenty-eighth birthday, an old lady walked into his department and told him that a tobacconist up the street was vacating his premises. John Lewis hurried there, signed a lease, and started up for himself. He was called 'Little Lewis,' to distinguish him from the then very important but now defunct Lewis & Allenby. He was able eventually to buy up adjoining shops, notably that of a greengrocer who in those days had the monopoly in London of bananas. The greengrocer had been at the corner of Holles Street and Oxford Street.

John Lewis was now becoming an important figure. Thrifty, cautious, painstaking, energetic, self-confident, masterful, and irritable, he continued alone for forty years in a position of absolute power, refusing always to take a partner or to convert his business into a company. Later he told his son Spedan that these years had been so monotonous and so lonely that he wondered how he got through them. He spent his evenings reading Alison's *History of Europe* in the basement of an old house in Harley Street which he shared with his staff and the rats who played on the hearth. When he finished the *History of Europe* he read it all over again. At rather more than forty he took a solitary holiday in the highlands, and on a steamer in the Caledonian Canal, fell talking to a stranger who turned out to be in the same business.

They discussed their early struggles, and John Lewis was mortified to discover that whereas it was not until his own remuneration had reached board and lodging and £40 a year that he was able to save his first £5, the stranger, Mills Baker of Bristol, had done that out of board and lodging and £20 a year.

This was the stuff our men of Oxford Street were made of. Let us be proud of them!

D. H. EVANS

The original D. H. Evans (his Christian names were Dan Harries) began with a small shop and two assistants in 1879. As the business grew Dan Evans acquired new property until he found himself with premises which, though facing Oxford Street, were divided by Old Cavendish Street. The business was formed into a company in 1894, and with the twentieth century D. H. Evans joined in that spontaneous desire to make Oxford Street one of the wonders of the world.

Between the wars the directors decided to give up the

east block and to concentrate on a 'one-building' business. Additional property was acquired in the rear of the western building until the entire island site between Chapel Place and Old Cavendish Street was theirs upon which to build the most modern store in the street. This magnificent building, whose immense ground floor, except for the lifts, has no dividing walls, giving it an almost French appearance, was opened in two sections, the first in February 1936 and the second in February 1937, with the coronation of the present king taking place between the two ceremonies.

The east block had been sold just before the war to Messrs. John Lewis, who by this acquisition could join it up with *their* west block and thus become possessed of virtually the entire island site between Old Cavendish Street and Holles Street. There was not much to change in the premises which D. H. Evans had sold them except to alter the name above the plate-glass windows. Whereas D. H. Evans had 'withdrawn' into the fastness of an island site, John Lewis, in addition to theirs, half of which was newly acquired, owned a west block on the other side of Holles Street. That was the position at the beginning of the war.

In the chapter on Regent Street I have described how the great fire raid during the night of 17th September 1940 destroyed so much of the island site which John Lewis had so lately made their own. The only buildings on the island to remain are at the back—a modern strip facing Cavendish Square and Henrietta Place. While the flames were at their height, the name John Lewis, which had been put above that of D. H. Evans on the Oxford Street façade, fell off, and because of this curious accident the Berlin newspapers announced the destruction of D. H. Evans which, in fact, because of the direction of the wind, was undamaged.

During the war the Ministry of Information organized exhibitions on the stricken island site, and John Lewis concentrated on their east block over which the Union Jack proudly floats.

SELFRIDGE'S AND THE GIANTS OF MARBLE ARCH

Curiously enough the area round the Marble Arch, in spite of its magnificent position, took longer to modernize itself at the beginning of the century than the part of Oxford Street on the other side of Marylebone Lane. Then, from across the Atlantic, came Gordon Selfridge, experienced, energetic, full of American ideas, who in 1909 opened the store which by 1927 was to dominate the entire street and spread its story of success all over the world. In November 1928 Mr. A. E. Abrahams finished building the giant Regal Cinema, now the Odeon, behind which the river Tyburn was once a pretty brook. On 12th December 1933 the Cumberland Hotel was publicly opened by Lyons, and in August 1934 came the Mount Royal, designed to give each of its tenants a kitchenette and facilities for shopping in the building. Now it has become an hotel.

During the period between the wars the figure of Gordon Selfridge became synonymous with Oxford Street. He was present at every first night in the West End. Flanked by the Dolly Sisters, he made the smart crowd at Deauville hold its breath. His social gatherings on the top floor of the great building he had so lovingly created brought together all who were famous in the land. By 1944 he had become, by a tragic turn of fate, the greatest forgotten man in London, and lived in a small flat overlooking Putney Heath with no servants, though sometimes a neighbour came in to do the cooking. He died soon afterwards as quietly as his life had been tempestuous, but one supposes that his ghost continues to haunt the busier and ever busier street upon which he has solidly left his imprint.

FAMOUS LANDMARKS

Certain other shops combine to add flavour to the name of Oxford Street. Is not John and Edward Bumpus one of the most famous booksellers in the world? What

English wife exiled to a tropical outpost does not, as soon as her son or daughter becomes engaged, cable to Buszard's for the wedding-cake? Does not the listening white dog of His Master's Voice add something to the street? And what about those stations of the romantic tuppenny tube?

THE BIRTH OF MUSIC-HALL

While James Marshall and John Snelgrove were planning to expand their little shop in the fifties, Charles Morton, the founder of the English music-hall, whose smoking concerts at the Old Canterbury were just then the talk of the town, was looking for another of those ancient inns to repeat his success. The 'Bear and Castle' in Oxford Street pleased him, and he opened the Oxford Music-hall on the site in 1859. There was a room where patrons could sup extremely well for half a crown and the whole place was lit by gas. The Oxford established music-hall in the West End, and though it was destroyed by a fire in 1868 people will continue to talk and write about its successes. After the fire a syndicate bought the Oxford and reopened it. It was destroyed a second time, but, with numerous vicissitudes, continued till 1925, when it was bought by Lyons and turned into one of their great restaurants.

THE PALLADIUM

Across the road, on the ashes of the Pantheon, the twentieth century had seen the building of a new hall destined to carry on this typical English entertainment long after not only the Oxford, but most of the other famous music-halls had either disappeared or gone over to stage or film. In 1908 a troupe of Italians were trying to entertain the public in a ramshackle building in Argyll Street, lately occupied by Hengler's circus. The Italians were doing such poor business that they had come down to threepence for the early door. Walter Gibbons, a young

Midlander, bought the building, pulled it down, and put up the Palladium, which had its gala opening in 1910.

A FOGGY EVENING, 1948

On Saturday, 6th March 1948, a thick fog settled over London. It turned the lights in Argyll Street orange and gave an air of mystery to the gables and half-timbering of Liberty's 1922 Tudor building on the other side of Great Marlborough Street. Costers with barrows full of oranges and grapefruit stood in front of the well-lit Quality Inn, while immense crowds seethed round the entrance to the Palladium, where the curtain would soon be rising on the 8.30 house.

This patient but excited crowd, these barrowmen, this fog, this corner of Argyll Street, these policemen moving like stealthy shadows in front of the variety theatre carrying on the tradition of Charles Morton—oh, how tremendously, gloriously London! Who said that variety was finished? Is this some special performance? But no! A notice said: 'Not a seat available until the end of next week.' Twice nightly and matinees twice a week, and not a seat available! The old stagers blink in the fog and remind us of Harry Tate in the pleasures of motoring, Vesta Tilley singing *Algy, the Piccadilly Johnnie*, Little Tich as the Gamekeeper and his big boots! Isn't it good to be alive on this foggy night and to watch all this animation, these people tramping on pavements running wet with the dampness of the fog!

A woman in the advance booking had found us three tickets for the stalls promenade which cost us, all told, half a guinea, a reasonable enough sum in these times of inflation, especially in view of the fact that the spivs were offering seats mysteriously at £4 each to the crowd. Danny Kaye was the great attraction. A few weeks earlier he had come from America and immediately London had given him that unstinted acclamation which it reserves for geniuses in every age. Obviously those who claimed that vaude-

ville was dormant because of the absence of Harry Tates
and Little Tiches, of George Robeys and Wilkie Bards
were right.   Bring the clown, bring the voice, bring the
song and the guileless smile, and Londoners flock to the
music-hall.   By the way, it needed but one year to celebrate
the centenary of Charles Morton's becoming licensee of the
old 'Canterbury Arms.'   That happened in 1849.   The
orchestra was playing *Night and Day*, the number of the
turn (as we arrived at the back of the stalls) was lit up
according to tradition in red lights, and there was a back-
cloth showing a red telephone booth, a red lamp-post, and
a red letter-box against the backsheet of a London street.
The atmosphere was very warm and the members of the
family standing next to us were beginning to peel oranges.
Scott Sanders, the delightful old philosopher, was fetching
the laughs with the old jokes: 'I have contacts in high
places.   I know a steeplejack!'   The tobacco fumes rose
in front of the boxes bathed in a warm, amber light, and—
well, it couldn't be anywhere else but where it was.   This
was the very essence of London.   A sense of well-being
crept up one's spine.   The curtain fell and rose again on
Hubert Cooke's ponies bearing drums and cymbals, clowns'
hats, and frills round their manes.   A woman standing at
the end of a long line against the wall kicked off her shoes
and lit a cigarette.   She didn't care who saw her in the
semi-darkness.   Against the pillar was a notice to say that
Mae West was playing in *Diamond Lil* at the Prince of
Wales's Theatre.   Outside, the fog would probably be
getting thicker.   The music quickened.   Here was a famous
song-hit from a musical comedy in the twenties, those
prosperous twenties between the wars: *Who stole my
Heart away?*   The ponies danced, boxed, did the prettiest
tricks, as other ponies doubtless boxed and danced in the
days of Hengler's circus.   The blonde trainer, in her black
dress covered with silver sequins, curtsied to the audience
and the ponies bowed.   The curtain went down in a roar
of applause, and as soon as it went up again half a dozen

searchlights were trained on Downey and Daye, the whirl-wind skaters. The swing doors behind us opened letting in the cold, foggy air and a group of rich-looking people who had obviously arrived just to hear Danny Kaye. Perhaps they had bought their tickets from the spiv out-side? It was very warm as soon as the doors closed, and the girl next to us was peeling another orange.

He came on almost immediately after the interval. One could feel the audience trying to sum him up. None had probably seen him before. They wanted to know if he was as good as the newspapers had said, and they looked up at him affectionately, waiting to be charmed. After the first uncertain moments he was sitting with his feet curled up under him in front of the footlights, saying: 'Let 's talk as if we were in a drawing-room. Can anybody give me a cigarette? Thanks. I think things will be better next year, don't you?' For forty-five minutes we remained obediently under the spell. Then the orchestra's drums rolled out the national anthem and we were again in the damp foggy streets. At the corner of Poland Street, once the eastern extremity of the Pantheon, was a great hole where a modern building had been blown away by high explosives during the night raids. Now, in the centre of it, was a pedestal, and on top of the pedestal a piece of sculpture showing an arm holding up a female head with the breasts alongside. Underneath were the words: FORTY YEARS OF MODERN ART. EXHIBITION NEXT DOOR. The first vans filled with Sunday newspapers drove cautiously through the fog to Paddington. The milk bars threw shafts of light on the pavements. Oxford Street was going to bed and it was best for us to hurry home.